How Difficult It Is to Be God

Critical Human Rights

Series Editors

Steve J. Stern ❦ Scott Straus

Books in the series **Critical Human Rights** emphasize research that opens new ways to think about and understand human rights. The series values in particular empirically grounded and intellectually open research that eschews simplified accounts of human rights events and processes.

The war between Peru's Shining Path revolutionaries and the state sparked a human rights crisis. Atrocities claimed some 69,000 lives, hit especially hard at native Andean peoples, and sparked mystery. How could a tiny Maoist sect in a remote highland region turn into a war machine that brought a whole society to the edge of collapse? How did it relate to youths and Indians? How did its cult of war affect the classic human rights doctrine of state responsibility? The late anthropologist Carlos Iván Degregori offered contrarian answers, and laid a foundation for Peru's Truth and Reconciliation Commission. *How Difficult It Is to Be God* is the only English-language book to provide his mature reflections on a tragedy that defied standard international scripts about human rights.

How Difficult It Is to Be God

Shining Path's Politics of War in Peru, 1980–1999

Carlos Iván Degregori

Edited and with an introduction by
Steve J. Stern

Translated by
Nancy Appelbaum, Joanna Drzewieniecki,
Héctor Flores, Eric Hershberg, Judy Rein,
Steve J. Stern, and Kimberly Theidon

The University of Wisconsin Press

The University of Wisconsin Press
1930 Monroe Street, 3rd Floor
Madison, Wisconsin 53711-2059
uwpress.wisc.edu

3 Henrietta Street
London WCE 8LU, England
eurospanbookstore.com

Printed in the United States of America

Library of Congress Cataloging-in-Publication Data

Degregori, Carlos Iván.
[Qué difícil es ser Dios. English]
How difficult it is to be God : Shining Path's politics of war in Peru, 1980–1999 /
    Carlos Iván Degregori ; edited and with an introduction by Steve J. Stern ; translated
    by Nancy Appelbaum . . . [et al.].
        p.   cm. — (Critical human rights)
        Includes bibliographical references and index.
        ISBN 978-0-299-28924-9 (pbk.: alk. paper)
        ISBN 978-0-299-28923-2 (e-book)
1. Sendero Luminoso (Guerrilla group)   2. Violence — Peru — History — 20th century.
    3. Political violence — Peru.   4. Peru — Politics and government — 1980–   I. Stern,
    Steve J., 1951–   II. Appelbaum, Nancy P.   III. Title.   IV. Series: Critical human rights.
HV6433.P4D4513   2012
985.06′4 — dc23
2012010942

Contents

Illustrations

Maps

Graphs

Tables

Charts

Translators' Preface

The book you have before you is a translation of the final work of a great Latin American public intellectual, the Peruvian anthropologist Carlos Iván Degregori, who passed away as a result of cancer in 2011. The original Spanish-language version was published by the Instituto de Estudios Peruanos in 2010.

Carlos Iván was our dear friend. We admired him not only for his ideas and originality but also for his warmth, sense of humor, generous spirit, and exceptional eloquence. We have come together to translate and edit this volume because Carlos Iván's writings on the internal armed conflict that convulsed Peru during the Shining Path era are of great value to an English-language readership. The English edition also serves to celebrate the enduring value of his life and work for all concerned with Latin America and with human rights.

The English edition of this book has been restructured modestly in an effort to maximize its utility for a non-Peruvian audience. Steve J. Stern has taken the lead in the editorial restructuring, and he has written an introduction. Eric Hershberg has managed the accuracy of translations, and the project and teamwork process that made this book possible. Each of us has undertaken portions of the translation, and Judy Rein has refined the translations to assure as much as possible that they speak in a single voice, as close to Carlos Iván's original Spanish as we can achieve.

We are grateful to Jo-Marie Burt, Rebecca Lichtenfeld, and from the Instituto de Estudios Peruanos (Institute of Peruvian Studies, IEP), Roxana Barrantes, Ramón Pajuelo, and Rosa Vera, in addition to the other many IEP colleagues who collaborated with and engaged the work of Carlos Iván over the years and are mentioned in his acknowledgments to this book. We are also grateful to the University of Wisconsin Press for its commitment to this project, and particularly to the support of Gwen Walker and Matthew Cosby.

Copyediting by Sheila McMahon and the editing team at UW Press has further enriched the final product. Ashley Miller and Amanda Sheldon assisted with formatting of the manuscript.

We dedicate the book to the memory of Carlos Iván Degregori. As sad as we are that he is no longer with us, we are heartened by the conviction that his ideas and commitments will live on, in Peru and beyond.

NANCY APPELBAUM

JOANNA DRZEWIENIECKI

HÉCTOR FLORES

ERIC HERSHBERG

JUDY REIN

STEVE J. STERN

KIMBERLY THEIDON

The chapters in this book are reprinted by permission of the author, and were previously published as follows: "The Years We Lived in Danger" and "How Social Sciences Failed" first appeared in the 2010 Spanish edition of this book. "The Maturation of a Cosmocrat and the Construction of a Community of Discourse" is the latest revised version and a new translation, based on the 2010 Spanish version, of an essay that evolved over the years. An early version first appeared in Spanish in *Quehacer* 79 (September–October 1992): 38–43, and in English in *The Legitimization of Violence*, ed. David Apter (London: UNRISD/Macmillan, 1997), 33–82. "Revolution by Handbook" was originally published in an earlier version in Spanish in *Revista Peruana de Ciencias Sociales* 2, no. 3 (September–December 1990): 103–26. "Youth, Peasants, and Political Violence" is the latest revised version, and the first English version based on the 2010 Spanish edition, of an essay that evolved over the years. It was first published in *Poder y violencia en los Andes*, ed. Henrique Urbano (Cusco: Centro de Estudios Regionales Andinos Bartolomé de Las Casas, 1991), 16–29. A subsequent revision was published as "Juventud rural peruana: Entre los dos senderos," in *Juventud rural, modernidad y democracia en América Latina* (Santiago: CEPAL, 1996), 153–82. "Harvesting Storms" includes a reworking of materials from Degregori 1991a. Before appearing in the 2010 Spanish collection, earlier versions of this essay were originally published in Spanish by the Instituto de Estudios Peruanos. This is a slightly revised version of the English translation first published as "Harvesting Storms: Peasant *Rondas* and the Defeat of Sendero Luminoso in Ayacucho," in *Shining and Other Paths: War and Society in Peru, 1980–1995*, ed. Steve J. Stern (Durham,

NC: Duke University Press, 1998), 128–57 (copyright © 1998, Duke University Press, all rights reserved, reprinted by permission of the publisher). "How Difficult It Is to Be God" is the latest revised version and a new translation, based on the 2010 Spanish version. The essay was published in several early versions in Peru by El Zorro de Abajo Ediciones (Lima, 1989 and 1990), and two additional versions appeared in *Nariz del Diablo*, no. 16 (1990): 33–44, and *Perú en el fin del milenio*, comp. Heraclio Bonilla (Mexico City: Consejo Nacional para la Cultura y las Artes, 1994), 119–38. An English version was published in *Critique of Anthropology* 11, no. 3 (1991): 233–50. "Epilogue: Open Wounds and Elusive Rights" was first published in the book *Memorias en conflicto: Aspectos de la violencia política contemporánea*, ed. Raynald Belay, Jorge Bracamonte, Carlos Iván Degregori, and Joinville Jean Vacher (Lima: IEP, IFEA, RED, and Embassy of France, 2004), 75–86. This is the first time it has appeared in English, based on the 2010 Spanish version.

Acknowledgments

The texts in this book were developed over many years in many places. As a result, my thanks are many.

First, I express my deep gratitude to the Department of Cultural Anthropology at Utrecht University. I am especially grateful to the department director Professor Dirk Kruijt, who served as the advisor for the doctoral thesis on which this publication is based, for generously providing me with the opportunity to work on the final version at Utrecht University with the support of its prestigious faculty. I am very grateful to Dr. Ton Robben and all of the faculty and colleagues at the Department of Cultural Anthropology who, during my three months at Utrecht in 2004, welcomed me with exceptional solidarity, offering friendship, knowledge, and the opportunity to discuss a broad range of issues. I am also indebted to the Centrum voor Studie en Documentatie van Latijns Amerika (CEDLA) and Dr. Michiel Baud for the use of their library in Amsterdam during my last weeks in Holland.

Returning to Peru and the beginning of my engagement with this research in Ayacucho, I express my unending gratitude to the friends and colleagues who made it possible for me to stay in touch with the reality of the region. At many points over the course of many years, they welcomed me and facilitated the collection of interviews, and they even gathered information for my research. I especially wish to thank Jaime Urrutia, José Coronel, Ponciano del Pino, Isabel Coral, Carlos Loayza, Teófilo Orozco, Herminio Huamán, Alex Muñinco, Celina Salcedo, Denise Pozzi-Escot, Juan Granda, Tila Castañeda, the former rector of the University of Ayacucho, Dr. Enrique González Carré, and the exceptional *retablista* Edilberto Jiménez.

My gratitude and recognition of a debt that cannot be repaid goes to those who agreed to share their stories—almost always heartrending—who out of discretion remain anonymous. I also acknowledge and pay homage to Julio

Orozco Huamaní, leader of the Federation of Peasants of the Apurímac River Valley (Federación de Campesinos del Valle del Río Apurímac, FECVRA) and United Left militant, from whom I learned so much about the Ayacucho jungle and who was disappeared in that valley, probably by Peruvian Navy operatives, in the terrible year of 1983. I also remember a group of *ronderos*, whose names I never knew, who accompanied us and protected us when we were stranded on the desolate plateaus of Tambo, Ayacucho, during the still dangerous times of early 1993.

In the early 1980s in Lima, I had one of my most intense experiences when I was a journalist for *El Diario de Marka*, where the central ideas were conceptualized for the article *How Difficult It Is to Be God*, the title of this collection. From those years I preserve the special memory of Eduardo de la Piniella, a young friend who was assassinated in a horrific manner as a result of his reporting in the Ayacuchan community of Uchuraccay. (De la Piniella was assassinated together with seven other journalists and their guide. One of them, Pedro Sánchez, also worked for *El Diario de Marka*.) Likewise, my thanks for everything that I learned from my colleagues in that journalistic adventure, especially to Sinesio López, Antonio Cisneros, and Ricardo Uceda, with whom I had the opportunity to collaborate many years later as a member of the editorial board of the weekly *Semanario Sí*. At that time he was the editor, and his reporting team discovered the bodies of the eight students and a professor who disappeared at La Cantuta University in 1992, one of the most shocking episodes of the conflict. My participation on the editorial board of the weekly *Amauta* with Santiago Pedraglio and Manuel Córdova allowed me to follow closely the expansion of the violence throughout the entire country from 1986 to 1989, and to contribute reporting on crimes and human rights violations committed by the groups in conflict, especially the prison massacres in Lima during Alan García's government in 1986.

Finally, in this vein, I am grateful to my friends at *El Zorro de Abajo*, the publication I ran from 1985 to 1987, especially to Carlos Tapia, for his many suggestions and the generous way he always shared information. I am grateful to Alberto Adrianzén for the library that he keeps in the encirclements of his brain, always at the disposition of users. I am also grateful to Sinesio López, Rolando Ames, Miguel Incio, and Óscar Malca. Many of the ideas that appear in the chapter "Revolution by Handbook: The Expansion of Marxism-Leninism in the Social Sciences and the Origins of Shining Path" grew out of the conversations and debates produced in that periodical.

And of course, and always, my thanks to my colleagues at the Institute of Peruvian Studies (Instituto de Estudios Peruanos, IEP), especially Cecilia Blondet, Julio Cotler, and Romeo Grompone, who encouraged me to persist in this research and offered me generous friendship, ideas, and advice. IEP first published many of the articles that are gathered here. Virginia García, head of IEP's library, was efficient and always willing to collaborate with my work, and Elizabeth Andrade, head of the bookstore, was an indefatigable promoter of its dissemination. Rita Márquez generously shared her valuable interviews with grassroots Shining Path militants from the mid-1980s. Finally, my former students at the National University at San Marcos, Rosa Vera and Rafael Barrantes, helped with bibliographic research, and Pablo Sandoval, a former student who became a colleague at IEP and San Marcos, offered invaluable friendship and generous assistance with bibliography and very helpful suggestions.

Through the course of all these years I have often enjoyed the support of colleagues and institutions outside of Peru, allowing me to develop my research and place it in comparative perspective. I am grateful to Coletta Youngers of the Washington Office on Latin America (WOLA), who invited me to return to the United States after nineteen years' absence, Jürgen Golte of the Free University of Berlin, and John Crabtree of the Peru Support Group in London. In all three cases, their invitations allowed me to participate in debates about Shining Path, at times with the organization's representatives abroad. I would also like to mention David Apter, coordinator of the working group on Political Violence and Social Movements for the United Nations Research Institute for Social Development (UNRISD); the chapter "The Maturation of a Cosmocrat and the Construction of a Community of Discourse" evolved from an article that came out of those meetings. Michel Wieviorka, another member of that working group and director of the Center for Sociological Action and Intervention (Centre d'Action et Intervention Sociologique, CADIS), developed the concept of "social antimovement," which was very useful to me. I am also thankful to him for the opportunity to spend time at l'Ecole des Hautes Etudes en Sciences Sociaux (EHESS), and to Anne-Marie Hocquenghem, who welcomed me to Paris. Additionally, my warm thanks to Steve J. Stern of the University of Wisconsin–Madison, with whom we organized the colloquium that produced *Shining and Other Paths*, edited by Stern, possibly the best collection of articles on the topic. Florencia Mallon, Marisol de la Cadena, Susana Lastarria, and many others made my stay in Madison very pleasant, especially Daniela and Carlín.

Many foundations supported my research. A John Simon Guggenheim Foundation Fellowship led to substantial advancement in the work; the Ford Foundation and the Swedish International Development Cooperation Agency (SIDA) also provided funding.

Finally, I would like to mention the project on Memory and Political Violence in the Southern Cone and Peru (1999–2002), organized by the Social Science Research Council (SSRC) and directed by Elizabeth Jelin, with whom

I worked for the last two years of the project. The ideas discussed there are not directly reflected in this book, except for the last chapter, because the articles were first drafted or written prior to the project. But what I learned there is an important element of my current and future thinking on the topic. For this I offer my profound gratitude to Elizabeth Jelin and Eric Hershberg, as well as to all the colleagues and students who participated in this exceptional project.

Except for notes, percentages, charts, and graphs, this book also does not reflect what I learned from serving on the Peruvian Truth and Reconciliation Commission (Comisión de la Verdad y Reconciliación, CVR) from July 2001 to August 2003. I believe that, in reality, this book closes a chapter; it allows me to settle a large pending debt and open the door to reflection that incorporates what I learned from the Truth and Reconciliation Commission, an experience that changed my life and that makes me think that the person sitting here at this moment writing these lines is a very different person from the one who wrote the texts that make up this book, and at the same time that it is the same person.

CARLOS IVÁN DEGREGORI

Lima, December 2010

Abbreviations

APRA	Alianza Popular Revolucionaria Americana (American Popular Revolutionary Alliance)
BR	Bandera Roja (Red Flag)
CAD	Comités de Autodefensa Campesina (Peasant Self-Defense Committees)
CCP	Confederación Campesina del Perú (Peasant Confederation of Peru)
CEDEP	Centro de Estudios para el Desarrollo y la Participación (Center for the Study of Development and Participation)
CEH	Comisión para El Esclarecimiento Histórico (Guatemalan Historical Clarification Commission)
CELS	Centro de Estudios Legales y Sociales (Center for Legal and Social Studies)
CEP	Conferencia Episcopal Peruana (Peruvian Episcopal Conference)
CEPAL	Comisión Económica para América Latina y el Caribe (United Nations Economic Commission for Latin America and the Caribbean)
CEPES	Centro Peruano de Estudios Sociales (Peruvian Center for Social Studies)
CENACAPES	Centros Nacionales de Calificación Profesional Extraordinaria y Producción de Material Educativo (centers of education and professional training)
CEPRODEP	Centro de Promoción y Desarrollo Poblacional (Center for Population Welfare and Development)
CGTP	Confederación General de Trabajadores del Perú (General Confederation of Peruvian Workers)

CIPCA	Centro de Investigación y Promoción del Campesinado (Center for Research and Promotion of the Peasantry)
CLACSO	Consejo Latinoamericano de Ciencias Sociales (Latin American Social Sciences Council)
CNA	Confederación Nacional Agraria (National Agrarian Confederation)
CNDDHH	Coordinadora Nacional de Derechos Humanos (National Coordinating Committee for Human Rights)
COB	Central Obrera Boliviana (Bolivian Workers' Union)
CONAI	Comisión Nacional de Intermediación (National Intermediation Committee)
CONCYTEC	Consejo Nacional de Ciencia, Tecnología e Innovación Tecnológica (National Council for Science, Technology, and Innovation)
CONUP	Consejo Nacional de la Universidad Peruana (National Council of the University of Peru)
COTESU	Cooperación Técnica Suiza (Technical Cooperation Switzerland)
CVR	Comisión de la Verdad y Reconciliación (Truth and Reconciliation Commission)
DESCO	Centro de Estudios y Promoción del Desarrollo (Center for the Study and Promotion of Development)
DINCOTE	Dirección Nacional Contra el Terrorismo (National Counterterrorism Directorate)
DNEC	Dirección Nacional de Estadística y Censos (National Bureau of Statistics and Censuses)
EZLN	Ejército Zapatista de Liberación Nacional (Zapatista Army of National Liberation)
FAO	Food and Agriculture Organization of the United Nations
FECVRA	Federación de Campesinos del Valle del Río Apurímac (Federation of Peasants of the Apurímac River Valley)
FEDETA	Federación Departamental de Trabajadores de Ayacucho (Departmental Federation of Workers of Ayacucho)
FER	Frente Estudiantil Revolucionario (Student Revolutionary Front)
FLACSO	Facultad Latinoamericana de Ciencias Sociales (Latin American Faculty of Social Sciences)
FOMCIENCIAS	Asociación Peruana para el Fomento de las Ciencias Sociales (Peruvian Association for the Promotion of Social Sciences)
FUE	El Frente Único de Estudiantes (United Front of Students)

IDL	Instituto de Defensa Legal (Institute of Legal Defense)
IEP	Instituto de Estudios Peruanos (Institute of Peruvian Studies)
INEI	Instituto Nacional de Estadística e Informática (National Institute of Statistics and Information)
MIR	Movimiento Izquierda Revolucionaria (Movement of the Revolutionary Left)
MRTA	Movimiento Revolucionario Túpac Amaru (Túpac Amaru Revolutionary Movement)
OAS	Organization of American States
ONU	Organización Naciones Unidas (United Nations)
PAC	Patrullas de Autodefensa Civil (Civil Self-Defense Patrols, Guatemala)
PCP	Partido Comunista del Perú (Peruvian Communist Party)
PCP-BR	Partido Comunista del Perú–Bandera Roja (Peruvian Communist Party–Red Flag)
PCP-SL	Partido Comunista del Perú–Sendero Luminoso (Peruvian Communist Party–Shining Path)
PCP-UNIDAD	Partido Comunista Peruano–Unidad (Peruvian Communist Party–Unity)
PUM	Partido Unificado Mariáteguista (Mariateguist Unified Party)
SAIS	Sociedades Agrícolas de Interés Social (Agricultural Societies of Social Interest)
SEPIA	Seminario Permanente de Investigación Agraria (Permanent Seminar on Agricultural Research)
SIDA	Swedish International Development Cooperation Agency
SIN	Servicio de Inteligencia Nacional (National Intelligence Service)
SUTEP	Sindicato Unitario de Trabajadores en la Educación del Perú (Unitary Union of Education Workers of Peru)
UNIR	Unión de Izquierda Revolucionaria (Union of the Revolutionary Left)
UNRISD	United Nations Research Institute for Social Development
UNSCH	Universidad Nacional de San Cristóbal de Huamanga (National University San Cristóbal de Huamanga)
WOLA	Washington Office on Latin America

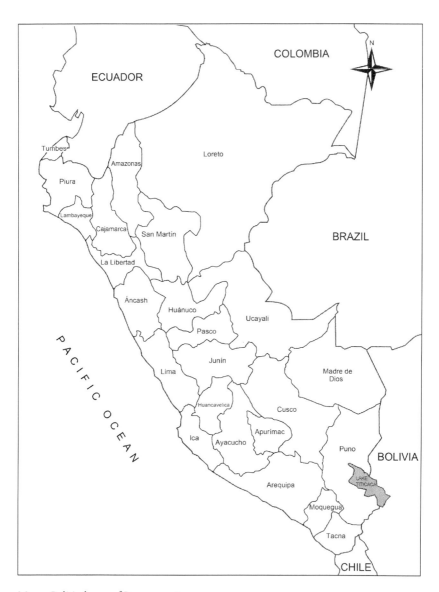

Map 1 Political map of Peru, ca. 1980

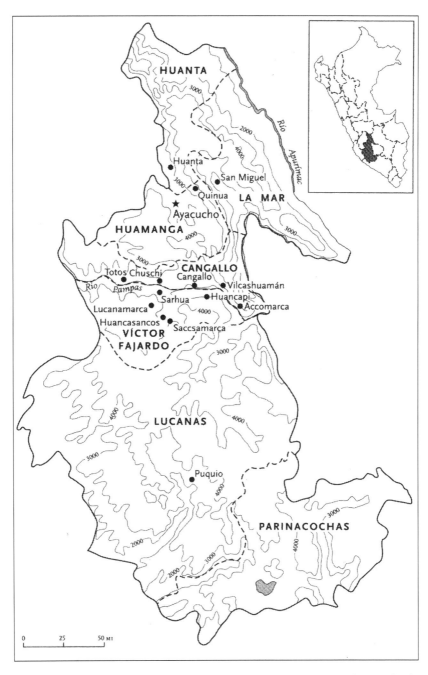

Map 2 Department of Ayacucho, ca. 1980 (contour lines represent meters above sea level)

How Difficult It Is to Be God

Introduction

Beyond Orientalism in Twentieth-Century Peru: Carlos Iván Degregori and the Shining Path War

STEVE J. STERN

This book presents, for the first time to English-language readers, the multifaceted thinking of the late anthropologist Carlos Iván Degregori (1945–2011) on Peru's Shining Path insurgency—its origins, inner culture, and appeal; its relational dynamics, especially with youth and indigenous peasant communities; its legacy, when considering the consequences of Peru's civil war for society, politics, and social science knowledge. The war crisis convulsed various highland regions in the 1980s, brought Lima to the edge of collapse by 1992, and did not wind down decisively until the mid-1990s. During 1980–99, armed conflict took some 69,000 lives, destroyed political third paths between the poles of violent revolution and a militarized state, and drastically transformed the country. Cities and the informal economy swelled with refugees; a once-strong Left imploded politically and lost capacity to support shantytown communities and their leaders; the fearful tenor of life sparked new sensibilities, sometimes contradictory, about state authority, violence, and citizen rights. The bloodshed drew international interest, and sparked a national Truth and Reconciliation Commission process during

2001–3. During the crisis and the subsequent reckoning with truth, Degregori emerged as the world's foremost expert—in the combined role of scholar and public intellectual—on the Shining Path experience and its legacy.[1]

Shining Path, a Maoist political party, declared a revolutionary war in 1980 in the central-south highland region of Ayacucho. (Shining Path, or Sendero Luminoso in Spanish, was the widely used abbreviated name for the Communist Party of Peru–Shining Path.) At the outset, the idea of a revolutionary war waged in a region of the high Andes far away from the capital city of Lima on the Pacific Coast, and considered economically and socially backward, seemed to many Peruvians an improbable flight of fantasy. Ayacucho was an impoverished region, mainly rural and Indian. Notwithstanding the economic stagnancy of haciendas and a crumbling oligarchy, and the rise of a vibrant university in the regional capital since the 1960s, the region's economy had languished. It had not experienced a great modernizing takeoff, and a legacy of "semifeudal" or colonial-like values still seemed strong. The region's long history of landed and racial domination on the one hand, and defensive Indian community authority structures on the other, still exerted a shaping influence on social relationships of rule and expectation in the countryside. Sendero's initial act of war in May 1980, moreover, did not amount to much. Militants burned ballot boxes in Chuschi, a pueblo in Ayacucho, to protest Peru's return to electoral politics. How could a small group of revolutionaries from one of Peru's most backward regions, and so out of step with the rest of the Left's acceptance of electoral transition from military rule to democracy, redirect the course of national political life?

Likewise, the propaganda symbols to announce the war in Lima later that year—dead dogs tied to lamp posts and traffic lights, with signs denouncing "Deng Xiaoping, Son of a Bitch"—seemed absurd. How could sectarian condemnation of the architect of counterrevolution in China amount to a political rallying cry in Peru? The gesture was enigmatic and exotic.[2]

However improbable, a war took off and proved far more serious than expected. Within three years, the conflict between Shining Path and the state was sparking slaughters by both insurgents and the military against Ayacucho's Quechua-speaking communities—and dynamics of fratricide within communities. The Shining Path proved formidable in its ability to organize cadres and build their ideological faith, to establish a beachhead of militants and sometimes a social base in rural communities, to overwhelm the local police, and to use lethal violence to enforce and expand complicity in "liberated zones." A presidential emergency decree in December 1982 allowed the armed forces to take direct command in the Ayacucho region and to unleash an indiscriminate "dirty war" to stamp out subversion during 1983–85. The regional violence was so fierce in this period that the Department of Ayacucho (see maps 1 and 2), whose population in 1981 amounted to less than 504,000 persons, suffered the death or disappearance of an estimated 26,259 persons. Yet all this failed to bring the war to quick resolution—or to confine it regionally. On the contrary, by the mid to late 1980s, the war expanded not only south but also north—into the central highland regions perched above Lima and serving as its granary and hydroelectric power base, and into the northeastern Andean slope regions that descended toward the Amazonian jungle and offered connection to coca money. In addition, another guerrilla group—the MRTA (Túpac Amaru Revolutionary Movement)—sought to promote its own armed revolutionary project along the eastern slope districts of the central sierra.[3]

Shining Path's expansion, which emphasized rural populations in accord with Maoist strategy of war and revolution, did not remain confined to the highlands. Eventually, the encirclement and strangulation of Lima would have to follow. In 1989, Shining Path declared it had reached "strategic equilibrium." By 1990–92, the war reached directly into metropolitan Lima, through a combined campaign of penetration of shantytown communities, including assassination of grassroots leaders, and select bombings in prosperous districts to inspire terror.[4]

The fall came precipitously, even as Lima entered its most precarious stage. As historian Nelson Manrique has observed, Shining Path resorted to "fleeing forward" to Lima at a time of fierce organized resistance by many peasant communities in the central and southern highlands. The irony was that Sendero Luminoso pushed the nation toward collapse by overextending its own politico-military capacity—thereby rendering itself more vulnerable to intelligence work by the anti-terrorist police (DINCOTE). On 12 September 1992, Abimael Guzmán, the leader and cult figure of Shining Path, was captured in a Lima safe house. Nine-tenths of the top leadership was also captured in 1992. Within a year, the insurgent mystique had crumbled. Media events reduced Guzmán to a fallible human being, suddenly open to compromise. In 1993, he petitioned President Alberto Fujimori for peace. By 1995, the hard-line insurrectionists who had reorganized as "Sendero Rojo" (Red Path) could only resort to symbolic maneuvers. Occasional bombings and assassinations announced their presence and a determination to intimidate. But such incidents no longer added up to a serious war.[5]

❧

How were people to understand the violent crisis of society? The war caught most Peruvians by surprise. In Lima, the media capital and intellectual center of the country, it produced mixed sensibilities of indifference and astonishment. The former was more common in the early 1980s, when the illusion existed that the war was a matter confined to a faraway highland department, but became less tenable over time. The transitions from indifference to speculation about the astonishing, and finally, to solid analytical research and interpretation, did not come easily to intellectuals grounded in Lima.

In a society divided by race and geography, where the colonial experience of Spanish rule continued to exert a profound legacy, and where the insurgents themselves seemed mysterious and exotic, the temptation of Orientalism knocked at the cultural door. Here Orientalism, adapted from Edward Said's famous 1978 study, refers to an extreme Othering that originated in Spanish conquest of indigenous American empires and their peoples. The colonizing sensibility defines the exotic and may even romanticize some aspects, but it also creates self-affirming contrasts of humanity that legitimate power and aggression. In postcolonial times, such a sensibility found new life within the internally divided nation whose high elites, intellectuals, and political leaders tended to concentrate spatially within the capital city and relatively compact coastal regions, and whose relationships with the internal Other of Andean highland regions oscillated between impulses of neglect, violent domination, and civilizing mission. Whether framed as a great tragedy that required paternal uplift and education of backward Indians, or as a great injustice that demanded social transformation to liberate colonized Andean peoples, or as a naturalized problem to be contained rather than solved, the national question was unresolved—imprisoned within the profound historical division of society between the West and the Andean, the European and the Indian. Whether despised or romanticized, the Andean Indian was Peru's historical and mythologized Other, in contrast to the world of power, wealth, knowledge, and modernity concentrated in Lima.[6]

Said conceptualized the problem on a grand intercontinental scale, but as Jane Schneider and Barbara Weinstein have observed for Italy and Brazil, respectively, "Orientalism in one country" may arise in societies whose national histories produce extreme regional contrasts. One territory concentrates material development and power while the other languishes. Yet the contrast is also cultural, and yields a traffic in ideas, images, and symbols that naturalizes the inferiority of a region and its people, without precluding fantasies of desire, authenticity, or revindication that may cut the other way. In such cases, the modern "nation" rests on a fractured premise. The internal Other—the social universe comprised of a backward territory and its predominant population—is the foil of misperception that defines the self-affirming, advanced community. Dynamics of this sort shaped the "Southern Question" of Italy, and the emergence of São Paulo as counterpoint to the Brazilian Northeast. Postcolonial Peru constituted another such case, albeit with its own particularities. Lima's place as seat of the civilizing and colonizing mission had a long history—since Spanish conquest in the sixteenth century. After independence, the traffic in photo-images of highland Andean peoples in the nineteenth and early twentieth centuries, the *indigenista* (redemptive pro-Indian) movement that unsettled the civilizational divide between coast and sierra in the early to mid-twentieth century, the relentless quest of highlanders to strip away the stigma of Indianness and acquire education and city life in the twentieth century, in distinct ways all bore witness to the Othering, accompanied by symbolic geography, that created "Orientalism in one country." In the case of Peru, there was even a literal aspect to the metaphor of Orientalism. Lima, perched on the Western Pacific Coast, looked upward and eastward when contemplating (rather than ignoring) native Andean peoples of the highlands.[7]

Put differently, in a society where historical dynamism radiated from whites and mestizos on the coast and in select highland cities and valleys, indigenous peasant communities of Ayacucho and other center-south and southern sierra regions constituted the last bastion of *lo andino*. They embodied the complex of community values, social relationships of reciprocity, indigenous language and memory, economic adaptation to the mountain environment, and organization of communal authority that constituted a kind of Andean cultural essence—a structure of life eroded and under siege by colonizers and modernizers for centuries, yet stubbornly resistant and persistent. In a society where Othering constituted a kind of common sense, *lo andino*—an idealized cultural core preserved against the odds, somehow transhistorical, and in need of defense—also constituted a kind of common sense.[8]

During the 1980s especially, to map the mysteries and shocks of the Shining Path phenomenon onto the well-worn cultural terrain of the exotic and stoic Andean Other offered paths that might transform the strange into the familiar—and tame astonishment with a restored sense of cultural order and explanation. The Orientalist impulse emerged in several ways. One path associated Sendero and its peculiarities with indigenous peoples and their cultural values. Early versions reduced Shining Path—whether its millenarian or messianic values, or its violent anger—to expressions of native Andean culture and resentment.[9] A more intellectually nuanced and politically responsible approach, brilliantly developed by historian Alberto Flores Galindo, stopped short of such direct association. It explored the values, memories, utopias, and frustrations that constituted long-running currents of Andean history—and that created climates of historical desire and expectation that influenced non-Indians, too. In this vision, Sendero was a political nightmare not made by Indians but influenced by a cultural history of recurring utopianism anchored in the embattled experience of the colonized, and extending beyond Andean peoples as such. This vision took the Orientalist impulse as a historical creation and fact of life but turned its implications upside down.[10]

A third path focused not on Sendero Luminoso as such but on the shocks of war. The marginality and ignorance of Indians was not only the essential tragedy of Peruvian life and history but also the key to understanding their role as victims and perpetrators of violence. A shocking media spectacle had come relatively early, in January 1983, when *comuneros* of Uchuraccay killed eight Lima-based journalists who thought they were visiting to investigate the war. The *comuneros* thought the visitors were Senderistas. A national investigatory report led by novelist Mario Vargas Llosa and assisted by Peruvian anthropologists invoked a familiar dichotomy—the modern Westernized and well-informed society of the coast versus the parochial ancient culture preserved in the high Andes—to explain how Indians fell into the trap of mistaking and killing journalists for terrorists.[11]

Engagements with the Orientalist temptation, whether complacent or critical, did not constitute the only approaches to the insurgency crisis. One might focus narrowly on Shining Path's leaders and active cadres, thereby creating a precise journalistic account of the inside story behind unfolding events. This was an important achievement but also carried the risk of reducing the problem to a handful of demonic actors who had come together—thereby sidestepping a larger social analysis of recruitment and appeal, grass-roots connections, and rootedness in historical trends. Alternatively, one might focus broadly on social issues that the insurgency made unavoidable, such as the role of violence and racism in Peruvian society and history. Such analysis provided insight into the social climate and dynamics that pervaded the insurgency and the state's dirty war campaign to suppress it. But it also risked bypassing a deeper or more specific understanding of the origins and inner culture of Shining Path and of its relational politics with communities.[12]

Put differently, such approaches were insightful and important but did not by themselves dismantle the Orientalist temptation. What actually happened inside Andean communities at war, how to comprehend Sendero's appeal to its own base of militants and sympathizers, how to understand the complex evolution of relationships between Senderistas and Andean peasants, these topics were politically and intellectually urgent, yet elusive. Intellectuals and activists needed to search for a realistic analysis—grounded in research and field experience—of both Sendero and the communities in which it had established a presence.

Carlos Iván Degregori ended up playing a major role in that search.[13] The role emerged partly by accident. He happened to have been present at the creation of Sendero's project and recruitment of militants in the 1970s, and he knew the regional birthplace well. His role also emerged partly by design, in the sense of individual intention and cultural expectation. In the Latin American context, the intellectual with special knowledge or perspective also carried responsibility, in times of civic need, to act as a public intellectual. Human connections pushed Degregori in the same direction.[14]

The son of Ayacuchanos, Degregori returned to the region in 1970 after undergraduate studies at Brandeis University. From then until 1979, precisely the period when the Shining Path group led by Abimael Guzmán consolidated its ideology and political strategy, Degregori taught anthropology and social science at the Universidad Nacional de San Cristóbal de Huamanga, conducted research on the region, and engaged the political debates and social movements that shaped the university and wider region. He knew Sendero up close, as political adversary but also as human beings within a familiar social landscape. He could insert Shining Path within a wider context—the full range of competing actors, social movements, and political projects that shaped the university and city of Ayacucho and the surrounding countryside.

When Degregori moved to Lima to take up a new line of work in the 1980s—as journalist at the influential Left newspaper *El Diario de Marka*, as researcher at the prestigious Instituto de Estudios Peruanos, and eventually as professor at Lima's Universidad Nacional Mayor de San Marcos—he was not especially preoccupied with the Senderistas. The transition to electoral politics and the future prospects of the United Left (Izquierda Unida) coalition seemed more important. But as armed clashes and dirty war unfolded, Degregori's knowledge and relationships in the region turned him into an unusual resource within the media and intellectual worlds of Lima. He was a grounded source of expertise, with capacity to discover more. For him, Ayacucho was not a remote place, nor was indifference an option.

Degregori started going back and forth to Ayacucho to research and talk with people, and began writing journalistic and analytic articles about Shining Path. Human as well as political and intellectual sensibilities came into play. He knew people in the region who were killed or disappeared in the 1980s, and also lost two colleagues at *El Diario de Marka* who comprised part of the group that went to Uchuraccay. As an independent voice within the Left who had known Sendero up close, he bore the special responsibility that came with knowledge. Shining Path could not be tolerated ambiguously as a misguided sibling of the broader Left. In the 1980s, a zone of ambiguity could arise because historically, the radical Left considered armed insurgency a sometimes legitimate and necessary strategy of revolution. Nor could the violence and political ideology of Shining Path be trivialized as a secondary problem, compared to state repression and other outrages inflicted on Peruvians.[15]

Thus began Carlos Iván Degregori's long journey—driven partly by circumstance, partly by civic sensibilities and cultural expectation—to seek a deeper understanding of the Shining Path war and its consequences. His writings combined an unusual range of skills—the intuitive insight that comes with the intimacy of field experience, the evocative metaphor that arises from a literary imagination, the analytical finding that results from painstaking research and reflection. The journey continued into the 1990s and beyond, even as the burdens of intellectual and international prominence multiplied. In the 1990s, Degregori directed major multiyear research projects on themes such as ethnicity, democracy, and violence; took on key leadership roles in Peru and abroad (e.g., Director of the Instituto de Estudios Peruanos, 1991–95; membership on the Executive Council of the Latin American Studies Association, 1995–98); and interspersed his teaching in Peru with visiting professorships abroad (Columbia University, 1993; University of Wisconsin–Madison, 1995; Johns Hopkins University, 1997). He embraced the opportunity to compare and contrast Peru's experiences with other cases. He stretched himself intellectually by mentoring Latin American students from six different countries (through a Social Science Research Council training fellowship project, co-directed with Argentine sociologist Elizabeth Jelin, during 1998–2002) on the emerging interdisciplinary and transnational field on social memory in the aftermath of atrocity.[16]

The increasing density of transnational engagement did not cancel out a profound drive to understand what had transpired in Peruvian politics and society. On the contrary, it set the Peruvian conflict and tragedy within a provocative field of comparative and theoretical thinking and conversation. The culmination of Degregori's journey to research, analyze, and disseminate the truth and consequences of what had happened came when he served as a member of Peru's 2001–3 Truth and Reconciliation Commission. The nine-volume report was a model of deep collaborative research and reflection on an overwhelmingly large experience—grounded in a mixed methodology of oral testimony, field research, and documentary and statistical investigation; written in clear language and analytically balanced between a narrative of national and regional trends on the one hand, and select in-depth case studies on the other;

informed by an awareness of other truth reckoning and transitional justice experiences, but without relying on mechanical application of formulas to Peru. (A fine one-volume summary, for broader distribution, soon followed.) In the work of the commission, Degregori had played a critical role in organizing the research and editorial teams, searching for justifiable common ground when differences arose, and taking responsibility for the quality of narrative strategy, consistency, and content.[17]

Degregori was the logical person to take on such a large role, not only because of his intellectual acuity and clarity, nor only because he had knowledge and experience of the Ayacucho region as well as Lima. He was also logical and credible because his writings—the essays in this book—had demonstrated an uncommon capacity to analyze and demystify the Sendero phenomenon. Whether one wanted to understand Sendero's inner culture and mystique, or wished to analyze the grass-roots dynamics and ambiguities of relationships in a countryside at war, Degregori's work was the starting point. He had moved the discussion far away from the Orientalist temptation.

〰

Taken together, the essays in this book capture the fundamental insights developed by Degregori during a quarter-century of reflection. Most have never before been available in English translation.[18] One dimension of Degregori's work was the negative task of undoing mistakes—to de-Indianize the analysis of the mysterious Shining Path insurgency and its social base, to differentiate Shining Path from most of the Latin American Left. Within the Left, one needed to dismantle the impulse to gloss Shining Path as misguided comrades within a larger revolutionary project or family. Within the human rights community, one needed to go beyond the temptation to reduce the atrocities of the war only to a familiar narrative of state terror. Unlike the overwhelming responsibility (well over 90 percent) by state agents and aligned paramilitary agents in dictatorships and wars elsewhere in Latin America in the 1980s, the Peruvian Truth and Reconciliation Commission would find that Shining Path had inflicted about 54 percent of deaths suffered in the conflict.[19]

The other dimension was the positive work of building an analytical portrait. Degregori sought to specify the ways Shining Path constituted, notwithstanding its perversity, an authentically Peruvian and authentically political phenomenon. It derived from within the country's historical currents, even as it propagated a revolution to release society from the grip of its past. It found its core social base in teachers and youths of the highlands—a certain kind of provincial intelligentsia in search of a solution. It did so for reasons that could be explained by Peru's trajectory of youth, education, and intellectual formation in the mid to late twentieth century, but which did not require reductionist, one-dimensional analysis. The same trends that produced Shining Path did not imply an absence of competing political and social projects, nor an absence of positive developments related to the influence of Marxism. In this perspective, the Shining Path phenomenon could not be reduced to an import from Communist societies abroad, nor to a calamity that came out of nowhere— mysteriously imposed by a handful of determined demonic criminals. Nor could Shining Path be interpreted properly, regardless of ideological pretense, as a vanguard proletarian party. In this perspective, too, one could begin to map a nuanced analysis of the ups and downs of adaptation and resistance in rural indigenous communities where Shining Path established a presence.[20]

At its core, what makes this book important is not simply its documentation of Degregori's thought, but its insightful focus on the politics of the insurgency, both in its internal sense (ideology, organization, and social base) and in its external sense (relationships with other relevant social actors). The key issues analyzed in the essays include the following:

(a) the relationships between the Shining Path and other key social forces, including university youth, indigenous/peasant communities, and competing social or political movements;
(b) the ideological dimension of Shining Path, and its connection to cult-like leadership, and formation of a community of insurgency with strong coherence and spiritual commitment;
(c) the social and political consequences of the war as it unfolded over time, especially in grass-roots Andean highlands contexts; and,
(d) the national and transnational dynamics that made possible but also placed at risk the work of the Peruvian Truth and Reconciliation Commission.

A guide for readers may be useful. The book has been modestly reorganized and abridged to minimize undue repetition across essays, to render the argument more accessible to nonspecialists, and to trim details of narrative and debate that have become less relevant over time. The essays published here represent Degregori's mature reflections of the 1990s and 2000s rather than the initial working out of key ideas in the 1980s.[21]

The chapters are divided into two sections. Part 1, "The War That Surprised Us: Why Shining Path Happened," explores what happened—and why what happened surprised so many people who thought they understood the country. It emphasizes the social actors who waged the war, and the intellectual actors who misunderstood it. Chapter 1, "The Years We Lived in Danger: The

Armed Conflict, 1980–1999," provides readers an introductory chronology of the war within its larger sociopolitical context, and including the evolution of Abimael Guzmán, the chief leader of Shining Path, after his arrest and imprisonment phase in 1992.

Chapter 2, "How Social Sciences Failed? On the Trail of Shining Path, an Elusive Object of Study," turns to the vexed topic of intellectual understanding. Here Degregori analyzes the persistent counterpoint between what "really happened," and scholarly and cultural mythologies about what happened. The chapter shows how poorly social scientists and others were prepared to understand a situation where insurgents ended up doing most of the killing of Indians and other citizens, notwithstanding mass atrocities also inflicted by the state. Intellectuals and citizens thereby proved vulnerable to a reading of Shining Path as something utterly exotic, and to relying on stereotypes of Andean indigenous culture to explain what would otherwise seem opaque.

This chapter is an important critique of how knowledge operates amid the human rights crises of civil war. It includes a frank reflection on the human experience that served as a point of departure for Degregori's distinctive perspective and sensibility. It provides a sobering caution for scholars and activists. When a ready-made paradigm of human rights, in which the state is the key violator, converges with the Orientalist mythologies and social practices of a racially divided society, one may wander into a desert of misunderstanding. The nature of the problem—let alone the solution—turns into an intellectual mirage. Once one comes closer, what once made sense evaporates.

The following chapters of part 1 address the ideological dynamics of Abimael Guzmán as leader, and of educated youth who became disciples. Chapter 3, "The Maturation of a Cosmocrat and the Construction of a Community of Discourse," adapts David Apter's concepts about communities of discourse to understand Shining Path's decision to go to war, its capacity for effective follow-through, and its transformation of Abimael Guzmán into a prophet. It shows in this context how Guzmán and Shining Path split off from and became alienated by the formidable social protest movements of Peru in the 1970s, thereby gaining more ideological coherence and more capacity for lethal action.

Chapter 4, "Revolution by Handbook: The Expansion of Marxism-Leninism in the Social Sciences and the Origins of Shining Path," shows how the social demand for education as the road to progress soared in Peru in the 1960s and 1970s, and created a new sociological and political phenomenon—in spite of state retreat from support of higher education. The new phenomenon was explosive growth of radicalized educated youth of humble community and racial origins, attracted to the study of social sciences, yet with poor future prospects for work and professional development. Many believed in a myth of education and found their "truths" in schematic textbooks of Marxist analysis, many of them originally published by the Soviet Academy of Sciences. The essay avoids reductionism by also noting the positive consequences of expansion of Marxist thought in a country as unjust as Peru, and by analyzing with sympathy the social tensions experienced by youth trapped between social worlds.

Part 2, "Harvesting Storms: Why Shining Path Failed," turns toward the social dynamics of war, from the perspective of grass-roots communities and from the perspective of the internal dynamics of the movement, that eventually brought Shining Path down. Shining Path turned into a cultlike force whose worship of reason converged with worship of violence, and provoked a resistance it could not suppress. Chapter 5, "Youths, Peasants, and Political Violence: Ayacucho, 1980–1983," uses the concept of "resistant adaptation," in tandem with study of generational and kinship/friendship dynamics, and attention to social fear, to understand how youths and communities in some regions of rural Ayacucho at first accepted Shining Path, even as they retained a sense of their own objectives. Eventually, peasant youths and their communities did indeed move toward a more alienated stance.[22]

The essay is important not only because of its original analytical approach to a nuanced political zone, shaped by *ambivalent* support or acceptance, in contrast to a simple dichotomy of support versus resistance. It is also important because Shining Path indeed expanded rapidly in many rural communities in the early 1980s, and because the essay includes the extraordinary testimony of "Nicario." Nicario was a person attentive to both the appealing and repulsive aspects of Shining Path, and his story also tells of the attractions of alternative roads to progress through migration—in other words, a bypass of the war.

Chapter 6, "Harvesting Storms: Peasant *Rondas* and the Defeat of Shining Path in Ayacucho," analyzes how the vision and the social practices of Shining Path clashed profoundly with Andean community cultures. The clash happened not at the level of idealized ideas of Andean social utopia or of grand values sometimes imagined by intellectuals but at a more mundane, practical level. The local understandings of punishment compatible with community economy and continuing human energy, the ties of kinship and labor exchange that sustained life and cut across economic strata, the expectations of social protection that shaped the legitimacy of authority, the connections to markets required to keep the community going, these practical values defined Andean everyday life and culture and sparked tension. Degregori's analysis facilitates an understanding of the rise of community self-defense patrols determined to keep Shining Path at bay and inclined to collaborate with the military.

Why did Shining Path prove so blind to the political implications of events on the ground? The party and its base experienced erosion of support and outright opposition in the countryside by the late 1980s, but those inclined toward reflective retreat or self-critique could not carry the day. How could the party rally so forcefully around the idea of strategic equilibrium, and flee forward by aggressively pushing the war into Lima?

Chapter 7, "How Difficult It Is to Be God: Ideology and Political Violence in Shining Path," offers useful insight by returning to the inner culture of Shining Path. Here Degregori seeks to understand the hypercult of reason, so strong that it converts reason into passionate desire. This yearning to transcend the rottenness of a crumbling "semifeudal" world of social tyranny and backwardness in the provinces defined a context in which education and knowledge had become objects of intense desire. They were weapons for progress and transcendence, so powerful that those who owned the key to scientific advance could turn into provincial tyrants—and reproduce the social domination they theoretically rejected. This line of analysis helps one understand the cult-like fascination with Guzmán as a god-like leader whose iconography stressed his role as teacher and intellectual. It also illuminates the mystique of a cleansing violence, justified as reason and science, but powerfully self-defeating in the long run.

The book's epilogue, "Open Wounds and Elusive Rights: Reflections on the Truth and Reconciliation Commission," steps back from the war experience to consider the truth and reconciliation process since 2001. Degregori shows how human rights groups who came together during the war created a prehistory of networks and experience that later enabled the work of the commission to proceed, notwithstanding powerful memories that glorified authoritarian strong-arm rule by Alberto Fujimori as the president who saved the country from terror. In this way, Degregori links the truth commission process to the histories described in the earlier chapters and demonstrates how a politico-cultural space opened that allowed for a truth commission process. At the same time, he offers insight into the ultimate irony of the Truth and Reconciliation Commission. The commission gained legitimacy among much of the national population and created new possibilities, but it also contended with great fragility—strong countermemories, vanishing support by political elites, and increasing pressure to shut down spaces for truth telling, justice, and social repair.

The essays in this book are not the last word on the history of Shining Path and war in Peru. They are at once works of enduring scholarship, and historical documents—essays of original insight and research by a pioneering scholar, conceptualized in times of crisis that blurred lines between the roles of scholar, activist, and public intellectual. Although Degregori became Peru's leading expert on Shining Path and the war by the turn of this century, he did not reduce his own intellectual project to these topics only. His early work included a trenchant study of rural-to-urban migration and shantytown life, and his mature work included acute analysis of national politics and symbolism.[23]

The essays in this book, moreover, sparked useful debate. Gonzalo Portocarrero wondered whether Degregori fully appreciated "a common cultural horizon" among elites, student militants, and peasant *comuneros*. Degregori thought the critique somewhat misplaced. The myth of education and progress indeed constituted a shared cultural horizon, within which the Shining Path phenomenon was one among several currents and options. This horizon, however, was a relatively recent creation, in notable contrast to the common assumption that a long-standing traditional community life, a version of *lo andino*, provided the fundamental cultural compass.[24]

Nelson Manrique offered another important critique. He argued that Degregori erred in drawing a parallel, in "How Difficult It Is to Be God," between Senderistas and petty non-Indian tyrants (*mistis*) of an earlier era of landed domination. The Senderistas aimed not to benefit from a landed order but to destroy it. Degregori agreed that the era of *gamonalismo* in the highlands, so dominant in the early twentieth century, had definitively crumbled as a socioeconomic fact of life, and as a basis for regional rule. Indeed, peasant movements since the 1950s had played a major role in the demise. (*Gamonalismo* refers to rule by provincial landowners and their allied merchants, authorities, and intermediaries over Indian peasants and servants. The term evokes "feudal-like" relations of human ownership and physical abuse buttressed by ethnic hierarchies. At the micro-level, the non-Indian *mistis* who became petty versions of *gamonal* masters within local communities could include local mestizos or "whites" of tainted social origin.) Degregori accepted the demise of the socioeconomic basis of *gamonalismo* as a specific historical era, and the distinct intentions of Senderistas. For him, however, these did not preclude ironic resurrection, at a local level, of political methods and symbolism evocative of an earlier era. The old culture and methods of *gamonalismo* had not quite disappeared.[25]

Degregori's style of work and thinking was collaborative and open minded. He welcomed debate. He criticized the limits of his own work, notably the tendency in some writings to adopt an overly idealized depiction of peasant community patrols (*rondas*) that had organized self-defense against Shining

Path. He understood what had been left aside in these essays but required more searching analysis, for example, about the roles of the armed forces and the state as such. Without abandoning his own analysis, he knew how to learn from others, and to draw on research and concepts from other scholars or fields, to refine his thought. He wore his prominence lightly, disguising it with a modest personal style and a sense of humor. These attributes left room for two-way dialogues—not only with his colleagues in Peru and abroad, and with the students he mentored, but also with the citizen-witnesses and staff professionals who collaborated with the truth commission process his country sorely needed. The fundamental insights about the Shining Path experience published in this book, built through his collaborative and open style of research and thinking, remain valid.[26]

Perhaps the most enduring contribution of these essays, however, is that they build critical distance from the Orientalist temptation that knocks persistently at the cultural door. In a country such as Peru, that temptation is powerful. It is rooted deeply in history. Perhaps no one can fully escape it. The Senderistas certainly succumbed to it, notwithstanding the discourse of revolutionary equality and justice. As one leader put it, after a vengeance attack against the troublesome Quechua *comuneros* of Uchuraccay, "We have swept out those *chutos* [savages] made of shit."[27]

One of the most disturbing findings of the Truth and Reconciliation Commission drove home the point. Quechua or another indigenous tongue was the maternal language for less than one-fourth of the national population but accounted for three-fourths of the dead and disappeared. Even within Ayacucho, one of the most heavily Indian regions of Peru, the violence bore down disproportionately on Quechua speakers. Non-Spanish maternal language accounted for about three-quarters of the regional population but nearly all victims (forty-nine of fifty). In times of fear and aggression, Quechua-speaking *comuneros* were the stigmatized Others of choice.[28]

These essays ground the origins and inner culture of Shining Path, and the ups and down of its links with youths and peasants, within specific historical contexts of lived experience, desire, and relationships. In this perspective, one may engage the Orientalism that pervades the national question in Peru and relationships with native Andean people. But one also comes to see it as one aspect within a more diversified and realistic narrative of politics, culture, and society. Carlos Iván Degregori pointed the way toward acknowledging the reality of Orientalism while moving beyond it.

Part 1

The War
That Surprised Us

Why Shining Path Happened

1

The Years We Lived in Danger

The Armed Conflict, 1980–1999

The night of 17 May 1980, in the small village of Chuschi in Ayacucho, a group of young people burst into the place where ballot boxes and voting lists were being stored for the national elections taking place the following day, and burned them in the public square. The news was published a few days later in some newspaper, lost among the avalanche of information about the first presidential elections to take place in Peru in seventeen years. In the following months, as the press reported the theft of dynamite in some mines, isolated petards started to explode in unlikely places: the tomb of General Velasco in Lima; a school parade in Ayacucho; a peasant assembly in the same city (DESCO 1989).[1] The situation acquired touches of sinister folklore when toward the end of the year, early rising *limeños* (residents of Lima) found dogs hanging from traffic lights with a sign around their neck that read: "Deng Xiaoping son of a bitch." The government as well as other political forces, including the parties that made up the United Left, downplayed the importance of these events.

If no one paid attention to the first war skirmishes, it was because up until 1980, Shining Path seemed like a small regional organization. It was not visibly present among the large social movements and national strikes that shook the country during 1976–79, hastening the military's return to the barracks. Even in Ayacucho, where Shining Path was born, its social influence appeared greatly eroded. Until the very moment it launched its armed actions, Sendero's backbone consisted overwhelmingly of professors, college students, and rural teachers. According to party documents analyzed by the Truth and Reconciliation Commission (CVR) and to conversations with Guzmán himself:

> They were always few in number. They wanted to be few.[2] There were 51 militants in the whole country and twelve in Ayacucho at the moment when the faction led by Abimael Guzmán . . . decided to follow its own path in 1970. Including militants and close sympathizers, there were 520 at the start of the armed conflict in 1980 and about 2,700 militants around 1990, without counting those in the Huallaga Valley,[3] when the violence reached its greatest expansion and intensity. (CVR 2003, vol. 2, chap. 1, 23)

Nevertheless, twelve years later, Shining Path, which claimed that then-remote 17 May as the start of the "people's war" in Peru, had become the most important armed movement in contemporary Peruvian history and certainly the most unusual to arise in Latin America in recent decades. During 1980–82, Shining Path expanded vertiginously in the rural zones of Ayacucho.[4] In response, the civilian government of Fernando Belaúnde (1980–85) entrusted the counterinsurgency fight to the armed forces. In 1983–84, the military unleashed a brutal counteroffensive that resulted in about one-third of the victims killed in the entire conflict, most of them civilian (graph 1). Compared to similar conflicts elsewhere in Latin America, what is astonishing is that during this period, the two adversaries treated the civilian population with equal brutality, especially the indigenous peasantry, as can be observed in graph 2.

Several chapters in this book analyze in more detail the reason for this egregious behavior. In this initial overview, I will expand only on the information provided by graph 2 with the justification offered by Abimael Guzmán after one of the first of the most brutal peasant massacres committed by Senderistas in Ayacucho, when the peasants in Lucanamarca (Ayacucho) rebelled against the Shining Path in early 1983.[5]

> Confronted with the use of armed bands[6] and reactionary military action, we responded decisively with one action: Lucanamarca. Neither they nor we will forget it, of course, because there they saw a response that had not been imagined. There more than 80 were annihilated, that is the reality, and we say it, here there was excess, as was analyzed in 1983, but everything in life has two aspects: our problem was to give a bruising blow to restrain them, to make them understand that the thing was not so easy. . . . The main point is we gave them a decisive blow and we reined them in and they understood that they were facing a type of combatants from the people that they had never fought before, this is what they understood;

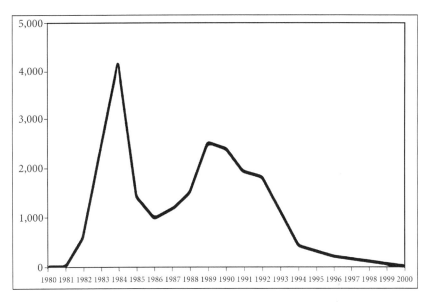

Graph 1 Number of deaths and disappearances reported to the truth commission, Peru, 1980–2000

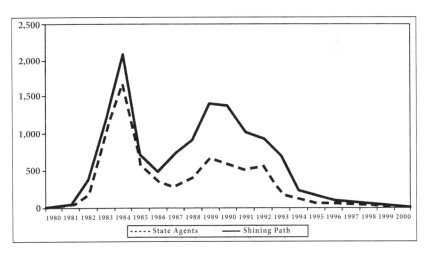

Graph 2 Number of deaths and disappearances reported to the truth commission according to agents principally responsible, Peru, 1980–2000

the excess is the negative side. Understanding war and based on what Lenin says, keeping Clausewitz in mind, in war the masses in combat can be excessive and express all their hate, the deep feeling of class hatred, repudiation, condemnation, that was the root; that has been explained by Lenin, very clearly explained. Excesses can be committed; the problem is to reach a certain point and not go beyond it, because if you do you get off course, it is like an angle, up to a point it can open up, but not beyond it. If we were to give the masses a set of restrictions, demands and prohibitions, in effect we are keeping the waters from overflowing; and what we needed was for the waters to overflow, for the mudslide to come in, confident that when it comes in it will raze things to the ground but then go back to its course. . . . But, I reiterate, the principal thing was to make them understand that we were a hard bone to chew, and that we were ready to do anything, anything.

Ready for anything against unarmed civilians, one should add.[7] However, while Shining Path was boasting that "the party has a thousand eyes and a thousand ears" and knew where and who to hit, the military engaged in blind repression. As a result, in many parts of Ayacucho, the contradictions between Shining Path and the peasantry that had started to surface at the end of 1982 were deferred. Appearing to be the lesser evil, Shining Path was able to survive and break the siege in Ayacucho. It opened other fronts, especially in the central sierra northwest of Ayacucho, and the Huallaga Valley, which in those years was the principal producer of coca leaf in the world, as well as in Lima (see map 1). In 1986, Shining Path recovered from the massacre in the Lima jails of almost 300 militants accused of terrorism; and in January 1988, it held its first Congress. Soon after, having acquired the cult name "President Gonzalo," Abimael Guzmán gave a very long interview to *El Diario*, his official mouthpiece.[8] The following year, Shining Path started to talk about the transition to "strategic equilibrium" in its war against the "old State."

A Million Deaths to Seize Power

In the closing days of Alan García's government (1985–90), 32 percent of the territory and 49 percent of the population of the country were under military control (Senado de la República del Perú 1992). Hyperinflation bordered on 60 percent monthly, the economic crisis brought havoc to the population and was destroying the state and the social fabric with as much or more efficiency than the insurgency itself. In elections held that same year, the discredit of the political parties led to the triumph of Alberto Fujimori, an

The Years We Lived in Danger

outsider whose hard-hitting neoliberal adjustment threw a significant part of the population into extreme poverty. "May the strategic equilibrium shake up the country more," declared Shining Path, which in 1991 believed to have reached such equilibrium. The Shining Path leadership then decided to accelerate the end of the war and to relocate the axis of its actions from the countryside to the city, increasing its pressure on Lima (PCP-SL 1991; Tapia 1997; CVR 2003, vol. 2, chap. 1).

It was around this time that Shining Path also started affirming that the triumph of the revolution would cost a million deaths. It is very possible that one of its objectives was to provoke the armed forces into reproducing the bloodbath that took place in Ayacucho in 1983–84 to an even greater extent, so that Sendero again could appear to the population to be the lesser evil. In any case, the military left them literally "out of the game" when instead of increasing indiscriminate repression they developed a strategy of selective repression, which could be defined as "non-genocidal authoritarian" (Degregori and Rivera 1993). This change of strategy did not signify the end of the dirty war. For three years (1989–91), Peru ranked first in the world among the countries that reported detainees/disappeared. Nevertheless, since the end of the 1980s, this more selective repression was accompanied by a new policy of rapprochement toward the peasantry, which started to or wanted to organize itself into Comités de Autodefensa (Self-Defense Committees, CAD). This rapprochement was difficult, especially because of the military's mistrust of the peasantry and its desire to subordinate it to the strategy of the state.[9] This time it was the armed forces that appeared to be the "lesser evil," and the CADs multiplied over vast areas of the Andes and Amazonia. Thus, Shining Path would suffer its first strategic defeat at the hands of whom it least expected: the poor peasantry, who should have been the "natural" ally of the revolution. This strategic weakness was not noticed in its entirety because of the pressure that Shining Path started to exert over the cities during those same years.

The year 1992 was possibly the worst year in Peruvian contemporary history. Along with the economic crisis, the Shining Path violence increased exponentially. Scores of peasants organized in CADs were massacred in Ayacucho and other Andean provinces. In the cities, the murders of community leaders and local authorities choked and paralyzed social organizations, already very weakened by the crisis. The explosions of powerful car bombs, in middle- and upper-class neighborhoods as well as in poorer areas, "Beirutized" the capital and facilitated the success of the so-called armed strikes, during which Shining Path used panic to immobilize Lima, a chaotic metropolis of some 7 million inhabitants in whose poorest neighborhoods there were more than 100,000 people displaced by the conflict.

Concern about the situation began to transcend Peruvian borders. There was talk of Shining Path or pro–Shining Path cells in Bolivia, Chile, Argentina, and Colombia. Sendero, for its part, started to imagine/wish/warn about a possible North American intervention. Graffiti with the slogan "Yankee go home" appeared on walls in various parts of the country, although in reality the Yankees had not arrived.[10] In March, the U.S. Congress held hearings on the Peruvian situation, during which the Assistant Secretary of State for Inter-American Affairs, Bernard Aronson, warned about the danger of the "third genocide of the twentieth century" if Sendero prevailed.[11] Shortly after, in a report for the Rand Corporation, one of the witnesses at the hearings, Gordon McCormick, announced the possibility of a siege of Lima and the collapse of the government. In his overblown words: "Whether Shining Path triumphs or fails in this effort will depend much more on Shining Path as an organization than any realistic set of responses on the part of the Peruvian government, which has shown scarce understanding of the insurgency and even less ability to stop it" (McCormick 1992, 78).

As if to prove McCormick right, on 22 and 23 July, a fierce armed strike shocked Lima. Sendero's cells all celebrated a toast to the "consolidation of strategic equilibrium." Days later, during an interview for the German weekly *Der Spiegel*, the spokesman for Shining Path in Europe, Luis Arce Borja, declared euphorically: "We are about to take power. The enemy is demoralized . . . cornered. There is no choice but to surrender unconditionally. There is nothing to negotiate."

Shortly before, on 5 April 1992, the besieged Peruvian democracy had teetered, pushed by the president, who dissolved Congress with the support of the armed forces, and took over the judicial branch and regional governments, concentrating power.

In August 1992, energized by its advance in the cities, which papered over its Achilles' heel in the countryside, Sendero's Central Committee approved the initiation of its Great Military Plan VI, which would lead them to "fight for power in the whole country" and to "consolidate the strategic equilibrium at the national level." On the political plane, this meant "making the country ungovernable."[12] Submerged in a kind of fatalistic paralysis, Lima awaited the new Shining Path offensive, which was programmed to coincide with the elections for a new Constitutional Congress that President Fujimori had been forced to convene under pressure from the Organization of American States (OAS) and the United States.

In contrast, to the average Shining Path militant, Guzmán truly appeared capable of interpreting the laws of history and of molding it with the precision and ease of a virtuoso. The revolutionaries had found the fourth sword; they were on track to make an irreversible revolution that would not repeat the mistakes of those who preceded them. The retreats, the partial defeats, the strategic mistakes, and the geological faults of the Sendero project were not noticed or were ultimately left as the smooth edges of what looked like the curve of an ever-increasing slope. Within that long march, Guzmán was placed at the highest peak. He was "the most grandiose fruit of conscious matter, engendered and forged by the class, by the communist proletariat: the leader of the worldwide revolution . . . synthesis of a million wills, light, teacher and guide of communists and revolutionaries that make up the people . . . leader of the oppressed and the exploited to their emancipation" (*El Diario*, 13 December 1991).

Gonzalo appeared not only as the interpreter of the laws of history but also as the military leader unreachable by the repressive apparatus of the "old State." He was everywhere and nowhere: "They looked for him simultaneously abroad, among the workers, peasants, intellectuals, everywhere. But he can be found in every Shining Path cell, in every unit of the Popular Guerrilla Army (EGP), in every People's Committee. . . . He is personally directing the revolution, he is presiding over the Popular Republic of Peru that advances towards the final victory."

And then, the night of 12 September, Abimael Guzmán was captured without a single shot being fired by agents of the National Counterterrorism Directorate (DINCOTE), a specialized branch of the National Police.[13] Never in contemporary Peru did the fortune of a single individual change in such a sudden and profound way, literally overnight, the mood of the country. The sensation of relief that swept over Peru, in all its geography and social diversity, was proportional to the fear and demoralization experienced until the day before. Because by then, with the exception of very discrete demographic and geographic pockets, Shining Path had been repudiated by the vast majority, especially due to its increasing violence against the peasantry in the countryside (graph 2) and its terrorist acts in the cities.

With Guzmán fell two of the three members of the Permanent Bureau of the Central Committee, the highest level of leadership, as well as voluminous party archives.[14] In the following months, the captures proceeded in rapid succession. At the end of 1992, nineteen of a total of twenty-two members of Shining Path's Central Committee were in prison.

In twelve days, Guzmán was convicted and sentenced to life in prison by a military tribunal under draconian laws, not recognized by the international community, that had been promulgated by Fujimori's government after the self-coup of 1992.[15] On 24 September, the government's clumsy psychological warfare maneuver of showing the convict to the press inside a cage wearing a striped prison uniform was taken advantage of by Guzmán to harangue his followers to ratify the application of the Great Military Plan VI: "May the strategic equilibrium shake the country!" After the speech he was taken to a high security prison to spend the remainder of his life.

Defending the Life and Well-Being of President Gonzalo

As proof of their stubborn political will, by early 1993 the national leadership of Shining Path had been rebuilt to some degree. Subsequently, and in much smaller waves than in the previous months, they re-initiated military actions, but their political and psychological impact was not the same. The elections to the Constitutional Congress were held without incident in November 1992; in good measure, so were the municipal elections in January 1993. Sendero was similarly able to mobilize its small but active international solidarity network.[16] "Committees for the defense of the life and well-being of Dr. Abimael Guzmán" were formed in various places.

In September 1993, Shining Path mobilized to mark the first anniversary of the capture of its leader. While its military apparatus attacked in different areas of the country, several cities in Europe and the United States held solidarity meetings for the "most important political prisoner in the world."[17] Although it did not reach the level of the 1992 actions, the offensive served to lift the spirits of the followers of Gonzalo. "What good has it been for the puppet Fujimori, twisted oriental snake, to imprison the greatest living Marxist-Leninist-Maoist? Nothing, since the popular war advances unstoppably," they declared defiantly (*El Diario Internacional* 1993).

They did not suspect that on 1 October 1993, fate, or perhaps "the laws of history," had a new surprise in store for them. In his speech to the General Assembly of the United Nations, Alberto Fujimori read a letter sent to him by Abimael Guzmán, addressing him as President of the Republic and asking for peace talks. The letter stated:

Mister President: We come to you as leader of the Peruvian State to ask that you convene talks that lead to a Peace Accord, the implementation of which may lead to the conclusion of the war that the country has endured for over thirteen years. We take this transcendent step based on our class ideology and class principles, securely confident in its historic need and with a clear understanding that it reflects what has become the need of the Peruvian people, nation and society as a whole. Please, Mr. President, consider and accept our request / Callao Military Naval Base, September

15, 1993. / (Signed) Abimael Guzmán R. (President Gonzalo) and Elena Albertina Iparraguirre Revoredo (comrade Miriam). (various Peruvian dailies)

The request to initiate talks was absolutely unexpected considering that one of the pillars of Shining Path's identity was to consider any negotiation synonymous with treason. To address Fujimori as president was also exceptional, since Sendero never recognized his legitimacy; they considered him a representation of the "old State" in contrast with the authentic "President Gonzalo."[18]

Shining Path's response was as fast as its battered logistical machine would allow. In a Declaration dated 7 October, the new leadership rejected the letter as an "absurd and ridiculous story that no one with half a brain could take seriously and that will vanish like its predecessors in the whirlwind of the People's War." At the same time, with even greater hyperbole they stood by their recognition of "our beloved, heroic and respected President Gonzalo, the greatest Marxist-Leninist-Maoist living on earth . . . [who] with his unfading light, the almighty Gonzalo Thought . . . has brought us here and leads us to the golden and resplendent communism with a firm and secure hand" (PCP-SL 1992b).

By then, however, a second letter had appeared, in which Guzmán not only reaffirmed his request to establish peace talks but also recognized the merits of the self-coup of 5 April 1992. This second letter started by justifying the Shining Path insurgency against "a state system of bourgeois pseudodemocracy and outmoded parasitic political parties; a society from whose oppression and exploitation the people have suffered for centuries." He then criticized the government of Belaúnde, who "after calling us 'cattle thieves' unleashed a bloody repression of the people"; and Alan García, who "after saying he would not fight 'cruelty with cruelty' followed a genocidal path all the same, plunging the country into the worst economic crisis in its history." Next, the greatest of surprises:

> And then you come to power. And the facts show that your management has achieved objective advances, especially after the events of 5 April 1992, a situation that was clearly arriving as necessary for the Peruvian state, to which end the foundations for the economic process and for advancing the readjustment of the state have been established; and as far as what concerns us directly, from that date and under your political direction, it has developed a coherent and systematic strategy implemented at various levels, especially in the field of intelligence, achieving real successes, especially in the capture of cadres and leaders, including the signatories of this

letter, which is evidently the most important success of the Peruvian state under your leadership during these thirteen years of war. (*Caretas*, 14 October 1993, 12–13)

The letter, which criticizes the democratic governments and praises the authoritarian government resulting from the self-coup of 1992, in addition to illustrating how extremes can touch each other, suggests some sort of Stockholm syndrome with traces of masochism. As with the first letter, it was signed by Guzmán and Elena Iparraguirre, admitted that Sendero's situation could not be resolved for a long time, and ended by calling for "a new historic decision": fight for a peace accord, given that "peace has become a need for the people, the nation and Peruvian society as a whole" (ibid.).

The suspicions that Guzmán had been tortured psychologically and undergone "brainwashing" arose not only among Senderistas but also among opposition groups. In order to convince the nonbelievers, Abimael himself showed up days later on TV, leaner but healthy, wearing a Mao style jacket instead of his striped prison uniform, with beard and hair trimmed and apparently dyed. It was not enough. Some Shining Path leaflets talked about a double, a look-alike that was usurping the personality of president Gonzalo, who might well be dead. But the Red Cross was able to access the prisoner and confirmed that he was in good condition.

El Diario Internacional (September 1993) then published a special issue whose main feature was titled "President Gonzalo replies." In four pages of interview format, the arguments laid out in the letters were refuted based on texts that Guzmán himself had written between 1980 and 1992.

—What is dialogue for President Gonzalo?
—. . . dialogue is a sinister trade . . . [that] seeks to undermine the people's war. (Guzmán 1991c, 16)

—What would be Shining Path's condition for dialogue?
—. . . we do not want a Peru of the north and Peru of the south, we want one Peru. That is our condition, exact, complete, and absolute surrender. (Guzmán 1988)

—Is it correct to call the coup perpetrator Fujimori "President of the Republic"? Is it perchance a legitimate regime?
—Fujimori has placed himself outside of the Constitution. . . . Article 82 of the Constitution establishes that no one owes allegiance to a regime that is unconstitutional and that the right to insurgency applies . . . (Guzmán 1992, 2)

—What is the position of Shining Path on Fujimori's military coup?

—... the *coup d'etat* of April 5 is one more step in the process of absolute centralization of the Peruvian reaction. . . . The genocidal dictatorship of today will sow more hunger and more repression against our people . . . (Guzmán 1992, 1, 4, 5)

—Could there be a political motive that would lead Sendero's leaders to stop and paralyze the revolutionary war?

—The leadership could be disappeared, in part, not all of it, but those who remain should and can continue with the plans, the fight, the people's war; we are forged in the revolution that does not stop, does not paralyze. (Guzmán 1993, 3)

—What would be the historical result of going back on the armed struggle?

—We have preached, call to arms. . . . Our voice has not fallen on the desert, the seed fell on fertile ground, it is starting to sprout. . . . Those to whom we said stand up, rise up in arms . . . they respond: we are ready, guide us, organize us—let's act! . . . Either we carry out what we promised or we will be a laughingstock, unfaithful traitors. And that we are not. (Guzmán 1990a)

The party can no longer develop any more but through war, through the armed struggle. (Guzmán 1990b)

Nevertheless, on 28 October 1993, on the eve of a referendum convened by the government to approve a new constitution, Guzmán appeared again on television.[19] This time he was accompanied by five members of the governing body of Shining Path, several of them moved to Lima from the high security prison of Yanamayo (Puno), at the far southern end of the country. The imprisoned command had signed a letter composed after a meeting with Guzmán in which they accepted their leader's turnabout and called on their free comrades not to fall into "provocations" and to "fight for a peace accord" (Lima newspapers and magazines).

This time the response came from the "Committee of relatives of political prisoners and war prisoners and the disappeared of Peru," which in a communiqué condemned "with categorical class hate, the sinister action of this handful of well-known and proven capitulators, informants, cowards of low morals that would not offer their lives, excrements of a revisionist bitch, lackeys of Yankee imperialism and of the genocidal and treasonous dictatorship . . . [who attempt] in vain to sow surrender in our heroic people, liquidate the party and annihilate the people's war" (Lima newspapers and magazines).

In the following months, however, reality in all its grayness started to impose itself over the Senderistas. Guzmán not only wrote letters but also apparently prepared documents for the celebration of a Shining Path Congress II (which could only take place with the acquiescence of the National Intelligence Service). In an extensive document that was leaked to the press, Guzmán expanded on the arguments of his second letter and called to "Accept and Fight for a New Decision and a New Definition" of similar importance to that taken by the party in 1980 when it decided to initiate the armed struggle: to fight for a peace accord and move on to a new stage of "political war" (Guzmán 1994b).

The letters of October 1993 and the "new great decision" to fight for a peace accord had a devastating effect among the Senderista ranks. Those who subsequently recurred to the law of contrition numbered in the hundreds, because by soliciting a peace accord—something that for any other armed group in Latin America would have been considered within the realm of possibilities, or at the very least would not be viewed as sacrilege—Guzmán brought to the foreground one of the most profound fractures within Sendero's identity as it was constructed in the 1977 to 1980 period: the intensification of a double register, simultaneously scientific and mystic.

Because what for Guzmán constituted, at least in part, an intellectual construct was assumed for thirteen years by the militants as a religious identity and lived almost as a mystical rapture. It was faith that in the final instance moved the Shining Path "war machine." In this context, the leader's imprisonment did not signify the end. Many divinities and many mythical heroes have spent "a season in hell." Nor was prison an irreversible condition. Sendero organized a brigade in charge of Gonzalo's rescue (*Semanario Sí*, 24 April 1993). Not even death would have meant the definitive defeat. *Gonzalo, el mito* (Roldán 1990, 53) would have fed the imagery of the hard-line Shining Path core a long time after his physical disappearance.[20] Thus the astonishment when the god of war decided to become a human being again, a run of the mill politician, to be more precise.

The Last Temptation of President Gonzalo, or a (Partial) Return to Realism

And you leave, holy shepherd
your flock in this valley
deep, dark
with loneliness and tears
Fray Luis de León

In the wake of his letters there was talk about the presumed cowardice of Guzmán, about his incapacity to withstand solitary confinement; also about possible psychological tortures and brainwashing. Even if there was some truth in these statements, they fail to explain the core: his bureaucratic side, overshadowed for a long time by prophetic discourse and war, was what made Guzmán's great turnaround in prison possible. If we remember him in 1970, holed up in the university and employed by a regime that he labeled as fascist, some of his current behavior is apparent. Back then he talked about the "defense of the university"; today he writes about the "defense of the party." In both cases, it was also about the defense of his self. He wants to return to the tactic of the 1970s while disregarding thirteen years of *jihad* and the deification of his personality.[21] By manipulating Christian symbols and Marxist concepts he constructed a quasi-divine image,[22] fed it to the point of paroxysm, and when he judged it convenient, decided to leave it as if changing skin. He decided to come down from the cross, paraphrasing Nikos Katzansakis in *The Last Temptation of Christ*. That was possible because the prophet was never able to subordinate the Stalinist politician in him. Intellectual construction, manipulation, whatever the term and whatever the degree, the deification was always instrumental.

Mao's affirmation, "except for power, everything is an illusion," always had a central place in "Gonzalo Thought." If that were true, then the party, privileged instrument of the conquest of power, was the only real thing. Society became an illusion. That is why when he/Shining Path decide(s) that a peace accord is convenient, suddenly everything changes. The accord becomes "historical need of the people, of the nation, even of Peruvian society as a whole" (second letter to Fujimori, in *Caretas*, 14 October 1993, 12–13).

Imbued with a sudden realism, as if after a hallucinatory voyage, the cosmocrat appears at long last to see what was long clear to ordinary mortals. His interpretation of the critical world juncture is upended. Until 1991, Shining Path affirmed that we were living "the strategic offensive of the world revolution" (PCP-SL 1991). After 1992 it recognizes that the initiation of armed actions in 1980 was not the start of the strategic offensive of the world revolution (!) and that we are experiencing "an international context of a general imperialist offensive, of a general political retreat of the world proletarian revolution, that must be counted in decades, at least more than one" (PCP-SL 1993).

Guzmán's success in gathering his followers around the new great decision was uneven. It was better received among the imprisoned militants, not only because he had access to them directly or through his already convinced lieutenants but because prisons are the habitat par excellence for Guzmán, who never operated in open spaces. He was undefeated in debates and party events attended only by small nuclei of leadership, unmatched in the handling of Stalinist teachings, and tireless in "pounding" ideas into the mind of militants until they were completely enclosed in circular arguments, trapped in the spider web of a closed discourse made with the sticky thread of confirming citations. It is there, moreover, where coercion of the group over individuals could be exerted with better success and where the superior could exercise in more direct manner his influence over the lower rungs of the hierarchy.[23]

Guzmán also had more success among followers who were the most committed to the vicissitudes of the political line. He was also successful among Sendero's old guard, especially those from the ancient Stalinist Peruvian Communist Party, heirs to the Communist Parties of the Third International, who, as is well known, were accustomed to the most abrupt turns and the most surprising pacts. Finally, Guzmán's new discourse enjoyed higher acceptance among those who were members of the party apparatus than among those who were part of the military apparatus. He could convince these groups not only because of his longstanding and undisputed leadership but because they shared an identity and the basic language that have remained unchanged.

The new great decision did not imply, in turn, an abandonment of the dogma. The turnabout took place within the frame of the strictest orthodoxy, resorting simply to other citations, to the Lenin of *Left-Wing Communism: An Infantile Disorder*, for example. That is why Guzmán asserts that the peace accord "does not imply and cannot imply capitulation, surrender, much less reneging on our class ideology." The people's war has only been suspended "temporarily," since class war has two forms: "First bloodless: 'politics is war without bloodshed' and second: bloody, 'war is politics with bloodshed'" (PCP-SL 1993).

The shedding of skin would be, then, only an appearance. To his followers, he continued to be the cosmocrat, capable of masterfully interpreting the laws of history. It is history that commands now, through Guzmán's mouth, to wait a few decades. Those who do not understand him are "a handful of military punks hung-over on political adventures . . . spilling their drool of defeat [to President Gonzalo]" (Guzmán 1994b).

To an external observer, however, the religious superstructure built by Shining Path had crumbled. But in contrast to other experiences in Latin America or Eastern Europe, the Stalinist dogma remained as a geological bedrock. And it is here that as the prophet steps down from his pedestal, what remains is an antediluvian politician who speaks only of "the temporary suspension of the people's war" turning it for the time being into a "political war," and though he may well ask for a "peace accord," he confirms his rejection of elections and representative democracy (Guzmán 1994b).

In Search of the Fifth Sword

The division that, in spite of everything, was produced by "the new great decision" was a serious blow to a party that with Guzmán as a "cosmocratic" figure had achieved the feat of exacerbating the "fight between the two lines" of Maoist tradition to an unprecedented degree, and that at the same time had managed to avoid the classical divisions of the Left, forging instead a unity that appeared unbreakable, organic. As a grassroots militant in the 1980s affirmed:

> I do not think as a person any longer. One feels the party as oneself, I am the party . . . and everything we do and think is part of the party. Such is the political mutual understanding that we have, that we draw the same conclusions no matter how far we are from each other. It is the same thing in politics, and better still in the military realm. There may be a column that wanders off because the enemy besieges and divides it. Those two commands know what to do. The unit is so strong that we all have the same initiative. Without coordinating, we coordinate. (Roberto)[24]

Under the leadership of Alberto Ramírez Durand ("Feliciano"), the only member of Sendero's politburo who was not captured in September 1992, the dissidents called themselves first "Red Path" (Sendero Rojo) and later the faction "Carry On" (Proseguir). Red Path tried to continue the war under the worst of conditions: pursued relentlessly by the armed forces, infiltrated by the state intelligence apparatus, running against the demoralization that corrodes the periphery and even the cadres that remain free, with the fear of being denounced by members of Black Path (Sendero Negro), as those aligned with Guzmán are called, overwhelmed by the weight that he conserves after thirteen years of deification. "President Gonzalo is the armed struggle," according to the Shining Path hymn. No one can fill this vacuum, because no one could become a cosmocrat and accumulate so much symbolic capital in such a short time.

Feliciano's followers have proceeded to recast themselves timidly, attempting to delink "Gonzalo Thought" from the concrete man Abimael Guzmán. But this turns out to be very difficult since the "gonzalistas" answer that "only President Gonzalo is capable of generating Gonzalo Thought" and accuse those who want to continue the armed struggle of "committing a monstrous crime against the party, the class, the people and the revolution." Deaf to these criticisms, the felicianistas have tried to hide the sun with one finger and "continue the people's war . . . developing the strategic equilibrium for the conquest of power in all of the country" (*Semanario Sí*, 25 April 1994), as if nothing had changed.[25] But any possibility of achieving this disappeared early on. According to reliable statistical indicators, already in 1994, Sendero's armed actions had dropped to 1982 levels (IDL 1994).

This sad reality filters through, in spite of all their precautions, into Red Path's documents; for example they reproduce a quote from Lenin that reads: "We march in a small united group along a rocky and difficult road, tightly holding hands. We are surrounded by enemies on all sides, and almost always we have to march under fire" (*Semanario Sí*, 25 April 1994, 93). And we have become orphans, they should have added.

By the mid to late 1990s, Red Path became silent, concentrating all its strengths on mere survival. The silence became even denser after the capture of the national leaders surrounding Feliciano. Those who are taken prisoner are thrown like Daniel into the lion's den in the quarters of the "accordists" and, if necessary, are sent to President Gonzalo, who, with his new realism and the fascination that he still holds over his followers, proceeds to "hammer their hard heads until their speculations are shattered into pieces," until finally they are converted to the new great decision.[26] Thus, around September 1995, many long, monotonous self-criticisms by Feliciano's followers were broadcast on television—Margie Calvo, Rodolfo Cárdenas Ruiz—recognizing their errors like in an extravagant version of the famous Moscow show trials, in which the chief justice ends up being sentenced to life.

Those who do not die in combat or end up in prison will continue fighting; some isolated pockets of Red Path perhaps will prevail even after Feliciano's capture, like those Japanese soldiers lost in the islands of the South Pacific, who either ignored or refused to accept that the war had ended. But it will be impossible for them to serve as a basis to reconstruct a Shining Path project. Because it will be impossible in their lifetimes to find the "5th sword of Marxism." In Peru or anywhere in the world.

2

How Social Sciences Failed?

On the Trail of Shining Path, an Elusive Object of Study

During the period from 1980 to 1999, Peru experienced the most intense, widespread, and prolonged period of violence in all of its republican history. Nonetheless, despite the importance that this internal armed conflict came to have throughout the 1980s and the generalized crisis into which it plunged the country, Shining Path was, and to a certain extent remains, a little-studied movement. This is the case despite the atypical character of Shining Path when compared to other armed groups in Latin America. Not only was it the only important Maoist group on the whole continent but it was exceptionally lethal. Indeed when one reviews the bibliography of publications by Peruvians and by foreign experts on Peru, it is surprising how little attention was given to the issue of social and political violence in analyses of the situation in Peru before 1980; how slowly this issue was taken up in studies done after 1980; and the degree to which research about the internal armed conflict before the establishment of the CVR in 2001 was relatively undeveloped.

In my opinion, this lack of research, which led to speculations and mis-interpretations regarding Sendero's armed violence and the counterinsurgency response by the government, was related to various factors, including surprise, fragmentation, postcolonial distancing, and fear.

A Triple Surprise

Surprise for the Government and the Intelligence Services

Around 1980, Shining Path was a small group with few connections to the great social movements that had convulsed the country in the second half of the 1970s, possibly the most important such events in the Peruvian republic's history. The media and government intelligence services concentrated their attention on these movements and on the Leftist parties that were associated with them. The majority of the latter joined together starting in 1980 to create the United Left front, which became the second-largest electoral force during the 1980s but was considered by some government agents as a possible "legal arm" of subversion.[1] Given the very large social mobilizations that took place during this period, the government of General Morales Bermúdez (1975–80) and Fernando Belaúnde's second government (1980–85) could have anticipated the appearance of an armed movement in Peru similar to the ones in Central America or the Southern Cone—variants of the classic Latin American guerillas—but not something such as that which began to emerge in Peru in 1980.

Surprise for Political Parties and Social Organizations

The social and political life of Peru in the previous decades had been surprisingly peaceful by Latin American standards. During the 1958–64 period, Peru's most important peasant movement of the twentieth century developed. Thousands of peasants and agricultural workers organized and mobilized throughout the country, invading or recovering thousands of hectares from the hands of large estates and dealing a death blow to traditional large landholding in the Andes. Nevertheless, in these years, only 166 people died, less than the number who died in the armed conflict during the first ten days of 1991.[2] In 1965, the guerrillas of the MIR (Movement of the Revolutionary Left) and the ELN (Army of the Revolutionary Left), and especially, the government repression directed against these groups, added several dozen more people to the list of fatalities.[3]

In the 1970s, a second wave of land takeovers shook the country during the implementation of the most radical land reform in South America, decreed by the government of General Velasco (1968–75). The mobilizations were not very widespread, but the level of peasant organization reached its highest point in 1974 with the reorganization of the Peasant Confederation of Peru (CCP) and the creation by the military government of the National Agrarian

Confederation (CNA). Nevertheless, once again, the cost in human lives of these rural movements was very small.[4] In a country that was by then primarily urban, different types of organizations acquired more importance: workers' organizations and movements,[5] government employees (especially teachers), neighborhood organizations, feminist groups, and, especially, regional movements—the so-called Defense Fronts (Frentes de Defensa). This social effervescence led to the only two national strikes really worthy of the name—in July 1977 and May 1978—that contributed significantly (and almost without the loss of lives) to the weakening of the military government and the subsequent democratic transition.

This low level of violence amid great political and social effervescence was the result of new strategies, leaderships, and forms of organization of peasants, urban workers, and other social sectors, as well as the evolution of the Peruvian state and political parties. Only a few factors will be noted here. In contrast to military regimes in the Southern Cone, the Peruvian military government (1968–80) was not particularly violent. In addition, in 1956, the great Peruvian populist party, APRA (American Popular Revolutionary Alliance), had "left the catacombs" of illegality, where it had spent various decades, and participated in the formal political system. Finally, during the democratic transition (1977–80), the overwhelming majority of radical socialist and communist groups, many of which considered revolutionary violence necessary to achieve power, decided to participate first in the Constituent Assembly that drafted the 1979 constitution and later in the 1980 presidential elections. Very soon afterward, they joined together in the United Left front.[6]

This dizzying change of direction by the radical Left was permeated by ambiguities and tensions between its continuing revolutionary discourse and its very new electoral participation. These tensions visibly manifested themselves at the final campaign rally of one of the Leftist presidential candidates when he addressed the gathered crowd while clutching a wooden rifle and repeating his party's slogan: "Power grows out of the barrel of a gun."[7] The reasoning was that the great mobilizations of the time that had pushed most of the Left into legality and electoral participation could also be understood in the radical code as signs that a revolution was "around the corner" if only the political vanguard knew how to take advantage of them.[8] Nevertheless, despite the existing tensions, it would have been very difficult to predict the outbreak of violence in 1980.

Up until then, Shining Path also had not employed violence. As a Maoist group, it proclaimed that "prolonged popular war" was necessary for the revolution to triumph. But, as we have seen, many small radical groups proclaimed the same idea during the 1970s. Moreover, Sendero's dogmatism led it to oppose many of the large national strikes in 1977 and 1978 because they considered some of the participants "revisionists" or servants of "socio-imperialism."[9]

Surprise for the Social Science
Academic Community

Of the triple surprise, this one is certainly the most relevant to our argument inasmuch as the first two refer to the political and social context.

During most of the 1970s, the principal efforts of social scientists, both in Peru and abroad, concentrated on interpreting a previous surprise: the so-called Revolutionary Government of the Armed Forces, especially in its first phase, led by General Juan Velasco (1968–75), which was not only incomparably less violent than its peers in the Southern Cone or Central America but also undertook a process of radical reforms that earned it the label of "Nasserist."[10] The military government's transformations, especially the agrarian reform, monopolized the attention and energies of researchers. The structural character of the reforms and the anti-imperialist stance of the regime created additional incentives to base research on dependency theory and/or structural Marxism—theories that were predominant at the time.

At the end of the 1970s and the beginning of the 1980s, social organizations and movements, both rural and urban, were gaining preeminence in studies, theses, publications, and debates. This change in focus was not arbitrary since organization and mobilization, primarily urban, was the most conspicuous characteristic of those years, especially for social sciences that had veered away from dependency theory or Marxist structuralism (whether in its Althusserian or directly Leninist versions) toward other interpretations that, influenced by Antonio Gramsci or Alain Touraine, emphasized what the latter called "the return of the actor" (Touraine 1984).

"History is a process without a Subject or a Goal," Althusser is said to have stated in his polemic with John Lewis. Touraine (1978, 1) argued just as forcefully in the first sentence of one of his books that was very influential in Peru: "Men make their own history: social life is produced by cultural achievements and social conflicts, and at the heart of society burns the fire of social movements."

It is not that the most important Peruvian studies during these years considered these movements prepolitical, nonpolitical, or "primitive rebels." Thanks to Gramsci, there was an incipient consciousness of the close and complex relations between state and society,[11] between politics and culture; still, the emphasis was on social movements.[12] This was not only for academic reasons but also because of the *political* evolution of the social sciences community, which had a strong presence of persons linked to one form or another of Leftist positions who had abandoned Leninist vanguardism and embraced a Gramscian version of Marxism.[13] British Marxism and especially the works of E. P. Thompson about the formation of the English working class reinforced this shift in vision. "Social classes" stopped being a generalization. According to Lenin's classic formulation (first expressed in 1920), classes are defined "by the place they occupy in a historically determined system of social production," something that could lead to viewing subjects as simple "bearers of structure" (Lenin 1975). For Thompson (1972), "there are no classes without class struggle," that is, without historically and culturally situated actors.

The political U-turn that resulted from this theoretical shift (also influenced by so-called Eurocommunism, then at its peak) was the construction of a "party of the masses" with internal democracy. In those years, Peruvian academia adopted the concept of "popular protagonism" to support what was called a "Copernican revolution," in which Leninist party-centrism was replaced by a sociocentric conception.[14] This was a way to attempt to provide a basis for the constitution of the United Left as a party of "the masses," and it was postulated that the party must necessarily be democratized.[15] As is evident in this book, the violence unleashed by Shining Path represented a complete and total break with these conceptions, which did not achieve hegemony in the United Left.

When reading the chapters of this book, it should be kept in mind that some were first conceptualized from within an academic community that was highly politicized, militant, very much in the tradition of the Latin American "public intellectual." Consider also that in those years, the politicization of intellectuals was not limited to the Left, as evidenced by the role of Mario Vargas Llosa—the Peruvian intellectual par excellence—in the formation of the Libertad political movement in 1987, and his run as the presidential candidate of neoliberalism in 1990. Consider as well the constant uncertainty of Hernando de Soto—from 1987 until this writing, he has vacillated between his successful career as an international consultant and the recurring temptation to run for president.

I will end this section by citing two texts to illustrate the surprise generated by the initiation of the armed conflict and the slowness with which the issue of political violence in Peru was confronted. Both these studies are of high quality and importance.

Tomas de tierras en el Perú (García Sayán 1982) provides an assessment of the peasant movement and the transformation of the agrarian sector in Peru during the 1970s. In all of the cases the book describes, there is a perceptible desire of the peasants, and especially of their leaders, to avoid or minimize violence. This same caution is shared by the state and its repressive forces. Flores Galindo noted this prudence in the case of the land takeovers during the 1960s despite the fact that those were more intense mobilizations. In those years, "police and 'invaders' occupied their places and nothing more happened, to the exasperation of the landowners" (Flores Galindo 1988, 61).

García Sayán wrote his book at a time when the land takeovers, which had been the central concern of peasant organizations, had practically ended. In the last pages of the book, he asks the question: "What is coming next?" He then correctly points out several trends that increased in the following years, but he finishes by saying: "The currently existing [and increasing] contradictions *with large capital and the problem of democracy*, always present, seem to be the issues around which the actions of peasants and agricultural workers in general will revolve in the medium term" (García Sayán 1982).

Not one word about political violence. This manuscript was probably finished around 1980, and the text was published in 1982. Thus, here we just have an inaccurate prediction. But several years later, Rodrigo Montoya, in his important book *Lucha por la tierra, reformas agrarias y capitalismo en el Perú del siglo XX*, finished in 1986 and published in 1989, continued using the same parameters employed by García Sayán, although he put more emphasis on the struggle against capital than the struggle for democracy. In the chapter "Where Is the Andean Countryside Heading?" he argues that "the political scenario of class warfare in the countryside includes new enemies: the capitalist market and its political expression in the commercial class and the state as the articulating axis of capital" (1989, 227). But he says almost nothing about peasant violence or the internal armed conflict despite the fact that a bloodbath was taking place in Ayacucho in 1983–84,[16] and Shining Path was already in its phase of "conquering bases" and had extended its activities to other parts of the country beyond Ayacucho. In general, for Montoya, "the armed conflict initiated by Shining Path in 1980 is still in the shadows because little is known about it."

Indigenismo

Anthropology deserves special mention. As in many other countries, in Peruvian social sciences there was still a kind of division of labor in which anthropology, institutionalized as a university discipline after 1946,[17] concentrated on the study of peasants and especially indigenous people.[18] In addition, in Peru, anthropology as a university discipline is a direct heir of the important *indigenista* movement that reached its peak in the first half of the last century.

Indigenismo is a protean term, difficult to define. It implies a way of thinking about what until the middle of the last century were called "interethnic relations" between criollo-mestizos and indigenous peoples. More than a theoretical concept, it expresses anything from a state of mind and a structure of sentiments to a political discourse and stance that nourished the creation of works of art, essays, social research, and public policies. Among the multiple sharp criticisms and definitions of a phenomenon that was an important part of twentieth-century thought, political action, and cultural production in many Latin American countries, there are two characteristics that I consider central. *Indigenismo* is (a) an urban and therefore external vision and (b) a ventriloquistic representation of indigenous people.[19]

These two characteristics are shared by an ample and heterogeneous group of studies, proposals, and cultural products that can be situated inside what Juan Ansión (1994, 72) has called the *indigenista* paradigm, defined as "focusing the discussion around the idea that there is a great social and cultural divide between Indians and criollos or between the Andean world and the Western world. With this as a base, one can suggest very different theories." For Ansión, the *indigenista* paradigm is "a product of colonial society, to the extent that it accepts its terms although it inverts them" (ibid., 76). The paradigm was useful for making indigenous peoples' exclusion and discrimination visible, but it has serious limitations in the current historical context when "the reality that is being described is in a real state of turmoil" (ibid., 75).

Despite its variety, *indigenista* production tended to offer an exotic and essentialist vision of indigenous peoples. It took them out of history as if for them "history had become frozen" or "time had stopped" and proposed their protection or their "redemption" by criollos or mestizos—or else by the proletariat or the middle classes if one understood society in class terms. This "redemption of the Indian" would be achieved through a transformation of the conditions that had caused their supposed degradation: whether through acculturation (achieved primarily through schooling) or through changes in economic conditions achievable through self-sustainable development or the social and political organization of Andean peasants. If an external agent should protect them (or redeem them), it was because *indigenismo* tended frequently to negate the capacity for independent agency of indigenous people and to view them fundamentally as victims. Other *indigenista* approaches did recognize this capacity but viewed it as an agency that was also essentialist, whether inherently "good" or brutally violent. For this reason, in many political party programs, indigenous peoples were always viewed as subordinate allies.

During a long initial period shaped by *indigenismo* and North American and Mexican anthropology, Peruvian anthropology emphasized classic holistic studies of communities and traditional peasant culture. Additionally, influenced by Mexican "applied anthropology" and North American community development approaches, it focused on community development programs. In these studies and programs, nourished by culturalism and functionalism, integration took precedence over conflict. Later, other influences appeared: cultural ecology and substantivism, developed brilliantly for Andean countries by John Murra (1975), the so-called Andean rationality (Golte 1980), and structuralism. What is interesting is that *indigenismo*, converted more into an ideology and accepted wisdom than a theoretical position, could be compatible with all these tendencies. In other words, research rooted in different theoretical currents continued to be formulated within the *indigenista* paradigm, which appeared as a transversal axis underlying all of them to varying degrees.

Not even dependency theory and Marxism were able to shatter this paradigm in the 1970s. In most studies, these new theories transformed peasants and indigenous people mostly into victims of imperialism and the "development of underdevelopment." Dependency theory sought to conceptualize poor rural populations as simultaneously peasants and indigenous people.[20] Even hard-core Marxism (Leninist), which viewed indigenous people as simple poor peasants who were "natural" allies of the proletariat and the revolution, maintained a certain respect for Peruvian Andean culture and indigenous peoples. Thus, in contrast to Bolivia, for example, the majority of Peruvian radical Marxist groups became *campesinistas* and also Maoists.[21] One of the reasons for this was the influence of intellectuals such as José Carlos Mariátegui, who Morse (1982) called a Latin American "meteorite," a seminal figure of Peruvian socialism who dedicated one of his famous *Seven Interpretive Essays on Peruvian Society* to what was then called "The Problem of the Indian" and was labeled a *campesinista* by the Third Stalinist International (Flores Galindo 1980). Later, José María Arguedas also exerted an influence.

Thus, unlike in Bolivia, where the work of the Marxist Left centered on the Central Obrera Boliviana (COB), which had the mining proletariat as its base of support, in Peru, most radical Marxist groups became *campesinistas* as well as Maoists. This is why, in the 1970s, Maoism had an influence, to varying degrees, in the majority of small Leftist groups, in addition to Shining Path.

Levi Straussian structuralism, in turn, turned out to be more adaptable to the essentialization of Andean and also Amazonian peoples. Its emphasis on "simple and elegant models" that were, at the same time, ahistorical, led to the proliferation of studies attempting to prove the existence of a model of Andean (and also Amazonian) thought that had persisted through the centuries, practically without changes.[22]

In other words, in important sectors of the discipline of anthropology, among historians and, to a lesser extent, sociologists, there persisted an idealization of indigenous peoples and, in many cases, also of Andean and

How Social Sciences Failed?

Amazonian culture. The beginning of the genealogy of this idealization can be traced to the *Comentarios reales* written by Inca Garcilaso at the beginning of the seventeenth century (see Flores Galindo 1988). Although another important sector of anthropologists took other roads, incorporating issues such as social movements (Sánchez 1981) or creatively developing the thesis of John Murra (Fonseca and Mayer 1988; Golte 1980), no one was prepared for the outbreak of brutal violence that convulsed the Andes and sucked into its whirlwind these same idealized indigenous peoples, revealing them in their naked condition of human beings in an extreme situation—no one, that is, except a very small nucleus of anthropologists from Huamanga who were members of Sendero's political structure or leadership.[23]

Their views happened to also represent a brutal rupture with prevailing conceptions since they considered *indigenistas* "cry babies," Andean culture in toto as "backward," and Andean social structures as "leftovers of semifeudalism." The destiny of the Andean and Amazonian peoples could thus only be proletarization, whether voluntarily or by force. But the Shining Path social scientists did not eliminate the *indigenista* paradigm, they simply negated it; they "turned the tables," which converted them into a negative of the same image. This is why, among other reasons, they did not anticipate the consequences of their "popular war," which they imagined primarily as a peasant war against the state. In reality, as is argued in some chapters of this book, when the Shining Path initiated its war, it opened a Pandora's Box that it was unable to control. Its inability to admit that independent peasant agency was possible and its blindness to Andean organization and culture was among the principal causes of its defeat.

A "Peasant War" in a Fragmented Country

In contrast to the Southern Cone countries of Latin America where state violence was directed primarily against educated urban sectors and the middle classes, in Peru the majority of victims were poor, rural peasants, primarily indigenous and with little education.

One of the most striking statistics presented in the CVR's *Final Report* was that 75 percent of the fatalities resulting from the armed conflict were native Quechua speakers, while only 16 percent of the Peruvian population had Quechua as their native language according to the 1993 census.[24]

In addition, of the total number of fatalities reported to the CVR, 79 percent lived in rural areas and 56 percent were engaged in agricultural activities. In contrast, the 1993 census indicated that only 29 percent of Peruvians lived in rural zones and 28 percent of the economically active population was engaged in agriculture. Finally, in 1993, only 40 percent of the Peruvian population had not finished high school, whereas 68 percent of those who died in the armed conflict were not high school graduates.

Forty percent of the dead and disappeared were from the Department of Ayacucho, the region where Sendero was born and from which it launched its "popular war."[25] If the ratio of victims to the population of Ayacucho were extended to the whole country, the violence would have resulted in 1,200,000 dead and disappeared. Of these, 340,000 would have been from Lima.

This geography of violence and fragmentation, which was sociocultural as well as physical, was the most surprising discovery from the CVR's work. Until 2003, it was believed that the internal armed conflict had caused about 25,000 fatalities—30,000 in the worst of cases. When the CVR made public its projection that the total number of victims was around 69,000, this figure caused astonishment and led to a fierce polemic.[26] This tragic discrepancy between the real and imagined figures shows that not even the social science disciplines can transcend the fragmentation of the country and, in some cases, even contribute to reproducing them.

Thus, the great demographic changes in Peru, the rapid rise of social movements from 1950 to 1970, and the democratic transition (1977–80) led to research in hegemonic centers of knowledge production that was heavily oriented toward urban space and social movements, precisely at the time when Shining Path began its adventure in the rural zones that were not only the most isolated but—another surprise—those with the least development of new social organizations.[27] While Shining Path proclaimed a "peasant war," its actions did not start in any of the regions where peasant organization was the strongest, such as Cusco or Cajamarca (see map 1). To the contrary, Shining Path had serious difficulties gaining a foothold in those areas. Ayacucho, on the other hand, had few organizations and peasant mobilizations before 1980.

Later, throughout the 1980s, as internal armed conflict spread across the country, Peruvian social scientists increasingly turned their attention to the political scene, but they focused on issues of democratic transition—which at that time was a recurrent theme in Latin American political science—and modernity and citizenship. Thus, the social sciences concentrated on spaces that were more economically and politically integrated into the country, relegating to second place the peripheral areas from which Shining Path was eroding the "old state" and where that state launched a fierce counteroffensive starting in 1983.

While this was happening primarily in Lima, research studies became more and more rare in universities located in regions declared in a state of

How Social Sciences Failed?

emergency in the 1980s and subjected to the authority of Political Military Commands.[28] In the case of anthropology, the discipline retreated into folkloric studies, but not of the type that were renewing that area of study at the time, such as García Canclini's (1990) concept of "hybrid cultures." Rather, they returned to monographs on customs, festivals, and traditions in the style of works from the 1950s. Generally speaking, the armed conflict contributed in a much more notorious fashion to the academic ruin of national universities in these regions, and especially the University of San Cristóbal of Huamanga in Ayacucho, than did the cuts in government funding or the subsequent measures to privatize education.[29]

As a result, a large and important sector was split off from the social sciences academic community that developed during 1940–70. These were the social scientists who worked in areas declared in a state of emergency as well as more generally in the provinces.[30] The rest, located in Lima and more integrated parts of the country, were divided by contrasting visions about the armed conflict, all of which were nonetheless informed by the *indigenista* paradigm to some degree. Some remained trapped by the vision of the "good savage" who was the victim of the two opposing forces and incapable of exercising any type of violence that was not within the framework of ritual cultural norms, even in extreme situations (Ossio and Fuenzalida 1983; Ossio and Montoya 1983).

The other social scientists were too immersed in what could be called an "expansive" approach with an evolutionist undercurrent that was optimistic about the country's future. During the 1970s and 1980s, they concentrated their attention successively on the following issues: the consolidation of a class structure, revolutionary change, the national problem, "popular protagonism," new social movements, modernity, and especially so-called popular modernity, democracy, and citizenship. For an important sector of social scientists, this thematic journey also marked the transition from radical to social democratic positions although two of the three greatest publishing successes in the social and related sciences in the 1980s were also situated within this vision: *The Other Path* by Hernando de Soto (1986) and *Desborde popular y crisis del estado* by José Matos Mar (1984).[31] Several texts that were less widely circulated but of better theoretical quality, such as Franco (1991) or Nugent (1992), also fall into this category.

On the other hand, those who warned about the dangers of too optimistic an approach to the Peruvian situation tended to go to the other extreme. Thus, the spawning of violence led to the (re)emergence of a vision in which Peru was essentially and especially violent. Studies that combined anthropological and historical approaches as well as a novel utilization of psychoanalysis also could not escape another type of essentialism: a kind of structural fatalism that viewed the country as almost irredeemably trapped among colonial nightmares and ghosts with its face disfigured by contemporary "scars of poverty."[32] Among those who proposed the most extreme interpretations of this sort was the distinguished historian Pablo Macera (1986), who pitched historical probes that, crossing the millennia, wove together the ferocious jagged vaginas of Chavín sculptures (ca. 1000 BC); Mama Huaco, the warrior wife of one of the mythical founders of the Inca empire; Micaela Bastidas, wife of Túpac Amaru II, the great Quechua rebel of the eighteenth century; and the young Shining Path militant Edith Lagos, assassinated in 1982. With Peruvians thus overwhelmed by the weight of such an ancient tradition, the future invariably belonged to Shining Path and the armed forces. With different variations and nuances, this essentialized image of Peru also transcended the walls of academia; fed by the economic crisis and the unfulfilled promises of political democracy, it helped contribute to a paralysis that threatened to lead to a self-fulfilling prophecy.

Emotional Distance, Postcolonial Structure

The violence in Peru took place principally in areas of Peru that were emotionally as well as geographically remote from Lima, the principal center of academic production. This emotional remoteness may have contributed to the underestimation of the phenomenon and a certain indifference to the issue and the conflict itself. We academics cannot entirely escape blame for this indifference, which the CVR indicated was civil society's primary responsibility. Academics and intellectuals remained primarily within the "learned city" (Rama 1984), studying and debating about popular modernity, informality, "the other path," the opposition between populism and neoliberalism; or we lamented being a country that was violent by nature while the "barbarians," to extend Rama's metaphor, besieged the city walls.

Nevertheless, it is essential to add two caveats to the previous assertion. One is an extenuating circumstance of the Peruvian academic community's underestimation of the Shining Path phenomenon. The other can help provide a more complex view of the concept of the "learned city" that has been used so much recently. The extenuating circumstance: the processes that we preferred to study in the 1980s were very real and very important. The studies about urban organizations or the so-called popular modernity were not an expression of the capriciousness of an elite that was ignoring the nation but rather an interest in real and massive processes that were taking place during those years. But

How Social Sciences Failed?

these studies did not provide a complete understanding of the kaleidoscopic reality in which directly opposed tendencies coexisted. In the words of Manrique (2002, 65): the strongest guerrilla movement in South America, the strongest legal Left, and the most important reformist party on the continent (APRA) were in power. This was possible because of the "the high level of disarticulation of Peruvian society."

On the other hand, our learned city was (and continues to be) highly stratified and fractured along the lines of class, region, gender, generation, and culture. These fissures deepened during the urbanization process, which was at the same time a process of centralization of population, wealth, and cultural production in Lima.[33] Shining Path turned the struggle within the intellectual arena violent. It is critical to understand Sendero as an intellectual and educational program as well as a political-military project. As the work collected in this book underscores, no other armed movement in Latin America gave such importance to the intellectual component of their project and to the status as an intellectual of its top leader, *Doctor* Abimael Guzmán, glorified in posters and paintings with all the attributes of an intellectual: glasses, a suit, and a book under his arm. Mestizo intellectuals primarily from national universities and medium-sized cities in the Andes,[34] who made up a large part of Sendero's leadership, not only demanded all the political power but also all intellectual legitimacy in an exclusionary manner. The rest of us were "prescientific" and/ or sinister agents of the "old state." Thus, it can be said that a dissident sector, learned in a classic, almost Weberian sense of the word (*literati*), headed by a "philosopher king" sought to ally itself with "the barbarians," not in order to destroy the learned city but to take power within it in order to even more forcefully enforce the distinction between the learned (scientists) and the barbarians ("masses").[35]

If this is the case:

(a) It was not accidental that the choice topics for study were: popular modernity, "the other path" or citizenship, the process of *cholificación* or hybrid cultures.[36]

(b) Overcoming the insufficiencies and blind spots of this "optimistic" approach implied coming closer to the dark side of Peruvian modernity by emphasizing the colonial heritage and the persistence of elements such as the Andean utopia, as well as studying issues that had been neglected or completely left aside, such as:

(1) "Unfinished modernization projects and policies that, at the same time that they weakened traditional relations and life conditions of large sectors of the population, were not quite able to produce new conditions of integration and development."[37]

(2) The crises of the medium-sized and small cities where Sendero recruited much of its cadres; this space was totally neglected since research concentrated on Lima or on rural areas and indigenous people.

(3) The pre-existing level of conflicts among peasants and indigenous communities, a subject that was almost prohibited within the *indigenista* paradigm[38] but was indispensable for understanding the violence endemic in the countryside at the time.

(4) The deterioration of public education, where Shining Path had its roots, and the transformations and frustrations of school teachers and their union, the SUTEP (Unitary Union of Education Workers of Peru), which have not been researched to date.

(5) The role of regional and local intellectuals from whose ranks Shining Path drew its leadership and intermediate cadres.

(6) Youth, and especially, the transformations and frustrations of new generations of educated people from the provinces that formed the main breeding ground for Shining Path.

(7) The links between gender and politics, since Shining Path recruited a significant number of young and educated women.

Finally, returning to the issue of indifference, Félix Reátegui (2004), in a very thought-provoking paper, suggests that racism was not only evident in the actual acts of violence or in the discourse that preceded or accompanied them,[39] but that it also affected the military strategies of both sides in the conflict. I would add that this same racism also could have influenced the silences and the front pages of the media, the priorities of political parties, and even the academic agendas of the time, whether because of their ignorance regarding this issue or because of the way it was approached. One exception is Flores Galindo and Manrique (1985), who referred to racism very early on and in a very noteworthy manner.

This hypothesis requires a detailed analysis due to the complexity of the Peruvian "racial formation," where "a cultural definition of race" (de la Cadena 2004, 40) predominates in which education, especially on the college level, is one of the principal legitimators of hierarchies and discrimination.[40]

Very Concrete Difficulties and Fears

Starting in January 1983, after the massacre of eight journalists and a guide in the Ayacucho community of Uchuraccay, the Political Military Command of Ayacucho cut off access to the countryside for outsiders. It became very difficult to travel—and even more so, to carry out research—in the rural areas of Ayacucho and later in all the zones that were declared in states of emergency.

To these difficulties was added fear, not only of possible repression from agents of the government but also of possible attacks by Shining Path. In contrast to other Latin American guerilla groups and even MRTA, Sendero was extremely secretive.[41] Until 1986, the year it took control of the Lima daily *El Diario*, it did not always claim responsibility for its attacks except in flyers or its own press, published in mimeograph form and almost always only circulated internally.

For all these reasons, especially during the first years of the conflict, the production of most of the information and knowledge about the internal armed conflict fell to journalists, and most of all to those who lived and worked in the areas declared in states of emergency.[42] This is another area in which the Peruvian paradox mirrored the ruptures that traversed the country. On the one hand, again in contrast to the Southern Cone and Central America, a large part of the internal armed conflict (1980–92) took place under democratic governments and with a constitution that guaranteed broad freedom of expression—so much so that, as previously noted, in 1986–88 Shining Path published an unofficial publication that was sold in kiosks in Lima and other cities with newspapers and magazines. On the other hand, this freedom was de facto restricted, and drastically so in the areas declared in states of emergency. But even so, journalists played an important role discovering what was occurring. Some paid with their lives.[43]

Nevertheless, throughout the 1980s, a corpus of essays and academic studies was produced about the process of violence and Shining Path, which will be discussed in the next section.

"Senderology": The Subfield of Shining Path Studies

In contrast to Guatemala, where the conflict took place primarily under bloody dictatorships, or the Southern Cone during the 1970s and part of the 1980s where even teaching social sciences and psychology was directly affected and limited, in Peru, despite the previously mentioned limitations, it was possible to carry out many types of research. In addition to journalistic investigations, essays were published, human rights violations were reported, there were three congressional investigations (Senado de la República del Perú 1988, 1990, 1992), and a nongovernmental organization (NGO),

DESCO (Centro de Estudios y Promoción del Desarrollo), worked on a database of incidents of political violence that turned out to be very useful.[44]

Thus, academic research about the armed conflict started to create an embryonic "field of study." If we apply Bourdieu's (1999) strict definition, this concept was not quite applicable because of (a) the small number of researchers involved[45]; (b) the heterogeneity, permeability, and instability of this group; (c) the indistinct boundaries between journalism, essays, and academic research; and (d) the lack of debates within what we could, in any case, call a "sub-field." Nevertheless, toward the end of the 1980s, the press coined the term "senderólogos" (senderologists) to refer to social science researchers and opinion journalists who dealt with the subject. Due to the fact that most were critical of the behavior of the armed forces and other state agents, "senderólogo" was used as derogatory epithet, especially starting in 1990, during the Fujimori government. We were accused of talking about subjects we knew nothing about since the armed forces and the intelligence services supposedly had a monopoly on knowledge of the issue. We were "salon" or "café experts." Thus, as "senderólogos," we entered into the demonology of the regime together with human rights groups and the sparse independent press that survived into the 1990s.

The following section is a very short review of the social science literature on this issue. The discussion is centered on the internal armed conflict and especially on Shining Path. Only works published after 1980 and that concentrate on rural areas are included. This is not an exhaustive discussion.[46]

Violence in the Andes: Pachakuti or Chaqwa?

"Missing the Revolution" is the title of a caustic and controversial article by Orin Starn (1991a) in which he criticizes North American anthropologists for not having warned about the gestation of Shining Path violence in the countryside of Ayacucho during the 1970s.[47] This is not the place to assess the achievements and limitations of North American cultural anthropology. Rather, I would like to stress that the outbreak of the Shining Path war and its rapid expansion throughout the Ayacucho countryside during the first years of the conflict happened under the noses not only of North American anthropologists but also of Peruvian social scientists in general. In the following years, blackouts and small explosive devices seem to have blinded and deafened us, inhibiting us from the analysis of this very important phenomenon. So much so that the first analyses were carried out by foreign scholars (McClintock 1983, 1984; Palmer 1986; Taylor 1983; Anderson 1983; Favre 1984; Werlich 1984),[48] while we Peruvians limited ourselves to journalistic articles.[49]

The first incursion of Peruvian social scientists into war scenarios was unfortunate. It happened as a result of the massacre of eight journalists in the community of Uchuraccay in Ayacucho, an event that because of its emblematic character, because of the way that its handling demonstrated the continued acceptance of the *indigenista* paradigm, and because of its repercussions in the social sciences in Peru, merits a section on its own.

Uchuraccay

On 23 January 1983, the national press published the news of the deaths of an undetermined number of Shining Path members in Huaychao, a community on the high plateaus of Huanta, Ayacucho.[50] Just three weeks earlier, the armed forces had taken on responsibility for counter-subversive activities in Ayacucho and had initiated a counteroffensive that already appeared to involve indiscriminate attacks. Who, then, had assassinated the Senderistas in Huaychao: the peasants, as the official version claimed, or the military? A group of eight journalists from several media outlets in Lima and Ayacucho traveled to the area to find out what had happened, but on 26 January, they and their guide were assassinated in a horrendous manner in Uchuraccay, a community near Huaychao.

The national impact of the multiple assassinations led the government to name an investigative commission presided over by the famous author Mario Vargas Llosa. The commission included three well-known anthropologists, a psychoanalyst, a jurist, and two linguists. As Fernando Fuenzalida explained later (Ossio and Fuenzalida 1983, 6), the anthropologists agreed to take part because of a moral and professional commitment since this event "had occurred in an indigenous community and not somewhere else." Nevertheless, their presence gave professional backing to a very debatable set of conclusions.

Twenty years after the massacre, the CVR's *Final Report* recognized that in spite of limitations in the collection of testimonies,[51] the Vargas Llosa Report (IVL) did a credible job in describing the context in which the massacre took place: the tension and the generalized political violence in this zone resulting from the open conflict between the communities and Sendero militants. At the same time, the IVL accurately reconstructed the events that occurred from the time the journalists began to prepare for their journey until the tragedy occurred and concluded with "absolute certainty" that "the assassination of the journalists was the work of the Uchuraccay community members . . . without, at the time the killings occurred, the participation of the forces of order" (Vargas Llosa et al. 1983, 19).

The silence of the community members about how the massacre was carried out impeded the commission from establishing the details of what happened on 26 January, which is why the report presumed with "relative conviction" that the journalists "must have been attacked suddenly, massively, and without a previous dialogue" (Vargas Llosa et al. 1983, 15).[52] Later, the discovery of photographs taken by one of the journalists demonstrated that this presumption was incorrect.[53] For diverse sectors of public opinion, this discredited the whole report despite the fact that it went on to say that "the possibility cannot be ruled out that this effort to dialogue did take place and was not effective due to an excess of suspicions, panic, and fury on the part of the community members or some indiscretion or error during the conversation on the part of the journalists that aggravated the misunderstanding instead of dispelling it" (ibid.).

Although it was denied that members of the forces of order were present on 26 January in Uchuraccay, the IVL noted that the peasants were encouraged to use violence by the Sinchis who had visited the communities in the area a few days earlier.[54] The IVL determined that "an important and maybe decisive factor" in how the incident ended "was the certainty of the community members that they had authorization from the authorities, represented by the Sinchis, to act in this way" (Vargas Llosa et al. 1983, 20). Nevertheless, the commission concluded that this incitement was not systematic and was not part of a policy implemented by the Political Military Command, thus ruling out any responsibility on the part of military high commanders.

Nevertheless, the IVL provided an extremely controversial interpretation of the events investigated that had significant consequences in the context of the armed internal conflict of those years. The massacre was presented as the result of a misunderstanding created by the cultural differences that existed between Quechua peasants and urban Peru. In an interview published during the same time that the IVL report was submitted, Vargas Llosa spoke about Uchuraccay as part of a world that was completely different from the rest of the country, frozen in time, "backward and violent," with people who lived "still like in Pre-Hispanic times" (Vargas Llosa 1983). According to this vision, the cultural distance between the "two Perus," also understood as a historical distance, is formulated as the great national problem:

> That there is a real country completely separate from the official country is, of course, a great Peruvian problem. That, at the same time, there are people in this country who participate in the twentieth century and people like the community members of Uchuraccay and all the Iquicha communities who live in the nineteenth century, if not the seventeenth century. This enormous distance that exists between the two Perus is behind the tragedy that we investigated. (Vargas Llosa et al. 1983)

The emphasis on absolute cultural differentiation also informed the interpretations developed by the anthropologists advising the commission, who sought the key to the events they were analyzing in the magical-religious background to the massacre. The style of execution—with blows concentrated on the eyes and especially the mouth—as well as the form of burial—outside the cemetery, with two bodies in each grave, half-naked and face down—would indicate that the journalists were seen as "devils" or "beings who had made a pact with evil" (Vargas Llosa et al. 1983, 37) because they were buried "according to rituals intended for the 'unbaptized' or 'non-Christians' or 'antichrists'" (Ossio and Fuenzalida 1983, 64).

In addition, the IVL stated that an important factor in explaining the event was that the communities in the highland plateau of Huanta belong to the "Iquicha" ethnic group or "Iquichanos," supposedly heirs of a history that went back to pre-Hispanic times characterized by "long periods of almost total isolation and by their violent and out of control actions" (Vargas Llosa et al. 1983, 38). According to the report, the "Iquicha tradition" has an "atavistic attitude," characterized by rejection of external influences and the sporadic use of violence against outsiders: "The jealous preservation of their own jurisdiction, which, whenever they perceive it to be violated, pulls them out of their relatively peaceful and reclusive lives and leads them to fight with braveness and ferocity, is a constant in the Iquicha tradition and is the reason for this bellicose and indomitable personality that people at lower altitudes, especially in the cities, attribute to them" (ibid., 39)

However, the "Iquicha ethnicity" did not exist before the nineteenth century and was, instead, a creation of regional Ayacucho elites interested in marking a difference between themselves and indigenous peasant shepherds of the punas (high mountains).[55]

In accordance with this image of the extreme traditionalism of Uchuraccay, the report also constructed a legal otherness. The legal advisor of the commission stated that "the high altitude communities do not have a clear awareness of the Peruvian state; rather, they intensively experience their own ethnic identity, constituting true nationalities inside the nation" (de Trazegnies 1983, 152). Nevertheless, both the investigations of del Pino Huamán (2003) as well as those of the CVR make it possible to affirm that the people of Uchuraccay were always conscious of the existence of a national judicial system and its security organs. Thus, from October 1982 and until the very day of the massacre, they went at different times to the Civil Guard asking to be protected and for order to be reestablished, given the increasing presence of Shining Path cadres in the area.

On the other hand, the communal judicial system became invisible in the IVL in spite of the fact that in their testimony, the peasants themselves described the behavior of their lieutenant governors, presidents, *varayocs*, and other community authorities.[56] They went from peaceful rejection of Shining Path in October 1982 to its violent expulsion in December of that year, when the traditional authorities led an intercommunal rebellion against Sendero.

Despite this, the IVL came to the conclusion that the peasants resolved their conflicts guided by an almost natural survival instinct, practically without any kind of norms, and considered that in the midst of violence, they "believe, as a result of their tradition, their culture, the conditions in which they live, their daily activities, that in this struggle for survival anything goes and one should kill first or die" (Vargas Llosa et al. 1983, 33). The cultural distance of the people of Uchuraccay, in addition, put in doubt their condition as citizens and subjects of law: "Is it possible to make these legal distinctions, clearly and precisely established in our constitution and our laws, in relation to people who live in conditions of primitiveness, isolation and abandonment in Uchuraccay?" (ibid., 34). However, in the days before the massacre of the journalists, the Sinchis, the head of the Political Military Command of Ayacucho, and the president of Peru himself, who had no doubts about the obligation "to make clear and precise legal distinctions established in our constitution and our laws," praised the assassination of presumed members of Shining Path in Huaychao and encouraged the *comuneros* in the highlands of Huanta to take justice into their own hands.

In addition, in 1983, Uchuraccay was far from the image of a place frozen in time and unchanging that was presented in the IVL. The community had had a small school since 1959 that was financed by all its members and included the first grades of elementary school. It also had two small stores that sold basic foodstuffs: salt, sugar, noodles, canned goods. Two *comuneros* worked selling clothes; another sold electrical appliances, such as radios and sewing machines, which he brought from Lima and Huancayo. Others bought and sold livestock. The people of Uchuraccay had a long tradition of migration. Almost all the men had gone to do seasonal work in the valley of the Apurímac River, in the lowlands of Ayacucho, to harvest coca, cocoa, and coffee. Some families had already bought land in this valley. In addition, since the 1960s, some residents had been moving to Lima. Thus, while the people from Uchuraccay participated in the local market, migrated, and dreamed of "progress" although they lived in conditions of extreme poverty, the IVL thought that for them, "the whole idea of personal improvement or progress must be hard to conceive" (Vargas Llosa et al. 1983, 36).

How Social Sciences Failed?

The interpretations presented by the Vargas Llosa Commission dramatically illustrated the limitations of the so-called *indigenista* paradigm.[57] But in 1983, this reasoning was widespread within public opinion and the intelligentsia. Even the media and the judges who were later charged with trying the cases of the seventeen Uchuraccay community members responsible for the massacre reproduced this vision and sought explanations in the cultural differences between the Quechua peasants and the rest of the country as the fundamental cause of the tragedy.[58]

Indeed, within the *indigenista* paradigm itself, interpretations of the tragedy that differed from those of the IVL were suggested. The cultural and magical-religious aspects of the massacre that were presented in the report were also the theme of arguments employed by those who criticized its conclusions: the peasants could not have carried out the massacre because in the Andean world the dead are not buried half-clothed nor in pairs nor in shallow graves.[59] These essentialist interpretations did not take into account that the armed conflict was spreading rapidly, pushing many peasants into extreme situations and altering the cultural patterns of normal times. The CVR collected many testimonies that described acts of inconceivable violence committed by Quechua peasants in different parts of the country.[60]

It should be remembered that in 1983, this slaughter was just beginning. When the journalists were killed, very little was known about Shining Path. Significant sectors of public opinion, especially from the Left and Center-Left, viewed it as a guerrilla group that was misguided but motivated by the desire for the social transformation of the country. On the other hand, from the time that Ayacucho was declared in a state of emergency in 1981, there were more and more criticisms of the police forces and, especially, about abuses and mistreatment committed by the Sinchis.[61] In this context of Sendero's relative urban legitimacy and growing criticism of the police, the government ordered the armed forces to take over countersubversive activities. The massacre of the journalists, which occurred less than a month after the Political Military Command was installed in Ayacucho, galvanized public opinion, diminished confidence in the government and polarized the country.

Impressively, the resilience of the *indigenista* paradigm is evidenced by the fact that the same arguments continue to be employed 20 years later[62] and that the CVR's report about Uchuraccay (the product of meticulous fieldwork[63]) is the part of the report that has received the most criticism—criticism that came from within this paradigm and was not accompanied by additional evidence.

However, in Uchuraccay, Sendero's Maoism also had to confront the serious limitations of its interpretation of Peruvian society and of peasants for the first time. Because, to the surprise of many, it turned out that already in 1982 some communities had decided to rebel against what they considered the oppression of the "new power" of Shining Path. Because these were poor peasants who lived in a zone where, until the 1970s, there had been large "semifeudal" estates, Shining Path was convinced that they would be their most faithful allies. In addition, anthropologist Osmán Morote, one of Sendero's top leaders, had worked on his undergraduate degree (*licenciatura*) thesis in an Iquicha community, Chaca, located near Huaychao and Uchuraccay (Morote 1971). Thus, since they were incapable of learning from practice, it is not surprising *given what we now know* that during the following months, Shining Path carried out several punitive actions against Uchuraccay, assassinating dozens of *comuneros* who refused to put themselves on the side of the "laws of history," which the party supposedly interpreted.[64]

Millenarianism

The Uchuraccay events as well as the type of war that was developing in the Peruvian Andes provided abundant raw material for a kind of fascination with millenarianism that the emergence of Shining Path inspired in both foreigners and Peruvians, conservatives and radicals. This fascination, which reached its peak in the 1980s, even affected authors who had had nothing to do with the culturalist tradition in anthropology.

Thus, among the foreigners, McClintock (1984, 51) believed that Shining Path had been "incorporating symbols of the Inca insurrectional tradition in its viewpoint." According to Palmer (1986, 87), "in its plan for Peruvian society after achieving victory, [Sendero] resembles the indigenous millenarian movements and, especially, the precepts of a primitive and purely indigenous communism of José Carlos Mariátegui." Taylor (1983) took the destruction of Allpachaka, an experimental cattle farm belonging to the University of Huamanga, which took place in 1982, as an example of millenarianism and attributed it to Shining Path statements such as "the whites must be killed and the cities that have always exploited us destroyed" or "we need a government of Indians," without indicating the sources. Werlich committed a very serious error when, seeking millenarian components in Shining Path, he affirmed that "in 1970 Abimael Guzmán was expelled from Bandera Roja, accused of 'occultism,' or using local customs and messianic traditions to obtain support among the peasantry" (1984, 78–82, 90). He did not consider that in the Marxist-Leninist tradition, the term "occultism" refers to the refusal or incapacity of the party to carry out open or legal work, concentrating instead on secret ("occult") activities. This was the meaning of the criticism that was made at the time against Guzmán's group.

How Social Sciences Failed?

Among Peruvians, Ansión (1982) made a brief incursion into the subject of Andean messianism in relation to Shining Path. He rapidly retreated, but other authors from different disciplines and theoretical approaches persisted in the same kind of approach to the phenomenon of violence. The most important was Alberto Flores Galindo, who suggested in his significant book *Buscando un Inca* (*In Search of an Inca*, 1988) that Sendero was "a nightmarish version of the Andean utopia,"[65] to the extent that its symbolism and its practice aimed at an "inversion of the world." Because he emphasized the link between Shining Path and the Andean utopia, Flores Galindo committed empirical errors and relapsed into an opposition between tradition and modernity that anthropology had overcome a long time ago. Thus, to explain the initial support of Shining Path by peasants in Ayacucho, Flores Galindo argued that "the Ayacucho region had been hit by a series of earthquakes. Some believed that the *pachamama* [mother earth] could not stand more suffering on earth, that the world had to change. Entire villages hoisted red flags and became "shining," ready to march to Huamanga and Lima, not to ask for alms but to throw out the exploiters and create a new order" (1988, 333).

Later field studies provided a much more complex and nuanced version of these first encounters between Shining Path and peasants. Sendero offered an authoritarian order and dealt militarily with concrete problems of poor peasants, whose inclination to support Shining Path in many cases had to do with much more pragmatic criteria than the foundation of a new order and was rarely unanimous. On the other hand, Flores Galindo pointed out that there were limitations to Sendero's advance:

> All communities were not like Chuschi.[66] The rejection of progress and Western civilization can be compatible with backward villages in which reciprocity persists, governed by the *wamanis* and ritual experts, but it is not necessarily the case among *comuneros* who, like those of Huayopampa (Chancay), Muquiyauyo (Jauja) or Puquio (Lucanas), had access to modernity and had opted for the Western school, electricity, the road and the truck; for them, progress could be a palpable reality and power an illusion. They have something to preserve. (1988, 333)[67]

But Chuschi did not reject "progress and Western civilization" and had also "opted" for the school, the road and the truck (Isbell 1978), nor did it unanimously and enthusiastically embrace Shining Path. In addition, by 1967, a monograph on Huayopampa (Fuenzalida, Villarán, Golte, and Valiente 1967) was specifically titled *Estructuras tradicionales y economía del mercado* (Traditional structures and the market economy) in order to emphasize that modernity did not necessarily obliterate tradition. At least in Huayopampa—and other studies demonstrated that this was not an isolated case—re-created traditional Andean reciprocity continued to exist and communal institutions were not necessarily weakened by the incursion of the community into the market.

It turned out that "millenarian" interpretations were not based on solid empirical evidence. Except for Ansión's work on Shining Path symbolism, the majority were essays or just isolated affirmations included in articles on other issues. Their broad diffusion thus can be explained, at least in part, by the way in which many of us intellectuals still viewed the Andean world. Assigning a millenarian character to an armed movement assumed that it was indigenous in character or that there was significant indigenous participation. Just as Said coined the term "Orientalism" to refer to the essentialization of Arabs, Starn (1991a) used "Andeanism" to describe a similar phenomenon in relation to indigenous people and/or "the Andean."

In spite of the empirical evidence that was accumulating as the 1980s unfolded, some continued to define Shining Path as a messianic movement throughout the conflict, though now without the painful and agonizing search for a radical alternative notable in the work of Flores Galindo.[68] Nevertheless, in the 1980s, Shining Path did not "invert" the world but did uncover a hornet's nest. It does not represent the *pachakuti*, the inversion of the world that would occur every five hundred years according to the pre-Hispanic conception of time, but rather the *chaqwa*, a Quechua concept that signifies a state of chaos or confusion, extreme times during which it is not possible to know for certain who is who (Ossio and Fuenzalida 1983, 77), a loss of identity and of a sense of localization, a literal dismantling of the order of things (Kirk 1991, 9).

Laying Siege to an Opaque and Elusive Object of Study

Beginning in 1984, the first studies appeared that tried to answer three central questions: What were the historical and structural conditions that made the emergence of Shining Path possible? What was the sociocultural profile of Shining Path cadres? And how did Sendero construct a social base in the countryside?

For example, Alberto Flores Galindo and Nelson Manrique published *Violencia y campesinado* (Violence and the peasantry, 1985) with articles criticizing the "dirty war" taking place in Ayacucho since 1983. In their discussion of the causes and consequences of this type of war, they opened up various avenues of inquiry that were later heavily traveled. Manrique emphasized structural violence as a causal factor. And both he and Flores Galindo high-lighted political authoritarianism, ethnic upheavals, and racism that erupted powerfully as a result of the Uchuraccay massacre. At the time, and still to this day, including racism as one of the central causes of the violence went against the current.

In terms of consequences, both analysts pointed to forced migration. This was the beginning of displacement and the problem of internal refugees.[69] Finally, Flores Galindo points out that at the end of 1984, the war had become "an assault of the Western part of Peru against its Andean side" (Flores Galindo and Manrique 1985, 31). What he forgets to point out is that "both parties to the conflict" are ideologically within the "Western side" and that both spurn the Andean side. But in both articles, the silence, pregnant with ambiguity, about the actions of Shining Path is noteworthy, since by that time those actions were susceptible to analysis. Flores Galindo broke the silence in *Buscando un Inca*, where he stressed Sendero's nightmarish quality as well as its authoritarian character. But by emphatically separating the Andean world from the Western world and by placing Shining Path on the "Andean side," he commits a serious blunder. The utopias, the millenarianism and the messianism, he says, are incapable of overcoming an unjust order, and he adds, on the last page of the book: "Another outcome could become possible if modern socialism with its capacity to organize, produce strategic programs and act in the short term within the political context were added to the millenarian mystique. In other words, if passion is amalgamated with Marxism and its capacity for reasoning" (1988, 368).

But throughout the book, Flores Galindo had been treating "the millenarian mystique" of the Andean utopia as the backbone of Andean culture. That's why his final proposal is for the Andean world to contribute its passion and for Marxism (a product of the "West") to contribute reason. In this final phrase, the Indian continues to be this Other who inspired affection in some *mistis* and fear in others (1988, 239).[70]

Around 1984, various works had begun to employ other perspectives to analyze the historical and sociocultural context of the violence. The earliest were Henri Favre's article on "obscure horizons," in "Perú: Sendero Luminoso y horizontes oscuros" (1984); my study of violent mis-encounters, *Sendero Luminoso: Los hondos y mortales desencuentros* (1985); and the work of Aya-cucho anthropologist Manuel Granados (1987), which dealt with an issue crucial to understanding Shining Path: its ideology.[71] The first two texts included ethnic analyses but went against the grain of the prevailing culturalist and/or *indigenista* explanations and tended to situate Shining Path within the indigenous sphere of ethnic stratification.

According to Favre, the deterioration in Andean society and the country in general led to a new breach between the integrated and the nonintegrated that was much more important than the traditional opposition between classes. This thrombosis that clogged the channels for social mobility was the source of profound frustrations, fueling Shining Path violence (1984, 34). But, Favre notes, Sendero's principal potential social base in the countryside was the rural population of people who were no longer peasants and were de-Indianized while the more Indian and more peasant populations seemed less susceptible to Shining Path influences (ibid., 32). Later works proved that these hypotheses were on the mark.

Favre and Degregori denied that the Shining Path had an Indian, millenar-ist, and/or *indigenista* character. But both studies include very little analysis of peasant participation in the war. Along with this issue, an analysis of the structures and social actors in rural areas were explored in a set of case studies that appeared subsequently. These efforts also instigated analysis of local and regional differences in Shining Path activities and in peasant responses. The first such study was published in 1986—an article by Ronald Berg about Shining Path and peasants in Pacucha, Apurímac. Berg carried out fieldwork in Pacucha in 1981 and 1982 and was later able to return in 1985, which was very rare at the time.

Shining Path appeared in the area at a time when the contradiction between communities and haciendas that had mobilized peasants in the 1970s was replaced by peasant conflicts with cooperatives created by the agrarian reform and with merchants as the community economies deteriorated. In those years, resentment against the state ran high because instead of dividing up and distributing the land of the great estates, the government had created cooperatives that only benefited a minority and were plagued with administra-tive problems. Sendero also exploited resentment against the most important merchants, who were accused of hoarding lands and not participating in tradi-tional Andean reciprocity, of "behaving like *mistis*" (Berg 1986, 188). Because of this, Shining Path was able to gain some sympathy among the peasants.

Berg distinguishes between sympathy, passive support, and active support. The peasants' attitudes usually fluctuated between sympathy and passive support. The sympathy included a large component of vengeance against "the rich," who ignored the norms of Andean reciprocity. However, the objectives of the peasants differed from Sendero's, and these differences quickly came to light, especially when Shining Path executed people thought to be treasonous, which led some locals to say, "I have nothing against their killing rich people, but I don't like it when they kill peasants" (Berg 1986, 186). Nevertheless, the indiscriminate repression by the armed forces and police kept the sympathy for Shining Path alive until Berg's second visit, without turning into massive active support.

In a study about peasant responses to Shining Path, Isbell (1988) found the same historic opposition to the state and local powers in Chuschi, which was even expressed in the ritual sphere.[72] Also in Chuschi, the merchants who benefited from the Velasco regime reforms were outsiders or former community members who were in the process of losing their identities, both class and ethnic, and turning into mestizos (*mistis*).

The conclusions of these studies were confirmed years later by the CVR's research, which found that Shining Path took advantage of the micro-differentiations in local rural societies "both in access to resources [and] links to the mechanisms of local power. Into the conflicts of this new inequality (which were probably undetectable to an outside observer, for whom both a rich and a poor person would be in the lowest quintile of income distribution) . . . Sendero inserted its discourse and practice" (CVR 2003, vol. 1, chap. 2, 110).

Similar strategies of using microdifferentiations also have been observed in the case of the spread of the Khmer Rouge in Cambodia (Hinojosa 1992; Kiernan 1985). Additionally, these studies support some of my early hypotheses about Shining Path as a dispenser of justice that punishes the *mistis* not to destroy the old hierarchical dichotomy (*misti*/Indian) but to occupy a place similar to that which was previously occupied by the mistis.

In 1989, two new regional analyses appeared: one by Nelson Manrique about the central Andes and the other by José Luis Rénique about Puno (see map 1).[73] In both areas, the peasants were confronting associative forms of organizations that emerged from the agrarian reform, especially the Agricultural Societies of Social Interest (Sociedades Agrícolas de Interés Social, SAIS), a property and management structure for the former large estates, which was even more complicated than the cooperatives.[74] However, whereas in Puno a "peasant bloc" led by the Departmental Federation of Peasants (Federación Departamental de Campesinos) affiliated with the CCP was able to lead the struggle against the SAIS with a proposal for "democratic restructuring," in the highlands of Junín Shining Path blocked this same proposal, using force to impose its plan to destroy the SAIS. After distributing the equipment and livestock of the SAIS, Shining Path had nothing else to offer peasants in the economic sphere so it became, as it had in Ayacucho and other places, a guardian of public morality—executing livestock rustlers, controlling teachers, and punishing deviant behavior. "This is how it has to be," explains a comunero, "because we Peruvians are driven by evil." According to Manrique (1989, 157), in these declarations we can see how, faced with "the vertical and violently authoritarian paternalism" of Shining Path, peasants fall back on the "old habits of fatalism and passivity, long internalized since the Colonial period." Thus, Sendero satisfies other, noneconomic demands, fundamentally the demand for *order*.

Finally, Manrique returns to his interest in the ethnic dimensions of Shining Path violence. For him, the ethnic is "the negated factor" for Shining Path, which never mentions anything related to ethnicity in its documents. But this silence does not eliminate the ethnic factor in its practice, to which "it returns with an annihilating force that cannot be satisfied with just the elimination of the other" (1989, 168) and acquires characteristics of cruelty, terror, and "exemplary violence . . . intended to paralyze, disintegrate and liquidate all will to resist." In addition, its practice is intended to "reinforce the passivity and the fatalism that historically has been nourished by the conviction that any effort to rebel is, by definition, futile" (ibid., 167).

To complete this panorama, I would add that in 1989 and 1990, the first books by Peruvian authors about Shining Path were published.[75] A text by Biondi and Zapata (1989) that provided a semiotic analysis of Shining Path discourse was virtually ignored. However, a work by Denis Chávez de Paz (1989) about the social characteristics of those found guilty of terrorism turned out to be a key tool for turning attention away from the indigenous or millenarist image of Shining Path. The book demonstrated that the majority of prisoners in Lima jails convicted of terrorism were young people with a university education. The statistical data in this study supported the propositions in my first work on Shining Path, mentioned earlier. Finally, Gorriti Ellenbogen's book (1990) draws on an abundance of unpublished Shining Path documents to deal with Sendero's conflict with the police forces and the state from 1980 to 1982. The peasantry is practically absent, but excellent chapters, such as "La Cuota" (The Quota) and "Batir!" (Defeat!), began to shed light on Sendero's activities in the countryside and their particularly violent practices. "In *Batir!* the key is to demolish. And demolish means to leave nothing," in the words of the Shining Path leadership as early as 1982 (Gorriti Ellenbogen 1990, 283). This helps explain episodes such as the destruction of Allpachaka, an experimental farm at the University of Huamanga, and the executions of communal authorities and powerful locals, which the press presented as an expression of "Andean rage." The other book that appeared in 1990 was my study on the emergence of Shining Path (*El surgimiento de Sendero Luminoso*).

Subsequently, despite the enormous number of Shining Path documents that were published after 1987 and the group's collapse in 1992 to 1993, research on Shining Path and the armed conflict in general continued along the lines of the partial advances made the previous decade, but there were many gaps, and the studies failed to make the leap to works of greater historical importance, interpretative power, and theoretical ambition. In my opinion, this was related to various factors:

(1) The generalized crisis that Peru experienced from the end of the 1980s, when hyperinflation and corruption combined with terrorist violence to magnify the country's weak political and social institutionality.

(2) The breakup of the United Left in 1989—the worst point of the national crisis and the same year as the fall of the Berlin wall. These events had a strong impact on those intellectuals who, to varying degrees, identified themselves with the Left. During the 1980s, they were the leading voices in national intellectual debates and, aside from any particular bias or ambiguity, had shown the greatest interest in the internal armed conflict and produced the best studies on the subject.

(3) The will to forget and to "turn the page," which the government and economic elites imposed after the 1992 coup and the collapse of Sendero's national leadership. During most of the 1990s, this discourse was accepted by large sectors of the population who wanted order and were hopeful about the new neoliberal economic model that had been imposed. The new scenario played a role in influencing the abrupt turn of a significant number of intellectuals toward more professionalization and a retreat from critical thinking.

Among the works that stand out during this decade is a holistic attempt by Poole and Rénique (1992) to deal with the phenomenon of the violence in its entirety; it follows on their previous work that centers its critique on North American "senderólogos" (Poole and Rénique 1991). Collections of articles were also published. The most important appeared outside Peru: Palmer (1992), Bonilla (1994), and Stern (1999). The latter is the most sound among these. In the general introduction, Stern (1999, 13) situates the emergence of Shining Path "within" and "against" history: rooted in certain aspects of Peruvian history and political culture and, at the same time, opposed to Peru's principal political and social trends in the name of a Truth and a Knowledge that the vanguard acquired outside of history, as a kind of self-granted ontological privilege. Stern also develops a line of argument that emphasizes peasant agency. He had presented this idea previously in another collection of articles about the eighteenth century (see Stern 1990). His concept of "resistant adaptation" is very useful to understanding the principal peasant response during the conflict vis-à-vis both state agents and Shining Path. More recently, Manrique (2002) has assembled his articles published between 1986 and 1998 into a book.

Research published in the 1990s deepened understanding of specific aspects of the internal armed conflict and Shining Path. The role of women in Shining

Path was studied by Kirk (1993) and also by Coral (1997). The military strategies of Shining Path and the armed forces were analyzed in detail by Carlos Tapia (1997), whose book revealed Sendero's remarkable strategic weakness throughout the conflict and proposed that Sendero's "popular war" be viewed as a constant fleeing forward sustained by its members' momentum and individual and collective wills.

The role of the Peasant Self-Defense Committees (Comités de Autodefensa Campesina, CAD) also received attention and was debated widely, including in 1980s journalistic articles and case studies, such as those about the CAD in Ayacucho collected in the work by Degregori and colleagues (1996) or in the work on the central highlands (J. C. Guerrero 2002). The Peruvian CAD and the Colombian self-defense organizations or the Guatemalan Civil Self-Defense Patrols (Patrullas de Autodefensa Civil, PAC) were significantly different. In spite of their subordination to the armed forces and, in many cases, to the very concrete strategies of these state agents, the CAD had a greater margin to maneuver and, in this sense, more autonomy than the similar groups in Guatemala.[76] In contrast to the Colombian self-defense groups, the CAD did not become the hired killers for large landowners, who practically did not exist in Peru, nor for drug traffickers. Once the conflict ended, in most cases, the CAD were reabsorbed by the type of community organization that had existed in normal times and, in other cases, the leaders of the CAD successfully entered local politics, becoming mayors (see J. C. Guerrero 2002).

The most recent important issue to be incorporated into this area of study was the theme of memory, especially in the project "Collective Memory and Repression in the Southern Cone and Peru," in which a group of young Peruvian researchers participated. The project led to the publication of a collection of articles (Degregori 2003) that, in addition to introducing the theme of memory into the Peruvian debate,[77] dealt with a number of issues that had not been sufficiently studied despite their importance in the armed internal conflict. Among these were Pablo Sandoval's *licenciatura* thesis (2002) and article (2003) about the massacre of nine students and a professor from the National Education University known as "La Cantuta," which returned to the study of educational spaces and the armed conflict, an issue that had been largely neglected after the work of Chávez de Paz (1989).[78] The article by Leslie Villapolo (2003) about the Asháninkas and the internal armed conflict dealt with another issue about which there was little information. The Asháninkas of the Peruvian Amazon basin were the group that suffered the most from the violence. Until now, except for the work of Espinosa (1994) and M. Benavides (1990, 1992) about the Asháninkas' confrontations with MRTA, knowledge about what happened in this region is confined to journalistic articles. The same was true regarding the armed conflict in coca growing and drug trafficking zones.[79]

The discourse of and about Sendero was examined within a cultural studies perspective by Vich (2002), but other important issues remained practically unexplored during this period, which ended with the presentation of the CVR's *Final Report* in August 2003. Thus, for example, research about violence in the cities is underrepresented.[80] In addition, little has been written about the behavior of businesspeople, unions, intellectuals, or the media during the armed internal conflict[81] or about the repercussions of the conflict on the economy or social organizations, and local governments and rural institutionality in general.

If anything distinguishes this period, it is the end of ambiguity about Shining Path's project as well as the notable retreat of the so-called *indigenista* paradigm, which in fact did not completely disappear. It reappears, for example, in *Razones de sangre* (Portocarrero 1998), a book that, in the words of its author, emphasizes impulses and symbolic universes, incorporating the traditions of psychoanalysis, interpretive sociology, cultural anthropology, and history from a perspective similar to cultural studies (Portocarrero 1998, 12).

Perhaps because of his excessive emphasis on personal histories and family contexts to explain aggressive impulses, when he contrasts the biographies of four young people in the second part of his book, Portocarrero falls back on an overly simplistic contrast between Andeans and criollos. This is most obvious when we look at the two most contrasting life histories presented—those of Raúl and Julieta. Raúl is poor, of Andean origin, and as a child he was treated roughly by his parents, who were always reserved, as well as by the husband of his older sister who "hit him for no reason, was unjust and abusive" (Portocarrero 1998, 173–74). Raúl joined Shining Path.

In contrast, the parents of Julieta were from the coast, criollos. She was part of a culture in which "the outsider is well received, especially if not an Indian. In any case, [he/she] is not demonized. Another important value is joyfulness and good humor, partying" (Portocarrero 1998, 218). Although she is from the Left, Julieta rejects violence. However, Pancho, the navy infantryman whose story appears in Degregori and López Ricci (1990), was a criollo who liked to party and was still capable of the worst atrocities in Ayacucho in 1983. The same was true of the members of the Colina death squad, who were capable of the basest atrocities (see Uceda 2004).

The *Final Report* (2003) of the Truth and Reconciliation Commission marked a turning point in research on the internal armed conflict.[82] The report was not, of course, an academic study. It provided an enormous amount of information on the issues, and although it did not propose hypotheses in the strict sense of the word, it decided on a position from which to speak its "truth," which ended up discrediting not only many of the core ideas and accepted wisdom about the internal armed conflict but, more generally, about the history of Peru.[83] The importance of the conflict in the history of contemporary Peru, its roots in our "long existence," and the ambitious thematic breadth of the *Final Report* produced this effect.

As de la Cadena (2003, 9) notes, the truth that the CVR revealed for the first time in the history of Peru publically questioned the hegemony of discourses based on institutionalized contempt and discrimination "sometimes cloaked in benevolence and, ultimately, with a certain 'multicultural' and cosmopolitan tolerance." But the CVR itself pointed out the limitations of its work when it noted that it "understands truth as a reliable account, ethically articulated, scientifically supported, intersubjectively contrasted, well constructed in narrative terms, affectively sensitive and perfectible" both because of the appearance of new evidence and as a result of "new analytical or critical perspectives that would contribute to its constant rewriting" (CVR 2003, vol. I, 49–51). In this way, the report is presented as a huge repository and a new starting point to continue the debate and deepen knowledge about the violent years that Peru experienced.

An example of the empowering capacity of the report can be found in *La voluntad encarcelada* (Rénique 2003), a study based, in part, on the work of the CVR and written by a historian who participated in its research. The book analyzes an arena that was of exceptional importance for the consolidation of Shining Path identities: the prisons. The study audaciously suggests a link between the prison strategies of Shining Path and that of APRA during the first half of the twentieth century, thus linking Shining Path with central aspects of Peruvian politics, especially what the author calls the "radical tradition." Political will and tradition are intertwined in this analysis of Shining Path in the prisons: "If you think of tradition as a kind of arsenal deposited through time, will is the hand that stirs up its layers in search of tools for combat" (Rénique 2003, 17).

The scope of the internal armed conflict was so vast that many aspects have not yet been studied. I will mention only one whose brief treatment in the *Final Report* led to severe criticism (Parodi 2004, Teivainen 2004): the international factor. If we translate this insufficiency into the language of this review, I would say that the Peruvian experience still needs to be analyzed in comparative perspective. With the exception of McClintock (1998), who compares Peru and El Salvador; Kruijt (1999) on the counterinsurgency activities in Peru and Guatemala; Hinojosa (1992) on similarities and contrasts between Shining Path and the Khmer Rouge; and Deas (1997), who includes

How Social Sciences Failed?

comparisons between the violence in Colombia and Peru, little has been written on this subject.[84]

Finally, in contrast, for example, to the Colombian case, we still find ourselves far from having proposed relevant theoretical models for understanding the phenomenon under discussion and—why not?—for influencing the course of postwar events.

Archaeology of (Limited) Knowledge:
The Author and His (Con)texts

At this juncture, I conclude with some considerations regarding the other dimension of this volume's "place of enunciation": the most personal. The essays in this book are not immune from being the "testimony of a witness." They are united by a "sensitive and painful" subject and analyze events that, at the time I wrote about them, were too close: chronologically, geographically, and, above all, emotionally.

My parents were from Ayacucho, and in the 1970s I was a professor at the Universidad Nacional de San Cristóbal de Huamanga (UNSCH). During the first part of my stay at this university, Abimael Guzmán was the Director of University Personnel. I never imagined that the sedentary professor who behaved and dressed in such a formal manner would later become the future "President Gonzalo." During my years at the UNSCH, I was a member of political groups that in those times opposed Shining Path from Leftist positions that were also quite dogmatic. I was a witness to and also took part in the confrontation of social and political organizations that, toward the end of the decade, seemed to be taking over the space in which Shining Path previously had hegemony.[85] I left Ayacucho in 1979, convinced that Sendero's announcements it would soon begin its "popular war" were one more fantasy of Peter crying wolf; that Shining Path was a tiny, stagnant group that lived in the past; and full of hope that in the immediate future, I instead would see a strengthened United Left.

In 1980, I began work as a journalist for the newspaper *El Diario de Marka*. My first articles about Shining Path were published in that newspaper and its Sunday supplement, *El Caballo Rojo*. I also reported on Shining Path actions and covered some of its first assaults on police posts in Ayacucho, where I was sent because of my previous knowledge of the area. In the supplement, I provided more analytical discussions about Sendero's subversive activities and the response of the state.[86] During the first years of the conflict, I also visited the area as a former professor at the university. Colleagues, friends, former students, social leaders, and peasants all told me about their experiences. The stories accumulated, and when I decided to work on the issue in a more detailed way, many of these people helped me collect other stories of people and places that I could no longer access because of the brutality of the conflict. I started to study these issues because I wanted to overcome my state of shock and figure out what had been happening under my nose without my noticing it during my years in Ayacucho. I also wanted to share the little that I knew about Shining Path with those who wanted to listen to me.

My work as a "Senderólogo" was laced with a variety of emotions: *indignation* about the "dirty war"—the furious violence of Shining Path and the indiscriminate repression of the armed forces—and about the slovenly manner that governments dealt with the issue and their blindness when they treated those of us who were critical of state actions as enemies; *frustration* with many of those in the academic community and the Left who at the time—well into the 1980s—were reticent to put distance between themselves and Shining Path and to recognize unambiguously the group's regressive character and the increasingly terrorist content of its activities; *admiration* for those who continued to work in the war zones, for those who faced the terror with a dignity that was even more surprising than the cruelty of the conflict: former colleagues from the university, political party activists, human rights defenders, social leaders, local authorities, members of defense patrols, the military, religious orders, and lawyers, journalists, teachers; and *pain* when learning that acquaintances and friends had been imprisoned, tortured, or assassinated. Among the latter was Julio Orozco Huamaní, leader of the Federation of Peasants of the Apurímac River Valley (FECVRA), who according to overwhelming evidence was disappeared by the navy in 1983; Félix Gavilán, a journalist from Ayacucho; Eduardo de la Piniella and Pedro Sánchez, fellow journalists at *Diario de Marka*, who died at Uchuraccay; and Piura legislator Heriberto Arroyo Mío and María Elena Moyano, deputy mayor of Villa el Salvador, assassinated by Shining Path.

At this point, it is obvious that I do not aspire to positivist objectivity, which in any event is always illusory. The reader will judge if I have managed to achieve the distance necessary to offer materials useful for understanding the phenomenon being studied.

3

The Maturation
of a Cosmocrat and
the Construction of
a Community of Discourse

Up until 1977, Sendero Luminoso was one of numerous groups of the radical Peruvian Left that proclaimed the need for armed struggle to conquer power. This chapter analyzes the importance for this effort of the elaboration of a discourse, the appearance of a "cosmocratic figure," and the construction of a "community of discourse" around him. These phenomena help to explain the transformation of Sendero, which until then had been a tiny, marginal provincial group, into a "war machine" that would play a decisive role in Peruvian political life during the 1980s and 1990s, even after the capture of its leader in 1992 and its subsequent collapse.

There is no political violence without discourse, for people need to convince themselves or be convinced by others in order to carry out such violence. In this light, a little-known text by David Apter (1993; cf. 1997) draws on discourse theory to develop an approach to the phenomenon of political violence that seems especially useful to explain the transformation of Sendero and especially its leader, Abimael Guzmán, toward the end of the 1970s. That transformation was the key element that drove Sendero to unleash violence beginning in 1980, and it also helps to explain its virulence, capacity for resistance and growth during the 1980s, as well as its sudden collapse following Guzmán's capture in 1992.

To be sure, this discourse-based approach does not explain the entire Sendero phenomenon or political violence more generally. One cannot ignore the structural roots of violence or the historical and sociocultural contexts crucial, as I have argued elsewhere, to understanding political violence in Peru (Degregori 1985b, 1989b, 1996). But I share Pizarro's (1996) assessment that at the *initial moment* of violence, political will plays a decisive role. That initial moment is the subject of this chapter.

Discourse Analysis and the Violence of Sendero

According to Apter, the discourse necessary for political violence begins with events that serve as raw material from which a reasoned interpretation is elaborated. That interpretation emerges through a process that draws on certain ingredients, paradigms, or examples; doctrines, myths, and theories; magic or fantasy and logic; metaphor and metonym; narrative and text. It is through that linguistic alchemy, for example, that spontaneous uprisings, demonstrations, and mutinies may become self-sustaining movements. Without discourse, however profound or longstanding the anger of some people or how serious their grievances, these events can explode like fireworks: they shine for a moment only to peter out as quickly as they were ignited. It is when events are incorporated in interpretive discourses and embodied in what Apter labels "discursive communities" that political violence can not only feed on itself but also become self-validating and self-sustaining.

Some event, which in ordinary circumstances would hardly have produced any comment whatsoever, suddenly stops time in its tracks, and starts it all over again. The meanings take on significance cumulatively, and the event acquires symbolic density. The story is told many times and becomes socialized. Stories, once collectivized, have consequences. Converted into myths, they aspire to be history, and as history are reinterpreted as theories, and as theories they explain as history events that become metaphors within a narrative process, and metonyms for a theory.

A narrator is needed in order for this process to be consolidated and to transform it into political power. The narrator can be a Ulysses-type figure, a vagabond who gains wisdom in exile and after many trials returns home to reclaim his heritage. Or the narrator can become "the source," the father or the mother of the homeland, the phallocrat, all pistols, weapons, uniforms, a putative figure of fertility. But to consolidate a myth, to convert it into mytho-logical, it is essential to have a cosmocratic figure, a kind of Buddha within the tantric circle, Apter notes, while cautioning that many other representations are possible.

Such is the figure who finds the logic of truth in the narrative. Myths repeated by the narrator create a space for theoretical explanation. If not a cosmocrat, the agent can be prophetic, a vehicle for a voice higher than his own. In reality, the narrator, the phallocrat, the cosmocrat, and the prophet can be combined into one single person, who in that way creates not only a discourse but also a form of monopoly capital over truth and virtue. The outcome is a sort of pact whereby people give up a piece of their minds to the collective but cannot take out from that collective pact more power than they cede to it. This is the power of discourse. Apter identifies this as symbolic capital. The result of this process is what he labels "collective individualism." Individuals aggregate their individual stories in order to reinforce a collective narrative, and they extract more in interpretive capacity and power than they brought to the collective. To state it simply, the "triumphant project" constructed in this manner is at the same time individual and collective.

To be sure, not all political actors who choose the path of violence fit within this definition. If on the one hand we find producers of "inversionary discourse," at the other extreme we encounter those who engage much more directly in competitive exchanges of power through the force of arms, without significant changes in meaning, constructing what Apter calls a "model of violent exchange" that has more to do with economic capital. By contrast, the model of inversionary discourse has to do with the accumulation of symbolic capital.

The Cosmocrat and the Making of a Community of Discourse

In 1964, the Sino-Soviet polemic reached Peru, triggering the division of the Peruvian Communist Party (PCP) into two organizations that distinguished themselves through the names of their two newspapers, the pro-Soviet PCP-Unidad (PCP-Unity) and the pro-Chinese PCP–Bandera Roja (PCP-BR, Red Flag). The Ayacucho Regional Committee of the PCP-BR, led by the young university professor Abimael Guzmán, aligned itself with the pro-Chinese faction. Between 1964 and 1969, the Maoists in Ayacucho expanded considerably, gaining influence in neighborhood and teachers' organizations and, especially, among students and professors at the

Universidad Nacional de San Cristóbal de Huamanga (UNSCH). Sendero also promoted the formation and development of the Frente de Defensa del Pueblo de Ayacucho (People's Defense Front of Ayacucho), an organization that achieved significant social recognition.

Ideological discrepancies and rivalries among leaders produced successive divisions of Bandera Roja (BR) over the years. In early 1970, Abimael Guzmán headed up a splinter group that, aside from a handful of isolated groups elsewhere in the country, only gained control over the Regional Committee of Ayacucho. Thus was born Shining Path, a product of a double defeat: a defeat in the struggle within the BR, and a defeat with regard to social movements, since a year earlier, following a massive mobilization for free education in the principal cities of Ayacucho, the military government of General Velasco (1968–75) had unleashed a fierce repression that disarticulated the People's Defense Front and brought about the retreat of the social movement in the region, as well as the cadres of Sendero.

Yan'an in an Andean Campus

Thus, over the course of the 1970s, Guzmán and his miserable followers began their long march, taking refuge in the UNSCH, where they constructed what we can call an Andean Yan'an. (Editor's note: Yan'an refers to the Chinese town from which Mao Zedong built a revolutionary base of resistance to the Japanese, taking refuge with the party there after the Long March of 1934–35.) To do so, they drew on undisputed control over the university, whose leadership they influenced decisively from 1969 to 1973.

During the following years, the "handful of communists" clustered in Sendero managed to elaborate an absolutely coherent doctrine and an exceptional organization. The price they paid for doing so was to cut off all ties to social movements, precisely at a moment when these were gaining influence on a national scale. This was a time of land occupations, regional movements, and widespread social upheavals. In 1977 and 1978, teachers and workers carried out two nationwide work stoppages of greater impact than any others in contemporary Peruvian history. Sendero had no role whatsoever in any of this. To the contrary, since the promoters of these events included the pro-Soviet PCP-Unidad and other groups on the Left, Sendero criticized the strikes as "revisionist" and "at the service of soviet social imperialism." The most important document it published at the time (PCP-SL 1989b [1978]) makes only vague mention of "growing popular protest" and does so in order to justify the tactic of boycotting elections that, in part as a result of those movements, had been convened by the military government in 1977 in order to elect a Constituent Assembly the following year.[1]

In any event, Sendero would have had little to contribute to those work stoppages because it no longer was prepared for this sort of struggle. Little remained of the great influence that it had over social organizations in Ayacucho during the 1960s. However, as became evident beginning in 1980, these social setbacks did not mean that Sendero was stripped altogether of its capacity to engage in struggle. To begin with, it always maintained its power among those fronts that it had privileged over the course of the 1970s: teachers and students. Elsewhere I have argued that after the defeat of "the masses," Sendero pulled together a core of cadres that, despite having lost the capacity to provoke social mobilization, during the same period had managed to achieve an ideological hardening and organic cohesion to the point where it became "a sort of dwarf star in which matter is concentrated to where there is almost no inter-atomic space, reaching a heavy weight disproportionate to its size" (Degregori 1985b, 48). During the 1970s, Sendero developed ideological and organizational mechanisms that made possible this apparent paradox. The following pages discuss how there unfolded in the discursive sphere a dynamic that came to give them the density of a black hole.

From Bureaucrat to Prophet

Around 1977, Sendero believed that its line was sufficiently elaborated and that it had a core of coordinated cadres necessary to launch its "popular war." In June of that year, it approved a "National Plan of Construction" and "dozens of cadres [were] sent to the countryside based on the strategic needs of the popular war" (PCP-SL 1989a, v). But it was not easy to convince the militants. It was not easy to invite them to start a war outside of and removed from social movements, precisely at a moment when the latter were reaching their highest peak and the principal tendency among Leftist groups was to unite around those movements in order to "accumulate forces" before launching any military adventure. Moreover, partly because of those movements, at that very moment (1977–80), a complex democratic transition was unfolding. Citizenship was broadened with the extension of the franchise to the illiterate, a great majority of whom were poor, indigenous peasants. And political space was clearly expanding, especially on the Left, with the incorporation of a majority of the Marxist political parties into the democratic political game.

The difficulty was even greater for a Maoist party. The agrarian reform undertaken by the military government (1968–80) had finished erasing the "semifeudal" landscape of landowners and peasant serfs, indispensable for the sort of revolution that Guzmán had in mind. At the same time, Mao Zedong had just died in 1976; the Gang of Four, led by his widow, had been defeated;

and the Cultural Revolution, which fueled the imagination of much of the Peruvian Left and especially of Sendero, had come to an end. The following decade would witness Perestroika and the fall of "really existing socialism," the crisis of rigid ideologies and doctrinaire parties.

But while the bulk of the Left by now had accepted, however partially and late, what Nun (1989) called the "Rebellion of the Chorus" — that "the masses" had the capacity for political initiative — and had admitted that in the international arena there no longer existed a "vanguard party," Sendero denied the new realities and proposed instead an alternative: it would reject any leading role for the masses, and the party would decide everything. It denied the predominance of politics over war: violence is the essence of revolution. Moreover, since its frameworks seemed capable of resisting change in their surroundings, like Joshua Sendero sought to detain the sun, that is, to stop time. According to its definitions, Peru remained a "semifeudal" country and the democratic transition meant nothing, for the Constituent Assembly (1978–79) that preceded the democratic transition was only "the third restructuring of the landowning, corporativist bureaucratic state" (PCP-SL 1989b) and the civilian government that arose from the elections of 1980 represented "fascist continuity."

Given that Guzmán's triumphant project was situated above the vicissitudes of the moment, in order to overcome such an adverse environment, the Senderista leader had to go outside the long Marxist tradition of analysis of the political conjuncture, and to transition from scholastic disquisition to prophetic discourse. As if to compensate for the fragility of a political analysis that was so impoverished as to become brittle, he would have to resort to other registers. As if he had to counterpose the weightlessness of his reasoning with the exacerbation of passions. The result was a total rupture. Passage through the desert; burning of the sails. No metaphor seems out of proportion.

The scale of this rupture is evident in four crucial texts produced by Guzmán between 1979 and 1980. These are the years when Sendero reached takeoff speed, achieving critical mass for the fusion needed to produce an explosion. From an alternative perspective, it could be said that these are the years that Sendero radically cuts its mooring ropes, crosses over the border along which it had been navigating, and penetrates into the unknown territory of the hallucinatory. This incursion can be seen in the texts that I comment on. These are Guzmán's most striking texts. At the least, they are the ones with greatest symbolic density and "inversionary potential" (Apter 1993). The first surprise is the abrupt change in tone. Until this point, his writings, plagued with citations from the Marxist pantheon, were arid and obtuse.[2] But all of a sudden, the discourse is transformed. The texts lack a "rational" structure, and are full of vignettes, metaphors, and oft-repeated, impassioned appeals.

A Cosmocrat and Community Discourse

The change may be due to the fact that the earlier documents were mostly official texts, while these were speeches delivered in closed meetings with a circle of "apostles" on the verge of armed struggle. The imminence of combat gives a particularly epic tone to the speeches. But the greatest influence on their flavor seems to have been the bitter internal struggles Guzmán had to confront when he decided to launch the armed struggle. According to the party's official history, in 1977, Sendero "crushed" a faction of "rightist" dissidents who acknowledged that the government had carried out agrarian reform and proposed strategies not unlike those of the rest of the Left. The dissidents advocated that the party "organize the peasantry around the Confederación Campesina del Perú [Peasant Confederation of Peru]," where various Leftist groups were present. "And in the cities they pursued workerism, carrying the class into trade unionism and failing to carry out their vanguard role" (PCP-SL 1989a, v). In other words, they advocated participation in the Confederación General de Trabajadores del Perú (General Confederation of Peruvian Workers, CGTP) that had organized the successful work stoppages of 1977 and 1978. Later, in 1979–80, three "intense struggles" unfolded against party members who opposed launching the armed struggle (PCP-SL 1989a, vi).[3]

Some sense of reality still lingered within the party. It was in order to extirpate and defeat his adversaries that Guzmán had to convert himself into a cosmocrat and transform his party into a "pueblo del Libro" (people of the Book). It was necessary to drive out of this Jerusalem in construction all the fearful and the vacillating, to eradicate any lingering shadows of doubt, to culminate the creation of a community of discourse, an inner world blinded against an objective correlation of forces that was so overwhelmingly adverse.

La Nueva Bandera

The first text, "Por la Nueva Bandera" (For the New Flag), was written in June 1979, eleven months before the start of the war, and it begins with a Biblical phrase: "Many are called but few are chosen."[4] Echoes of the internal struggles resound in the phrase, as they do in others with equally deep Biblical roots, such as "The wind carries off the leaves, but the seed remains." It is interesting to see that in the party's decisive moments, it is the Bible that appears as the great storehouse of symbols. But the God of Sendero's Book is Matter, advancing irresistibly toward the Light, toward communism.

Through a clever rhetorical twist, Guzmán and his followers appear as embodying that movement of matter and thus becoming indestructible. As they gain cosmic strength, the opposition minority is reduced to "threads, spattered drops, extinguished voices, darkened sparks wanting to deny the bonfire." Why? Because of questions and aphorisms: "Can a spark rise up against the bonfire?" "How could seeds of grain stop the millstone? They would be turned into dust." "Foolish it is to want to destroy matter." "Fifteen billion years it has taken Earth to bring forth communism. . . . Arrogant bubbles. Is that what we want to be? An infinitesimal fragment trying to rise up against fifteen billion years? What vanity, what putridness!" (Guzmán 1989b, 144).

The speech is wracked with a certain fatalism: "Nothing can stop the revolution, that is the law, that is destiny."[5] We can thus understand a phrase repeated in slogans and proclamations and even in a poem written by a prisoner later murdered in the great prison massacre of 1986: "We have been sentenced to win / What a beautiful sentence."

But it was not easy to raise the flag of optimism. Who better to inspire than Paul of Tarsus? The speech continues, "What little faith some have, what little charity, what little hope. . . . We have taken the three theological virtues in order to interpret them. Paul said man of faith, hope, and charity."

To latch on to the carriage of history a total rupture is needed. Like Lot upon leaving Sodom, one must only look forward. There is no possibility whatsoever of turning back: "What is done is done, it cannot be changed." Once again, the grandiloquent language barely hides the nastiness of a fierce internal struggle. The votes taken in previous events, the accords that have brought the party to the brink of armed struggle, the possible maneuvers (in other respects, recourse to religious language to resolve political problems is not agile), all are raised into cosmic deeds that "cannot be questioned." "Are we to revoke what time has written, the deeds etched into matter?" All that remains is to "rise into flight" and move ahead. And there, ahead, is the revolution, to honor the Virgin Mary. "There is an old verse," says the cosmocrat, and he goes on to recite his version of the Magnificat: "Who is she that looketh forth as the dawn, fair as the moon, clear as the sun, and impotent as an army with fluttering banners?" (Guzmán 1989b, 142).

The rupture Guzmán presents to his followers is collective, but it is also personal, internal. "Two flags [struggle] within the soul, one black and the other red. We are the Left, let us make a holocaust of the black flag." To do so it is necessary to "cleanse our soul, cleanse it well. . . . Enough of putrid individual waters, of abandoned dung." All militants must share the cosmocrat's scorching intellectual battles, so as to emerge at last cleansed and born anew, like born-again Christians. Yet at the same time, "the individual is worth nothing, the mass is all, if anything we are to be, to be as part of the mass. . . . Our love, our faith, our hope is collective, they can be achieved, they are three in one sole flag." The soul can only purify itself within the community of discourse, because "the Party is the salt of the earth, the living tree, the others are parasites." The definition of the party is, evidently, a blatant plagiarism of

A Cosmocrat and Community Discourse

the Catholic Church's self-definition in the Gospel. This inevitably evokes the future cosmocrat's early training in a religious school in Arequipa.[6]

According to Gorriti Ellenbogen (1990, 53–54), after the meeting that gave rise to this text in June 1979, one of Guzmán's lieutenants broke with him, accusing him of being "Hoxhista," and managed to form around himself a dissident group from the Politburo and the Central Committee. "The group might have achieved a majority," Gorriti Ellenbogen writes, "and thus changed the nation's history, but it lacked cohesion and was crushed by the reverential fear of Guzmán" (ibid.). Defeated, the opposition leader abandoned the organization and left Peru.

Three Chapters of Our History

The second text is titled "On Three Chapters of Our History."[7] The speech was given on Guzmán's birthday, 3 December 1979. Victorious in his internal battle and eager to link inextricably his personal life with that of his political child, Guzmán took advantage of the date to give birth to the People's Army and to recapitulate not only his own history but Peru's as well. Here we find that Guzmán is very aware of his change in tone, for he tells his audience: "There are moments when men turn to speaking in symbols, in metaphors, or in forms that are not so directly intellectual. Instead, we prefer that our group of communist beings speak for us, directly and fully" (Guzmán 1989a, 145).

As if through an oracle, the group of communists is to speak through his mouth although, oddly enough, they will express themselves in symbolic rather than scientific language. To fulfill his role as medium, the narrator uses a rhetorical device, which we might call "the flash forward." He asks his listeners to "enter the field of revolutionary imagination" and put themselves in the second half of the twenty-first century. From there, they are to imagine history as written by future communists. After all, if victory is their destiny, nothing could be more natural. Guzmán tries in this way to abolish time and infuse his followers with faith in the certainty of triumph. The Goddess of History is on their side, and so is the Goddess of Matter, which is but another name for the same divinity. And so, having become a twenty-first-century historian, the cosmocrat begins his story: "There was a time when shadows prevailed."

Thousands of years of Peruvian history are condensed into three long chapters that lead us from darkness to light. The first, "On How the Shadows Prevailed," spans from the arrival in the Andes of homo sapiens until the beginning of the twentieth century. If anything startles us here, it is the meager attachment to the past and to the native land. He is not trying to reaffirm a nonprimordial parochial identity, or to recover some paradise lost. In a country with Peru's historical richness, the text's coolness toward the great pre-Hispanic civilizations is striking. In Sendero's strictly classist vision, the ethnic dimension plays no role whatsoever. What matters is the rise of the state and of classes during the Wari period (the sixth to eleventh centuries AD). The Conquest is but a change of one group of exploiters by another. "As [the Inca empire] was a decayed system based on exploitation, it was buried in the clash with a superior order." There are no tears. The text deals more with projecting ahead than recovering the past. Paradise lies in the future.

The second chapter's title is "On How Light Burst Forth and Steel Was Forged." It begins around the late nineteenth and early twentieth centuries when, along with the new imperialist order, "a new class, the proletariat, dawned." At first, José Carlos Mariátegui and Peru's young working class are the protagonists until, as in a cosmogony, out of the darkness "there began to emerge a purer light, a radiant light, the light we carry within our breasts, within our souls. That light fused with the earth, and that clay turned to steel. Light, clay, steel, the PARTY arose in 1928" (Guzmán 1989a, 148).

This is no longer only biblical language. It is a Bible with its own proletarian Genesis and a history of redemption with a classic trilogy of life, death, and resurrection: Mariátegui died at thirty-six, just two years after he founded the party. Thus "we had a possibility that came apart when the life of the one who founded us was extinguished." Nevertheless, "what could not be reality remained as Program and Plan," even though Mariátegui's germinating legacy "was denied, ignored, hidden." This was, without a doubt, a time in hell. The Holy Grail—Program and Plan—remained entombed by the traitors and revisionists who had seized control over the party. But it did not disappear, because "the class embodied it, its heartbeat continued within the combative class and people and within the communists." Until once again history speeds up to a dizzying speed. During the 1970s it reaches rapture because then:

> Our people were enlightened by a more intense light, Marxism-Leninism-Mao Zedong Thought; at first we were blinded at that first breaking of endless light, light and nothing more; little by little, our retinas began to understand that light, we lowered our eyes and began to see our country, to see Mariátegui and our reality, and we found our perspective: the Reconstitution of the Party. (Guzmán 1989a, 148)

Mount Tabor, Easter, and the Pentecost condensed into a single sentence. Revived by a sort of God the Father who lives in China, those disciples, marginal and functionally superfluous, are ready to "speak in tongues" and be the protagonists in a third chapter that begins the very day on which the cosmocrat is giving his speech. Plan and Program have been rebuilt. It is the day of resurrection, and hence this title for the third chapter, "On How the Walls Came Tumbling Down and the Dawn Unfurled." The narrator returns to the twenty-first century and from there writes the history of that precise moment:

> It shall be said: Our Party, forged of the strongest light and the purest steel, faced a moment of decision and generated the National Plan of Construction, and the Party, which was a piece of flag unfurled in the wind, grew until it illuminated our fatherland. . . . The communists arose and the earth shook, and as the earth shook the comrades advanced. . . . The few communists there were convened from different places, and at last they committed themselves and made a decision: to forge through deeds the First Company of the First Division of the People's Army. And so, the shadows began to roll back for good, the walls trembled and were breached; with their fists dawn opened, darkness became light. . . . Their souls were joyful and their eyes shone with the light. (Guzmán 1989a, 148–49)

The Communists congregate like the masses at the Sermon on the Mount, or more accurately like at Armageddon. Once having achieved the community of discourse, the new people of the Book are prepared to move forward. Nothing will stop them. To prove this, the narrator resorts to another flash forward, and continues his story from the distant future:

> A chapter will say: great effort was required, we shed our share of blood, and in difficult moments we buried our dead, dried our tears and continued battling. So it took place and on the day of the nation the Popular Republic was proclaimed. . . . Our America shines, and it is now a free world and it extends everywhere. Today old empires sink, they are dirty waters, decaying ash, whereas labor is making demands and the countryside flourishes in the Red Republic. . . . Such will be history; in this sense we are on the inevitable path toward communism, to arrive at full and absolute light. The blood of those who fell cries out: light, light, to communism we arrive! This will be written, this is what history will say. (Guzmán 1989a, 149)

Tearing Down the Walls

The third text is titled "Let Us Begin to Tear Down the Walls and Unfurl the Dawn." It was given as a speech in a key meeting, the Second Plenary Session of the Central Committee, which according to Gorriti Ellenbogen (1990, 49) began on 17 March 1980 and lasted until the end of the month.[8] In line with Guzmán's magisterial and sermonizing vocation, these meetings were generally long seclusions in which the leader was not only rhetorician, exegete, and prophet but also strategist and organizer. The texts that were studied and cited were not only biblical but rather predominantly from Marx, Lenin, Stalin, Mao, and, as Gorriti Ellenbogen points out, the Western classics. These were long meetings, in which the master progressively overcame all of the disciples' resistance, molding them in his own image. He worked more like a smith than a potter because, as he would repeat in varied ways for years, about those who were neither disciples nor enemies: "It will not be easy for them to accept. . . . They will need overwhelming facts . . . that hammer their hard heads, that break their speculations into pieces, in order for the reality of this, our fatherland, to take root in their souls" (Guzmán 1990a, 166–67).

This Second Session of the Central Committee was key because internal opposition persisted, although leaderless: the head of the opposition had fled the country but sent a document that was read "and defended" during this meeting (Gorriti Ellenbogen 1990). We can imagine the differences between youths dazzled by the cosmocrat's narratives who did not need hammer blows to open their souls to the triumphant project, and their elders, older militants, battle-hardened in the harsh struggles of the Peruvian Left during the 1970s, who also could perceive the cresting wave of social movements and the great strides that the rest of the Left was making. But we can only speculate as to the narrator's degree of cynicism when he appealed to cosmology in order to resolve internal problems of the party.

In any case, in 1979–80 the party experienced three internal battles. The first was against a "rightist opportunist line," which denied the existence of a revolutionary situation. They were expelled. The second was "against a new rightist line that believed it impossible to initiate the armed struggle." The third, which appears to have been developing in this particular meeting, concerned "divergences in the Left, in which nuances emerged concerning how to develop the popular war, establishing that the proletarian option was President Gonzalo" (PCP-SL 1989a, vi).

In any event, using Senderista terminology we can say that in this Second Plenary, Guzmán decided to "finish off with a golden seal" the internal struggle and "annihilate" his adversaries. If in the Ninth Expanded Session a fatherly tone had predominated, this time he is the God of Rage, thundering and threatening from the unquestioned stronghold of Matter. Blood invades the stage. Not for nothing does the meeting include reading excerpts of Macbeth, Julius Caesar, and Aeschylus's Prometheus (Gorriti Ellenbogen 1990, 57). "The blood of our people inflames us and boils within us." "We are blood, powerful and throbbing." Who is it that speaks through the mouths of the opposition? "The black jaws of oppression and exploitation, the black jaws full of slime and blood. Do not forget that the reaction needs to spill blood in torrents to appease the people, that is their dream of fire and iron" (Guzmán 1990a, 154).

In "For the New Flag," echoes of Genesis resound. The internal struggle separated darkness from light, day from night. Now the Apocalypse takes center. Fire replaces the light: "All that is left to us is to burn the old idols, to burn what has expired." The syntax at times turns frenetic: "Unacceptable, inadmissible: burn it, blow it up." Previously, rupture implied cleansing the soul, and the opposition was "silence," "aged scum," "an aged old sea rotted by time," "black waters decomposing." Now, as if in a fit of panic or hysteria, the cosmocrat demands more:

> Let us uproot the poisonous weeds. They are pure poison, cancer to the bones, they would corrupt us; we cannot allow it, it is putrefaction and sinister pus; we cannot allow it, particularly now . . . let us unearth those sinister vipers, those noxious vipers, we can allow neither cowardice nor betrayal, they are asps. . . . Let us begin to burn, to uproot that pus, that poison, it is urgent that we burn it. It exists, and it is not good, it is harmful, it is a slow death that could consume us. . . . Those who are in that situation must be the first to cauterize, uproot, burst their boils. Otherwise, the infection will spread. Poisons, purulence must be destroyed. The body is healthy; if we don't destroy them it will lose its vigor. (Guzmán 1990a, 155)

It is impossible not to mention here two ailments that forced Guzmán to leave Huamanga in 1974. One was polycythemia, a blood disease that makes living at high altitudes dangerous. The other was psoriasis, a skin disease that causes open sores (see Gorriti Ellenbogen 1990). This was like a slow death. And death, the great protagonist of the years to come, makes its appearance in Guzmán's words alongside blood. To complete the defeat of the opposition it is necessary "that armed actions confirm our preaching, that our blood merge with the blood of those who must spill it; we have no right for the other's blood to shiver alone, may its chill be mixed with the warmth of ours. Or we are not what we are" (Guzmán 1990a, 154).

To be, in death: "If our blood and life are demanded, let us take a stance: to carry them in our hands to surrender them." Because: "Our death for the good cause would be the seal of our revolutionary action." Death as the goal: "Tomorrow, matter will gather us into its bellicose peace, and there we will be able to rest definitively." Blood and death must be familiar to those who have decided to "convert the word into armed actions." The evangelical allusion to the Redeemer—"the word was made flesh"—is fully recognizable and not at all gratuitous. It announces Guzmán's and Sendero's attitude toward violence. Violence is the Redeemer. She is not the midwife; she is the Mother of History.

We Are the Initiators

The fourth and final text, and the most important one, is titled "We Are the Initiators." It was a speech delivered at the closing of Sendero's first military school on 19 April 1980 (Guzmán 1990b), less than a month before the commencement of armed actions. Once again, the narrator announces that he will speak "with his heart open, in the word of will and the reasoning of sentiment." But almost immediately, as if fearing that his apparently contradictory words might be misinterpreted by an audience accustomed to the "scientific" discourse of Marxism-Leninism, he adds: "This, too, has a strict logic" (the strict logic of sentiment). A cold passion that for the ensuing thirteen years would scorch Peru to the point of consuming it.

Once purified and ready to interpret past, present, and future, the born-again Maoists can now move on to action. In doing so, they will shock the world. Because, according to Abimael Guzmán, the beginning of their armed struggle in the remote Peruvian Andes marks a turning point in the worldwide correlation of forces, and means that "we are entering the strategic offensive of the world revolution."[9] The cosmocrat traces a thread that runs from the most ancient struggles of the masses, passing through the Paris Commune, the October Revolution, the Chinese Revolution, and the Cultural Revolution until reaching that day on which "all these glorious actions across the centuries have become concrete here. The promise opens, the future is unfurled: ILA 80" (Guzmán 1990b).

ILA are the Spanish initials for "initiating the armed struggle." Guzmán has the habit of condensing into initials, like algebraic formulas, an enormous amount of symbolic capital. If in earlier texts he accumulated that capital by moving between physics and cosmology, he now tries to do so on the terrain of analyzing the international political situation. Four reasons are given for why one can now speak of a strategic offensive in the world revolution: "the powerful international workers' movement, the cresting waves of the national liberation movement, the development of communist parties [and] Marxism's elevation to the great summit of Mao Zedong Thought" (Guzmán 1990b).

It is very difficult but not impossible to imagine that from Ayacucho, Peru, his listeners could not see the weaknesses of the international labor movement and the cracks in the movement for national liberation, buffeted at the time by wars between Vietnam, China, and Cambodia. But there is a blind spot in the analysis of someone who so closely followed the evolution of the Chinese Communist Party: the death of Mao and the defeat of the Group of Shanghai,

A Cosmocrat and Community Discourse

the Gang of Four. It is impossible not to suspect that this omission arises from the penumbra between consciousness and self-deception. Another, complementary interpretation is that in leaving behind traditional Marxist political analysis for prophetic discourse, Guzmán breaks with all traces of materialism. It did not matter that Mao had died and his followers had been defeated. What mattered was that the Marxist Idea had been elevated to the great summit of Mao Zedong Thought . . . and that he embodied that Idea.

"Rebellion is justified" was one of the main Shining Path slogans, inspired by Mao. It is worth asking whether the hardly concealed impulses of the leader might not cause us to reformulate the slogan as "rebellion against reality in the name of the Idea is justified." Although at first sight it may appear as a slow and patient effort, in fact Sendero's history from the 1970s onward can also be read as an ever-more bloody escape forward. The construction of a community of discourse as an impenetrable armor allowed them to ignore reality in the name of a dream and to overcome a brutally hard fact, which was that they had arrived late on the stage of history. Velasco's reforms and the massive peasant organization that did away with the peasant serf, the principal subject of his project; the 1978–80 democratic transition, which diluted the potential polarization of "fascist" dictatorship versus revolution; the end of the Cultural Revolution in China, which squelched hopes for a triumphant worldwide Maoist revolution: to what extent did Guzmán's decision to launch armed struggle reflect an influence through negation?

"We Are the Initiators" tries to sweep away every shadow of doubt and strengthen one conviction—the armed struggle is possible and necessary. The world situation is favorable and the national situation justifies it. So-called structural violence lies at the basis of that justification: "They in their old and bloody violence, in their peace through bayonets, in their accursed war that kills in the jails, in the schools, in the factories, in the fields, killing even children in their mothers' wombs. That sinister violence today has met its match" (Guzmán 1990b, 166).

Whereas earlier he ascended to cosmology, Guzmán now sinks into deep structures so as not to "see" either society or politics, so as to ignore the immense majority of the country, located somewhere between the mythical "they" and Shining Path. All that exist are the "revolution and the counterrevolution that prepare themselves for violence." At the core of this lies an analytical vacuum. He does not see that there are people rebelling in other ways. These were the years of Peru's greatest social mobilization of the twentieth century, of labor, peasant, neighborhood, and regional movements, of unprecedented women's movements and broader electoral competition. The Marxist Left reached 28 percent of the vote in the elections for the Constituent Assembly of 1978.

None of this matters; all other forms of struggle are denied and denigrated, and those who carry them out are accused of betrayal. This would bring painful consequences in the years to follow, when Sendero became a true "social anti-movement" (Wieviorka 1988). Those who were not on the party's side were identified with the mythical "they" of the state, the incarnation of absolute evil, and were deserving, therefore, of death, which Sendero took it upon itself to lavish ever more generously.

We could say that Guzmán's analysis is less vulnerable when it remains somewhere between Genesis and the apocalypse. But in reality it is no longer a matter of political analysis of correlations of forces but rather a discourse, a narration through which the pain of the functionally superfluous is converted into rage. Shining Path becomes the hand that writes on the wall in the middle of the banquet: "The reaction dreams of the blood of hyenas, disturbing dreams shake their dark nights. Their heart plots sinister hecatombs. They arm themselves to the teeth, but they shall not prevail. Their destiny is weighty and measured. The time has come to settle accounts" (Guzmán 1990b, 164).

ILA 80 marked the beginning of that settling of accounts, and ILA is made possible, according to Sendero, because there exists a strategic equilibrium on a worldwide scale. In the equilibrium:

> The people get riled up, arm themselves, and rising up in rebellion slip a noose on the neck of imperialism and the reactionaries, they grab them by the throat, they bind them; and necessarily they strangle them, necessarily. They will strip off the reactionary flesh, turn it into rags, and will bury these black scraps in the mire. What remains will be burned, and its ashes scattered to the winds of the earth so that nothing remains but the sinister memory of what must never return because it cannot and should not return. (Guzmán 1990b, 165)

The virulence of this language announces the coming violence:

> Their black troops will move against us, they will mount powerful aggressions, great offensives. We will respond, we will tear them into pieces, we will divide them. Their offensives we will convert into countless small offensives of our own, and the surrounders will be surrounded, and the would-be annihilators will be annihilated, and the would-be victors will be defeated and the beast at last will be trapped, and as we have been taught, the thunder of our armed voices will make them shake with horror and they will end, dead from fear, converted into a few black ashes.

If man is made of the material of his dreams, then here we are faced with the product of an unmitigated nightmare. After ILA 80, the community of discourse had taken shape, the triumphant project vibrantly delineated. "The

A Cosmocrat and Community Discourse

destruction of 'the party' has been exorcised." The party has been reconstituted and its militants turn themselves into alchemists of light: "We are a growing torrent against which fire, stones and mud will be hurled; but our power is great, we will convert everything into our fire, the black fire we will make red and the red is light. That we are, that is the Reconstruction. Comrades, we are reconstructed" (Guzmán 1990b, 168).

Turned into supermen, anxious to start their long march to the Promised Land, the Levites of this new people of the Book then sign a pledge:

> We the communists of the first Military School of the Party, stamping the end of the times of peace and marking the commencement of the people's war, place ourselves in combat readiness as its initiators, assuming under the leadership of the Party and tied to the people, forgers of the invincible legions of iron of the Red Army of Peru. Glory to Marxism-Leninism-Mao Zedong Thought! Long live the Communist Party of Peru! Along the path of comrade Gonzalo, let us initiate the armed struggle! (Gorriti 1990, 67)

The "millenarian war" was about to begin.

From Prophet to Messiah, or a High C to Change the World

During the 1980s the exegetical tie that united the community of discourse developed along three intertwined lines: the cult of death, the abolition of the ego, and the exaltation of the leader.

The cult of death deepened in each new stage of the "popular war." In the Fourth Plenary of the Central Committee, held in May 1981, Guzmán pointed to the need to pay "the quota" of blood necessary for the revolution's triumph. From then on, the militants made a pledge, which among other points included "to struggle and give one's life for the world revolution" (Gorriti Ellenbogen 1990, 67). The logic that upheld the cult of death was that "blood doesn't stop the revolution, it irrigates it." When Sendero proposed to achieve "strategic equilibrium," Guzmán began to speak of a million deaths, and the possible usefulness of a "genocide" in order to achieve that equilibrium (Guzmán 1988).

Consolidation of the cult required the negation of individuality and, thus, of the value of human life in general and in particular the lives of the militants, who had to "carry their lives in their fingertips," be willing to "pay the quota" and "cross the river of blood" necessary for the revolution's triumph. The devaluation of sentiments, of love and of sex, flow naturally in this context. This is why for Laura Zambrano Padilla, one of Sendero's national leaders, love was to be found "at the service of popular war" (Zambrano Padilla 1985).

After his capture, Guzmán seems to have defined sex as a "physiological anxiety" (*Semanario Sí*, 24 September 1992). A military cadre interviewed in *Semanario Sí* (2 November 1992) used these same terms. Corollary: Deuteronomical, Pavlovian norms ruled the sexual life of the combatants.

These four key texts discussed earlier reflect a rabid willingness to obliterate individuality linked to the teleological vision that aids the triumphant project. In "For the New Flag," that will expressed itself in biblical contrapositions. In "On Three Chapters of Our History," the imaginary future took on a touch of science fiction: "Let us place ourselves in the second half of the next century. History will be written by us and those who follow with us, the future communists, because we are inexhaustible; and others and others will come, and those who come are us" (Guzmán 1990b, 146).

Note that everything is written—or said—in present tense and in first person plural. In this community of discourse, time, and therefore death, is abolished: "the future communists are us." That "us" transcends, and even more than in the Catholic Church or the theory of Gaia or the planet-organism of Asimov novels, individual life becomes irrelevant, something that can be carried in one's fingertips.

But at the same time, within that great We some are more equal than others. The cosmocrat is one whose ego is exalted through a personality cult of unprecedented precocity in the history of the communist movement.[10] Let us consider some examples. In the "Bases for Discussion" elaborated for the First Congress and published in El Diario in 1988, the chapters are not presented as the decisions of a collective—whether the Central Committee or the Politburo—in keeping with Leninist tradition or the more general practice of political parties, but as the "teachings of President Gonzalo."[11] Strangest of all, since the early 1980s militants had to sign a "letter of submission," not to the party or to the "revolutionary line" but to President Gonzalo and his thought. The following passage is not precisely a letter of submission but rather a report by a party militant to the Central Committee, written in December 1988. The language, nonetheless, is so absolutely canonical that it gives a fairly precise idea of the chain of "subjections" to which the militant was submitting himself:

> Dear Comrades: I express my greetings and full and unconditional submission to the greatest Marxist-Leninist-Maoist living on Earth, our beloved and respected President Gonzalo, chief and guide of the Peruvian revolution and of the world proletarian revolution. I express my greetings and full and unconditional submission to the scientific ideology of the proletariat, to Marxism-Leninism-Maoism, to Gonzalo Thought, principally to Gonzalo Thought, an all-powerful and unfading conception that illuminates our path and arms our minds. I express my greeting and full

and unconditional submission to the great, glorious, correct and victorious Communist Party of Peru, the high council of the armed revolution that it has magisterially led for eight years of popular war in our fatherland. I express my greetings and full and unconditional submission to the Permanent Committee, Politburo, Central Committee and the entire system of party leadership. I express my greetings and full and unconditional submission to the 1st Marxist Congress of the PCP Marxist-Leninist-Maoist, Gonzalo thought, a shining historic milestone, a milestone of victory, that Gonzalo thought has given us, and the base for party unity, to all of its accords and the tasks that emanate from them. Having expressed my greetings, dear comrades, I turn to the motive of my intervention" (quoted in Starn, Degregori, and Kirk 1995, 336–37)

It is as if the militants stripped off their egos and siphoned them to the leader, whose own ego would grow proportionally. Already in "For the New Flag," Guzmán had given an indication of how this mechanism might function, using a musical work to explain it:

The Ninth Symphony [Beethoven] has a characteristic: a soft, growing murmur, a light being forged until it bursts into a musical explosion. The human voice enters, the voice of the choral mass, it is the earth, which is becoming the voice. Over a background of the choral mass, four individuals sing. The mass has generated those four voices that sing more loudly, but one voice must rise still higher. Never before could it be sung, by anyone, but in this century, after many attempts, and what was once impossible was achieved. (Guzmán 1989b, 142)

Clearly, Guzmán identifies himself with that voice that manages to "rise still higher." In his obsessive pursuit of that dream, amidst a rising river of blood, the caudillo-teacher is increasingly transformed into a teacher-Messiah. Bit by bit, the references to Mariátegui disappear. "Presidente Gonzalo" becomes "the greatest living Marxist-Leninist-Maoist," the "Fourth Sword of Marxism" after Marx, Lenin, and Mao. He is the soloist of the Ninth Symphony, who takes up where Mao was defeated and who believes himself capable of sounding the note that will change the world.[12]

Epilogue: Violence, the Genie, and the Bottle

On 12 September 1992, on all of the television channels, closed up in an iron cage, a disheveled, bearded man, dressed in a striped prison suit reminiscent of days gone by, yells and gesticulates like a corralled beast.[13] It is Abimael Guzmán, finally in custody after 12 years of "popular war." All of the violence accumulated in the social body over centuries would appear to be concentrated inside of that cage, inside of the so-called President Gonzalo, who after his final harangue is entombed for life in a maximum security jail. The genie of the violence had returned to the bottle. A sigh of relief swept the country. Years later, as the official slogan intones, Peru is a country in peace and with a future.

Nevertheless, as happens in some horror movies, nobody predicted that at the moment when he left for his final place of residence, the rivers of violence concentrated in Guzmán would flow out of him, as if through the bars of his cell, and become embodied in other parts of the social fabric and in the government. In reality, the genie remained on the loose and continued to punish us, multiplying and taking on multiple forms, acting in manners that were more subtle but perhaps equally noxious. In effect, both the violence of political discourse, particularly in the media, as well as certain styles of political conduct exacerbated in the Peru of the 1990s were—at least in significant part— inherited from the "dirty war" confrontation between the armed forces and Shining Path, with the complicity to greater or lesser degree of the political parties and the mass media.

The Media Discourse

The violence of discourse in the media was especially blatant in the so-called *chicha* (tabloid) newspapers and in broadcast television, especially when the latter fell under the control of the government of Alberto Fujimori around 1998. Just as in the Senderista "popular trials," it was not enough for the condemned in the media trials to receive the maximum sentence. Equally imperative in this case was the destruction of their image, their symbolic death. What was needed was their annihilation. Just as Shining Path crushed its prey with stones, slashed throats with dull knives, dynamited and blew into thousands of pieces the cadavers of its victims, in this case as well it was essential to feast on them, to tear them apart on successive programs and episodes, to ridicule them and humiliate them in headlines. Both the popular trials of the Senderistas and the media trials of the Fujimoristas, or Montesinistas, produced "exemplary punishments" that had as their objective to intimidate and to vilify. The goal was to imbue the *polis* with fear, paralyzing it through the terror inspired by a hidden power that watched vigilantly yet invisibly from the shadows. The goal was to strike fear into opposition politicians but also into everyday citizens, to ensure that they "not stick their hands into politics."

Styles of Doing Politics

Peru remained for many long years sequestered in the times of the war against hyperinflation (1988–90), the "traditional parties," and subversion. Maintaining alive the phantasm of the war served to legitimate a regime whose fragile institutionality and bellicose style of doing politics exhibited traces of the violence in the midst of which it was born. The tactics of war and the ethos of demolishing one's enemies undermined the potential emergence of a democratic politics understood as consisting of accords, negotiations, or alliances; of democracy understood as the right of the majority to govern; of democracy understood moreover as citizen participation and protection of the rights of minorities. To convert its style of doing politics into common sense, the government pursued an intense struggle for memory that had among its objectives, on the one hand, to portray the Peruvian State and its armed forces as the fundamental victims of terrorist violence and, on the other hand, to create a memory in which the country had been saved by two principal actors: President Alberto Fujimori and his advisor Vladimiro Montesinos, with the armed forces and police as secondary actors. As for all other Peruvians, a few, particularly participants in the peasant *rondas*, figured as extras in the performance, trotted out on such occasions as military parades, but virtually the entire remainder of the country was reduced to a condition of passive spectator, by definition grateful to the pair of superheroes who had saved them. To achieve this double objective, to construct themselves as victims and to implant the memory of the president as savior, the state sought to atomize and consume society, to obscure its own violence and legitimize its dark side, embodied fundamentally in the figure of the advisor Montesinos. The consequences, as we know today, turned out to be disastrous.

4

Revolution by Handbook

The Expansion of Marxism-Leninism in the Social Sciences and the Origins of Shining Path

During the 1970s, a series of texts inundated Peruvian universities.[1] These were handbooks on historical materialism, dialectical materialism, and political economy produced by the Academy of Sciences of the USSR during the Stalinist period and republished numerous times over the course of what today is known as the "Brezhnevian stagnation."[2] This chapter analyzes this influx, which I call the "Revolution by Handbook." These texts helped to create and/or strengthen a common-sense understanding of social science as a closed system of universal truths, a common sense that appealed to the "principle of authority" to legitimate itself, and that considered politics fundamentally in terms of confrontation, head-on clashes, and elimination of the adversary. The existence of this common sense contributed to establishing the bases for the expansion of the Communist Party of Peru-Shining Path, among certain clusters of university youth, and to disarming ideologically many others in the face of the Senderista advance.

I would like to make clear, however, that this common sense did not originate solely in the "Marxism by Handbook." Obviously there were additional elements that explain both the existence of the handbook phenomenon and the emergence of Sendero. These included the misery and backwardness of the country, national political traditions and local authoritarianisms, the weight of the religious factor, and the feelings of insecurity among provincial university youth, among other factors.[3] At the same time Sendero was merely the most highly developed, extreme, and violent version of conceptions that, in their more general characteristics—in their authoritarianism, for example—underlie the entirety of the Peruvian political spectrum and that specifically as "Marxism by Handbook" persist to this day in some Leftist groups, achieving beachheads even in sectors of Aprista youth.

The Authoritarian Divide

The conversion of the various social science disciplines into university degrees formed part of the process of modernization of the state and society that gained momentum around the middle of the century. The first Instituto de Etnología (Institute of Ethnology) was founded at the Universidad de San Antonio Abad del Cusco in 1943, and three years later another was established at the Universidad de San Marcos. In 1956 the Instituto de Sociología (Institute of Sociology) was created in that same university. By 1960 there were already two schools of anthropology, two of economics, two in social work, and one in sociology (Bernales 1981, 33). Prior to that year there existed only nine universities and no more than 30,000 university students in the entire country (ibid., 32). But the pressure from middle and popular sectors on the university was growing. Enactment of Law 13417 resulted in the creation of twenty-three more universities, and enrollments quickly soared, from 30,000 students at the beginning of the decade to 108,000 by the end of the 1960s.

In parallel fashion, around the middle of that same decade, state invest-ment in university education reached its highest levels, accounting for 4.8 percent of the national budget in 1965, which signified a record expenditure (see table 1). Toward the end of the decade, there was nonetheless a decisive break in the relationship of the state to the university, the explosive growth of which had inundated the channels opened up by Law 13417. In what turned out to be one of its greatest errors, in February 1969, the newly installed military government enacted Legislative decree no. 17437 for the Peruvian university. The decree eliminated student co-governance, replaced faculties with academic departments and programs, and, in general, opted for an authoritarian and apolitical modernization of the system, ignoring the context of social democ-ratization and politicization of the university. Subsequent efforts to achieve greater flexibility through a statute for the Peruvian university and a General Law of Education failed to break with the parameters or to break down the barriers erected by the legislative decree. At the same time, the resources allo-cated to the university declined. In 1975, the university budget represented

Table 1 Central government expenditures on education and public
universities, 1960–85

Year	Education expenditures as percent of national budget	University expenditures as percent of education budget	University expenditures as percent of national budget	Public spending per university student[a]
1960	25.0	11.9	3.0	5,777
1965	24.7	19.5	4.8	12,886
1970	20.3	16.7	3.4	8,668
1975–76[b]	19.6	11.5	2.3	5,250
1980	10.1	19.3	1.9	3,517
1985	9.6	23.0	2.2	2,463

Source: CONAI 1986.

[a] In 1,000 soles at 1960 value.

[b] National budgets in the period 1971–76 were biennial.

only 2.3 percent of national spending, compared to 4.8 percent in 1965
(table 1).[4]

In that context, several fissures were generated. On the one hand, while
public universities sank into a general crisis, turned inward, and became radicalized, private universities grew in both number and quality. As part of a
trend, this split reflected the sharp divisions that separated upper sectors and
popular sectors, Lima and the provinces, Andeans and Creoles. It is at this
juncture that the Universidad de San Marcos ceased to play the role that, as
Macera has noted (1977), it had fulfilled between the 1920s and 1950s: a force
for integration of the intellectual and political elites of Lima and the provinces,
and of youth derived from the upper classes and their counterparts from middle
or petty bourgeois sectors.

The other divide arose as a result of the military government's most radical
phase in which, to a degree up to then inconceivable, it expanded the labor
market for professionals in the social sciences.[5] But this expansion took place
precisely when many of these professionals were undergoing a process of radicalization that brought them into militant opposition to the government. This
is when the split occurred between those who would "integrate into the process"
and those who resisted the call of the "philanthropic ogre" and tried to remain
in the universities. The latter group was able to maintain a certain ambiguity,
since given their autonomy universities are at the same time both within and
outside the state apparatus. The effects of this effort to maintain independence
vis-à-vis the state were perverse, in that it sharpened disputes within the

Revolution by Handbook

universities over professorships, the identification of academic programs with political parties, and the composition of governing councils.[6]

The Mexican anthropologist Guillermo Bonfil once referred to the relationship between the state and anthropology in his country as a long marriage that had endured for various decades.[7] In the Peruvian case, by contrast, we can speak barely of a conflictive courtship, a love/hate relationship that lasted throughout the government of General Velasco (1968–75). Even for those who became "integrated into the process," this was an *interrupted* honeymoon, because during the second, less radical phase of the military government (Morales Bermúdez, 1975–80), the social sciences began to be seen as "an ideological apparatus more than as disciplines of scientific rigor" (Bernales 1981, 110). Perceived as minimally productive, responsible for the radicalization of vast sectors of the population, hermetic for their reliance on complicated terminology, the social sciences lost favor during the "second phase" of military government, and the state began to reduce job openings and close off avenues for research in the social sciences.

In 1984, the second Belaúnde government promulgated a new university law, which to some degree softened the most authoritarian edges of the military period, for it reestablished university autonomy, revived the faculties, and again permitted student co-governance. But by not inscribing itself within a broader national project or reversing the trend toward economic strangulation, the public universities remained as "autonomous" islands without resources, abandoned to their fate.

In this manner, if the military government and its successors were not the only ones to blame for the obstacles holding back Peru's universities, their lack of understanding of the processes of ideology, politics, and the sociology of expectation and discrimination that were unfolding within them contributed decisively to their stagnation and deterioration. What were these processes?

Education: A New Myth

It is worth taking a brief digression that will enable us to understand, on the one hand, the importance that education and the university increasingly took on for the popular classes, emergent sectors, and, especially, for Andean migrants to the cities as the twentieth century unfolded, and, on the other hand, what those parents and their children who studied social sciences were looking for, how they understood their profession, and what demands they made of it.

Table 2 Growth of middle-income countries, 1960–82

	Income per capita (% growth) 1960–82	Agriculture (% growth) 1960–82	Mining (% growth) 1960–82	Exports (% growth) 1960–82	Youth with secondary-level education or more (%)	
					1960	1980
Peru	1.0	2.0	2.8	2.7	19.0	76.0
Other countries	3.6	3.2	6.2	3.8	17.0	52.0

Source: Webb 1987.

One useful explanatory axis is what I have labeled elsewhere "the shift from the myth of Inkarrí to the myth of progress" (Degregori 1985a).[8] Between the 1920s and the 1960s, and most of all after the middle of the century, among the majority of the Andean peasantry, until then the most important demographic segment in the country, the myth of Inkarrí was gradually replaced by the myth of progress, diffused without much initial consequence by new bourgeois and mercantile sectors. This shift reoriented Andean populations, who now no longer waited for the Inka and launched themselves instead with an unanticipated vigor toward the conquest of the future and of "progress."

The great peasant mobilizations as well as the massive migrations that transformed the cities also can be understood as products of this shift. The Andean populations on the move seemed to develop a strategy of protracted duration in which education became a medium and long-term intergenerational investment. Thus, the percentage of the population from six to twenty-three years of age who were enrolled as students rose from 40.6 percent in 1960 to 73.8 percent in 1980. At the same time, Peru's ranking for student enrollment within Latin America went from fourteenth place in 1960 to fourth place in 1980, surpassed only by Panama, Argentina, and Cuba (CEPAL 1985, 130). This growth was all the more spectacular considering that in terms of GDP per capita, Peru ranged from eleventh to thirteenth place in regional rankings (ibid., 226). Similar patterns are evident in life expectancy and infant mortality.

The Peruvian case seems exceptional not only in the context of Latin America. In a study carried out by Richard Webb for the United Nations (UN), we see that among the more than sixty countries that the UN identifies as medium-level development, in which most of Latin America is included, in only two decades did Peru experience a quite revealing evolution.[9] In effect, while during this period Peru lags in all economic categories, the growth of its youth population enrolled in secondary or tertiary education is remarkable. Between 1960 and 1980, the figure rises from 19 percent to 76 percent, whereas elsewhere it goes from an average of 17 percent to 52 percent (see table 2).

　　　　　　　　　　　　　　　　Revolution by Handbook

Table 3 Growth of student population in national and private universities, 1960–90

Type of university	1960		1976		1986		1990 (est.)	
	Number	%	Number	%	Number	%	Number	%
National	27,040	89.4	138,505	72.3	250,600	66.3	340,642	67.5
Private	3,207	10.6	53,099	27.7	127,600	33.7	164,058	32.5
Total	30,247	100.0	191,604	100.0	378,200	100.0	504,700	100.0

Sources: 1960 and 1976—Lynch 1984; 1986—INEI 1986, 59; 1990—INEI 1989, vol. 1 (estimated).

Educational aspirations of such force in a poor country with abysmal socio-economic, ethnic, and cultural differences no doubt have profound democratizing content. This is even more evident considering that after an initial stage when state and society pulled in the same direction, the former began to withdraw and from that point onward the social impulse moves in opposition to the state tendency to reduce its participation in education, especially following the outbreak of economic crisis in the middle of the 1980s. Thus, in 1974, the state spent 3.7 percent of GDP on education, and in 1980 that figure had fallen to 2.1 percent (CEPAL 1985, 138). If we go back to table 1, we see that the notable decline in educational spending continues in the 1980s, falling from approximately 20 percent of the budget in 1975 to less than 10 percent a decade later. The recovery of university percentages (from 11.5 percent to 23 percent) during this period reveals only the magnitude of the disaster in other levels of education, for although the university did indeed maintain around 2.2 percent of the national budget, the annual expenditure per student was reduced by at least half in this same period, with the amount allocated in 1985 being five times lower than that of twenty years earlier (see table 1).

When aspirations for greater educational coverage begin to collide with the limits of a state that is not only poor but that at that same time, moreover, does not prioritize education to the same degree, society increasingly takes education into its own hands. This is especially evident in the construction of infrastructure, which in small towns and rural zones is done by local initiative, through financial contributions and communal labor brigades.

At the university level, the retreat of the state is compensated by the growth of private education, though here the segmentation of Peruvian society is again notable, since after high-quality private universities emerged during the 1960s, there was a "third wave" of higher education expansion (Cotler, Grompone, and Rospigliosi 1988). These were universities of low academic quality, born of the new middle sectors' search for prestige and their fear of the politicization of the public universities. Thus, the percentage of students enrolled in private universities went from 10.6 percent in 1960 to 33.7 percent in 1986 (see table 3). The

Table 4 Growth of university population,
1960–90

Year	Total students	% compared to 1960
1960	30,247	100
1965	64,676	214
1970	109,230	361
1975	181,180	599
1980	241,816	799
1985	354,640	1,172
1990	504,700	1,669

Sources: 1960–80—Lynch 1990; 1985–90— Figures derived from data of
INEI.

percentage growth of private education was even greater if we include the figures for students enrolled in the countless centers of learning located in that uncertain and expanding terrain between the secondary and university levels. Part of this growth, the most formalized, appears in official statistics under the rubric of "non-university higher education," which includes only arts education, physical education, teacher training, and the ESEP (Professional Education Schools). In 1986 this sector included 103,500 students, whereas the universities boasted in that same year 378,200 (INEI 1986).[10]

The number of universities rose from seven in 1958 to thirty-three in 1970 and then to forty-six in 1989, without taking into account several more that sought legal recognition. And the number of university students rose from 30,247 in 1960 to 504,700 in 1990 (see table 4). In other words, there was an increase of nearly seventeen times the usual enrollment, whereas the overall population of the country during this same period only doubled. As a result, Peru ranked as the fourth-highest university population in Latin America, surpassing Colombia, which has more inhabitants (CEPAL 1985, 745).

The Growth of the Social Sciences

The demand for degrees in the social sciences rose along with the explosive growth of the universities. Thus the number of universities that offered training in this field multiplied (see table 5). The greatest expansion took place between 1960 and 1969. During the 1970s, the military government tried to rationalize this growth, but even as the pace of growth of new

Table 5 University programs in the social sciences and economics, 1960–85

Subject	1960	1969	1977	1985
Anthropology	2	5	7	8
Archaeology[a]	–	–	–	7
History[a]	–	–	–	6
Political science[b]	–	1	1	–
Sociology	1	8	13	12
Social Work	2	9	10	12
Total social sciences	5	23	31	45
Economics	2	20	22	25
Total social sciences and economics	7	43	53	70

Sources: 1960–77—Bernales 1981, 33; 1985—CONAI 1986.

[a] These fields began to emerge as independent of anthropology and letters, respectively, in the mid-1970s, but our source does not have data for 1977.

[b] The program that Bernales recorded in 1969 and 1977 does not appear in CONAI 1986.

Table 6 Number of students in social sciences and as percentage of total university students, 1960–88

Subject	1960	1965	1970	1975	1980	1985	1988
Total university students	30,247	64,676	109,230	181,601	257,220	354,640	431,040
Economics	322	2,792	6,626	20,302	22,046	27,130	28,535
Social sciences	349	1,447	3,417	10,322	14,276	18,896	18,751
Anthropology	64	169	365	1,108	1,521	2,170	2,112
Archaeology[a]	–	–	–	49	863	1,479	1,552
History	90	139	213	275	804	1,355	1,681
Sociology	70	573	1,084	4,188	4,768	5,930	5,604
Social work	125	566	1,755	4,702	6,320	7,962	7,802
Social sciences as % of university totals	1.2	2.2	3.1	5.7	5.6	5.3	4.4
Economics and social sciences as % of university totals	2.2	6.5	9.2	16.9	14.1	13.0	10.9

Sources: 1960–85—CONAI 1986; 1988—INEI 1989, vol. 1.

[a] Until the early 1970s, archaeology students were included within anthropology.

universities and new social science programs slowed (table 5), the student population continued to increase. The consequence was overenrollments in many of the programs established in the previous decade, as can be seen in table 6.

The most explosive growth took place during the 1960s, but massification was felt with greatest force during the following decade, when sociology enrollments reached ninth place among a total of sixty-nine degrees offered at the time by Peruvian universities (CONAI 1986). In addition, during the 1970s enrollments continued to increase in sustained fashion, with the percentage of students enrolled in higher education pursuing social science degrees reaching its highest level around 1975, when it approached 6 percent. If we include economics, at that time the second most popular degree, the figure is extraordinary: one of every six university students studied social sciences or economics.[11]

Student Profiles

The expansion of the social sciences during the 1960s and 1970s has to do, among other things, with factors that were emerging in society itself, such as the profile of the student body that was forming at the time and the evolution of the professions themselves.

During an initial stage, in the 1960s, the exponential growth of the student body was akin to the conquest of immense, virtually uninhabited territory. The demographic pressure of later years was still not felt. The students trained during this period in social sciences reflect in large measure the process of social democratization and massification that the Peruvian university had begun to experience at the time. The students consisted mostly of *mestizo* youth from the small and medium provincial bourgeoisie, searching for their roots. It is not by chance then that among the most outstanding social scientists of that phase, the majority would begin in anthropology, even when later on some of them would move toward other fields. Because anthropology was influenced by *indigenismo*, its object of study was almost exclusively rural and Andean Peru and, within that setting, the peasant community.

At the same time, that youth underwent a process of political radicalization that affected the entire university student body in a context of social effervescence and international events, such as the Cuban Revolution. Thus, the Movimiento Izquierda Revolucionario (Movement of the Revolutionary Left, MIR) split off from the Alianza Popular Revolucionaria Americana (American Popular Revolutionary Alliance, APRA), but in the universities the division of the old Communist Party in 1964 at the height of the Sino-Soviet polemic had greater repercussions. The pro-Chinese faction managed to gain hegemony over the Frente Estudiantil Revolucionario (Student Revolutionary Front, FER), the Leftist organization that was displacing the APRA from university federations across the entire country. The beginning of the Chinese Cultural Revolution (1966–76) deepened this radical sentiment at the time: revolution was something permanent and youthful.

In this way, beyond seeking roots and explanations, the students began to look to the social sciences as an instrument for revolution. If, as Lenin had said, there could not be "revolutionary practice without revolutionary theory," then the university would have to provide these theoretical foundations. Outside the standard curricula, in informal study circles mimeographed sheets of the Marxist classics circulated from hand to hand.

It was amid this climate that the government promulgated the already mentioned Law 17437, to which the forces of the Left were in general incapable of offering alternatives. Although I mentioned earlier the responsibility of the military government in degrading the condition of the universities in the 1960s, the intellectual and student Left of those years emerges as equally responsible for that deterioration. The university, overwhelmed by demographic pressure and by a radicalism that it could not manage to channel, entered into a phase of "massification without a project" (Lynch 1990). This began the collapse of the public university system and opened up a second phase in this evolution.

It was almost natural that there would emerge a youth opposition to an authoritarian reformism that was military and hierarchical and closed off avenues for political participation. What is curious is the *type* of opposition that emerged: an "economicist radicalism" that could be defined in a single phrase as the attempt to satisfy the expectations of professionalization and social mobility through the path of confrontation. Thus, for example, the most radical groups that in those years gained hegemony in the FER, and thus in the university, characterized the military government as fascist or, at the very least, as fascistoid, and anticipated "popular war" as the strategic path for the transformation of the country. But at the same time they mostly focused their attention on the struggle for easy income, special class schedules, and graduation without preparing a thesis. The extreme radicalism that expanded throughout the universities corresponded to a second wave of the massification of the university. Whereas the former had been driven by the provincial middle classes, this one was constituted by the children of rich peasants or of "*mistis*" from small towns, with a greater Andean component and generally both more popular in origin and poorer. These traits were accentuated in the provincial universities being established in the highlands at the time. The poorer the region, the clearer these characteristics were.

So much so that when we differentiate stages along types of students, we find *tendencies*. There is not a radical rupture between students of the 1960s and 1970s, but rather the accentuation of certain characteristics that to me seem highly relevant. Similarly, when I sketch the profile of the students of the 1970s, I know that it is not a homogeneous universe. My aim is to describe an ideal-type student that corresponds approximately to those who were active in politics and their leadership.

In the case of the social sciences, the social prestige that they acquired during the 1970s and their capacity to satisfy needs for social or political recognition enabled them to attract middle class and even urban upper-class youth. They differentiated themselves from the majority of their counterparts, especially in that they were concentrated principally in the Universidad Católica and, politically, in that they affiliated with the more "modern" parties (the Trotskyites and those that around 1984 comprised the PUM [Mariateguist Unified Party]). But, in general terms, also in the social sciences we notice the same broad tendency.

Revolution by Handbook

In the political arena this new wave of students was reflected in different branches of the FER, which triumphed in almost all of the public universities. In the ideological arena, the new wave for the most part adopted Marxism-Leninism in its Maoist version, which spread explosively in the universities after the failure of Cuban-inspired *foquismo*, and was fanned by the flames of the Chinese Cultural Revolution. (*Foquismo* assumed that establishment of a guerrilla beachhead in the countryside would suffice to spark a larger revolutionary insurrection.) During this time there flourished what I call "Marxism by Handbook." The vehicle for its mass diffusion was a series of texts produced by the Academy of Sciences of the USSR, circulation of which was legalized during the first phase of the military government. Their success was such that some pillars of the world vision that they offered became common sense among the majority of radical youth.

It is legitimate to ask why handbooks that were a slanted simplification of the Marxist classics, produced primarily during the Stalinist period, became university texts. I shall try to decipher some of the reasons.

The new waves of migrant youth who arrived at the university were looking not so much for their roots, for in some sense those roots are abundantly evident. But in the new context, in the hustle and bustle of urban life, they have become aerial roots. They seek, then, to *reaffirm* themselves. It could be said that the students of the 1960s, with a more stable beachhead into modernity, sought to consolidate or reconstruct the bridges that linked them to their Andean past, whereas the students of the 1970s, by contrast, have remained in a sort of no-man's land, caught between two worlds. On one side is the traditional world of their elders, described in an infinite number of ethnological monographs. Its stratifications cease suddenly to operate in the cities, and the students no longer share its myths and rituals, even though when faced with urban aggression, the students feel ethnically and culturally in solidarity with that traditional world (those who deny their roots seldom radicalize—the play on words between "root" and "radical" is apt here). On the other side is the Western world, or more precisely the urban creole world, which discriminates against them and rejects them and which they do not comprehend.

Caught between two worlds, this cohort of youth required an explanation not only for Peru but indeed for everything. It sought a new identity that could provide them with *security*. And it sought that identity in the context of a vacuum of "global political representations" (Macera 1977). The APRA, which in decades past had supplied these representations, had by this time confirmed its journey rightward, and the oligarchy had long been ideologically exhausted. Among the new middle-class parties, Acción Popular (Popular Action) and Democracia Cristiana (Christian Democracy), which never achieved a very high level of reflection, shipwrecked soon after reaching government in 1963. Meanwhile, the elaborations of social-progressivism failed to go beyond the intellectual elite to encompass a wider audience. The so-called new Left, in turn, arose with a pragmatic spirit, interested more in taking up arms than in developing a critical vision of Peru. Only after the defeat of the guerrillas of the MIR and the Ejército de Liberación Nacional (National Liberation Army, ELN) in 1965 would this attitude begin to change.

Marxism by Handbook thus encountered open and fertile terrain. Moreover, it represented a winning combination in that it offered all the explanations and all of the reassurances longed for by a generation that needed both. It was a system of "universal truths" expressed didactically and inscribed in the authoritarian tradition in which this generation of youth had grown up. It was validated by real existing social models and assured an ineluctable victory.

In the first place, the system of truths encompassed all scales—the universe, humanity, the country—and it included all fields of knowledge—philosophy, politics, economics, art, and culture. This *universality* proved attractive to those who found themselves in this sort of no-man's land and who needed, metaphorically, to start over from zero.

At the same time, the handbooks transmitted an authoritarian vision both of social transformation—vanguardism—and of a model of a new society—politically vertical (the single party at the apex) and culturally conservative, even in the name of the struggle against capitalist degeneration. Thus, at some levels to adopt Marxist-Leninist conceptions did not imply a rupture for provincial students, who came from a socially authoritarian milieu of still rigid stratifications and who clashed with "liberal" and "alienated" urban culture.

Not only was the content authoritarian, but so too was the form in which it was transmitted. The handbooks are inscribed within a traditional pedagogical conception, in which the authority of the book (of the author) and the teacher are unimpeachable. This also fit well with the prior school experience of the majority of students.

Even while authoritarian, the form of presentation was undoubtedly accessible, and it was didactic, a quality that was indispensable for youth with deficient prior schooling and cultural backgrounds distant from the urban intellectual baroque style. The handbooks by Georges Politzer and Martha Harnecker, with their flow charts, diagrams, and questionnaires at the end of each chapter, are the best examples of this didacticism.

Because of the consequences that it had, the most important element to note is the exclusionary character of a system of truths that presented itself as the *only* valid and genuinely *scientific* explanation. In this sense, the handbooks constituted a sort of defense mechanism against the avalanche of information that the students could not or did not wish to assimilate. Multiple schools of juxtaposed ideas and theories, each with its own jargon and more or less hermetic, overpopulated every discipline. By contrast, the handbooks offered a single explanation—historical and dialectical materialism; a single jargon—Marxist-Leninist; and a single conclusion—the inevitable arrival of socialist revolution. They become a sort of shortcut toward modernity for those "premoderns" who, without ceasing to be premodern, can consider themselves in possession of a science that is not only the most new and most exact but also *morally legitimate* in that it offers the key for the substantial and positive transformation of the world. Thus, the disorientation and feelings of inferiority that they run the risk of experiencing under the avalanche of information that they cannot process can be transformed, even into a feeling of superiority, through knowing that one is in possession of *the* truth.

As Rafael León explains (1991, 8), "In the '70s I had a friend, a militant in Bandera Roja, who when 'the ones at la Católica' started to talk with us in terms that were hard to understand, she'd sing to us a little rhyme that went like this: 'the people [*el pueblo*] don't need / for you to speak with them in theories. / what you told them today / the people already knew it.'"

This feeling of security and faith revealed itself in many student theses as well. Consider one of the best of the theses presented at the Universidad de Huamanga, in which the introduction included the following passage:

We are aware that Peru is undergoing a revolutionary phase. Compre-
hending the inevitability of the revolutionary transformation of our society
some social sectors and classes struggle to take the lead of the revolutionary
process. In the university, as an institution, these struggles are reflected at
an ideological-political level. It is thus that, suddenly, basic problems of
revolutionary theory begin to take on significance for intellectual sectors,
principally in the university. One of these problems and perhaps the most
important of all is that of the correct classification of Peruvian society, and
within that theoretical framework, the characterization of the agrarian
sector.

When we set out to develop this study, we endeavored to study the
latifundio from a materialist conception, that is, a perspective that will
provide a structural explanation of the sector and enable us in that fashion
to abstract its essence and identify the derivative aspects.

But in addition to the materialist [dimension] we wanted a dialectical
notion, with which we would achieve a study of the *latifundio* in its evolution, in its internal contradictions and in the general interdependence of
its parts.[12]

The content need not necessarily correspond with the initial declaration of
faith. In this particular case the thesis was a quality monograph with useful
quantitative data on the socioeconomic conditions of a rural district of
Ayacucho.

In the social science programs, by presenting themselves as the disseminators
of the only true science, the handbooks constituted themselves as the best
shortcuts to secure the degree most quickly and easily. All the more so if all
courses repeated more or less the same topics and texts, give or take a few
chapters. If *the* social science was condensed into these texts, everything else
was secondary and even superfluous, data, monographs, or techniques that
could, after all, be learned in the practice of the profession itself. The handbooks
constituted then the natural complement to *economicism*, of the struggle, as
previously noted, for easy entrance exams, special class schedules, and graduation without having to defend a thesis.

But at the same time, by conceiving revolutionary transformation of society
as a fact governed by laws that are fulfilled inexorably, the Marxism of the
handbook fueled radicalism in that it provided a total guarantee of victory.
This satisfied the longing for revolutionary change of a generation of youth
that suffered in flesh and blood from discrimination, poverty, and injustice.
The guarantee of victory had been ratified already in practice by the triumph
of the Russian and Chinese revolutions and by the advance of the struggles of
the peoples of the Third World, particularly in Southeast Asia. Thus, the

youth felt themselves to be in conditions to become protagonists in an inevitably victorious epic.

Despite the fact that the manuals came from the USSR, this possibility of heroic radicalism had the effect that in the Sino-Soviet polemic, the bulk of the youth adopted the pro-Chinese position. Faced with "revisionism" and the stagnation of the USSR during the Brezhnev era, China stood out as "the great proletarian cultural revolution." Its youthful red guards "bombarded the general fortress of the capitalist roaders" and promised successive cultural revolutions until the day that they would conquer communism: permanent youth. But equally or more important was the fact that Maoism offered a peasant-centered version of revolution for semifeudal countries. The leading role of the peasant and the image of Peru as a semifeudal country proved easy to accept for students who themselves—or their parents—came from primarily peasant zones, and where social relations, or at least ideology, retained strongly semifeudal content. The Foreign Language Editions of Beijing, which rivaled the publications from Moscow, contributed to the popularization of Maoism. They disseminated the *Complete Works* of Mao, in particular the *Four Philosophical Theses*, which revealed nothing less than the general laws of philosophy, quintessence of didacticism in comparison with the greater complexity of, say, Lenin. And they offered illustrated magazines, full of color and very inexpensive, that placed emphasis on rural development: "To Learn from Tachai in Agriculture."

Thus, through the Maoist peasantry the youth proceeded to an ideologically charged reconstruction of their ties with the Andean world, partially broken by the experience of passing through school, the university, and the city. Culture returned as ideology, everyday life as "science," the Andean man as "poor peasant of the lower sector."

In conclusion, the handbooks were a success among youth stressed by contradictions not only in the cultural arena but also in the social sphere: between their longing to radically transform a reality whose injustices affected them directly and the quest for social ascent through education, in enormously adverse cultural and ethnic circumstances.

The circular reasoning, the system of closed truths, and the mixture of economicism and authoritarianism reached special intensity among the students living in university housing and eating in the university dining halls. The university was their entire world, a closed universe where they enjoyed access based on clientelism: the party that controlled the dining hall and housing distributed access to these scarce goods in exchange for loyalties. It was no coincidence that the university office for social service activities in Ayacucho, on

Table 7 Expansion of university teachers of social sciences and economics, 1969-76

Subject	1969		1976	
	Number	% of university faculty	Number	% of university faculty
Social sciences	415	5.2	750	6.4
Economics	320	4.0	670	5.7
Total social sciences and economics	735	9.2	1,420	12.1
Total university faculty	8,013	100.0	11,749	100.0

Source: Bernales 1981, 39.

which the housing and meal services depended, was among the key positions for Sendero, which placed there one of its principal leaders, Antonio Díaz Martínez.

The Revolution by Handbook reached takeoff speed, in part, when its distribution expanded to include a significant number of young professors. As the number of universities training social scientists grew, so too did the need for instructors, and between 1969 and 1976, the number of social science instructors practically doubled (see table 7). We could go so far as to say that there were more positions available than there were applicants to fill them, because instructors were also required in order to teach students from other fields who now included social science courses, particularly in historical and/or dialectical materialism, in their study plans. There was also demand in the ESEPs or higher institutes in Lima and the provinces, where new graduates would head off to take teaching jobs; those new graduates were a product of a radicalized atmosphere, but their training had deteriorated rapidly. Neither Claude Lévi-Strauss nor Louis Althusser, to mention two of the most noteworthy figures of the decade, figured often on their horizons. Frequently absent as well was any of the Peruvian literature produced by "the elite." And even the manual by Martha Harnecker could be deemed excessively heterodox, as was the case at the Universidad de Huamanga, where the works of F. V. Konstantinov or Victor Afanasiev reigned supreme. Education was not only impoverished by massification without resources: it turns out that it was also rendered rigid by the rise of dogmatism.

The following account by an anthropologist who entered a provincial university as a professor at the beginning of the 1970s illustrates this dynamic:

When I was a student I was on the Left, but I'd done my studies before the handbooks were in vogue, I'd studied classical anthropology and all of a sudden I had to teach the Introduction to Social Sciences course, which actually was Historical Materialism I; actually, I think that at some point it even was called that. So they lent me the manual by Konstantinov and for me it was a relief. The whole course was right there, and for a young professor who had just started, it took a load off to not have to worry about what I'd teach, whether they'd understand it. Also there was the risk of being labeled reactionary. I'm sure that subconsciously one tried to offer "what people like," and what they liked was the easy stuff, for sure, everything neat and tidy. Ideally with a flow chart.

I remember that I was learning the night before the stuff that I was going to teach the following day. Reading for the first time that the productive forces were made up of . . . I don't remember . . . were the interaction of man and nature, but there was a very precise terminology that I'd just discovered that I'd forgotten. But in those days it all seemed the best. I tried to get ahead and would prepare several classes in advance, but I always finished all the points super quickly; I didn't have any examples, nothing concrete, or from my own experience, so it all didn't take too long. That was in 1970. Afterward, in my trip to Lima—it would have been '72 or '73—I discovered Martha Harnecker. In comparison with the Soviet rubbish, it was more of an easy read and didactic, she was Althusserian, though those parts to be honest didn't stand out for me because I didn't understand them: all the stuff about mode of production and social formation and synthesis of multiple determinations. My god! But the Sendero professors, we called them *oportos*, accused me in a polemic of being a Trotskyite revisionist.

Really I thought that I was discovering the key to the functioning of society, something as clear and irrefutable as the law of gravity. Can you imagine what that means to a twenty-five-year-old kid? It was to learn to handle a secret language, an abracadabra that let me open all the sesames.

The impact of the handbooks was greater still once they reached the schools of education and, through the teachers who had graduated from these programs, secondary school students as well. One must keep in mind, in addition, that many graduates from the social sciences found work in high schools and further reinforced this tendency.

Thus, little by little, the course plans of a majority of social science programs saw the historical/dialectical materialism couplet replace the standard Introduction to Social Sciences. Later it flowed beyond the limits of the social science programs and reached entire universities alongside courses like Dialectic of Nature and others along similar lines. Thus was produced, at the

Revolution by Handbook

beginning of the 1970s, a particular brand of curricular reform in most Peruvian universities.[13]

And Nevertheless . . .

Despite the many obstacles and troublesome divisions, during these years there were still important advances and clarifications. In the first place, with the massification of higher education came a certain democratization of the social sciences. In addition, the very social effervescence that Peru was living through at the time was conducive to attracting good students to orient their studies toward careers in social sciences so they were not only the port of call for those who could not find vacancies in other, more demanding professions.

On a theoretical level, in those instances where it managed to elude the most sterile extremes of dogma, the spread of Marxism fostered a critical vision of Peru and touched on themes that before that time had been forgotten by a harmonic and ahistorical vision of the country, inadequate to describe a country rife with structural contradictions, in which Marxism placed emphasis at the time: economics, social classes, dependency, and so on. That the shortcut provided by the handbooks was the path most frequently taken had clear causes, but that does not negate the advances, nor does it imply that everyone became totally "*handbook-ized.*"

Part 2

Harvesting Storms

Why Shining Path Failed

5

 Youth, Peasants, and Political Violence

Ayacucho, 1980–1983

On 17 May 1980, in the community of Chuschi (Ayacucho), the Communist Party of Peru–Shining Path (Sendero Luminoso) launched its self-proclaimed "people's war." At the time, Sendero was basically a regional party, with very small groups outside of its principal base, the Department of Ayacucho. This base largely consisted of university professors and students, and schoolteachers (based throughout the rural primary and secondary school system). In other writings, I have sought to explain how the encounter between intellectuals and young students in the Universidad Nacional de San Cristóbal de Huamanga (UNSCH, Ayacucho) occurred, and its evolution during the 1970s (Degregori 1985a, 1989a, 1990).

Although Shining Path began to send cadres to rural zones during 1977–78, by 1980 the organization was far from having a significant presence among the peasantry, even that of Ayacucho. However, when the armed forces entered and took political-military control of the Department of Ayacucho shortly after Christmas 1982, Sendero had already achieved the "semiliberation" of approximately 80 percent of rural areas in the northern provinces of Ayacucho, and was prepared to lay siege on Huamanga, the departmental capital.

How was it possible to expand the "people's war" so greatly in barely two and a half years? This text seeks to *begin* to answer this question, as well as to analyze peasant responses to the presence of Shining Path, responses that largely marked the limits of Sendero's advance. I draw on testimonies gathered from peasants, small merchants, professors, and secondary school students who lived through that experience in approximately a dozen communities in the provinces of Cangallo, Vilcashuamán, Sucre, Huancasancos, Huanta, and La Mar. Two of my informants were, for a time, Shining Path militants. The violence in the region impeded the systematic collection of testimonies. Some I have gathered personally, others via colleagues and friends in Ayacucho. The interviewees do not constitute a representative sample, and they answered questions only to the extent they chose, or were able, to do so. Given these limitations, and the fact this is a first reading of the testimonies, my claims here should be taken as hypotheses that will continue to be tested. Prior to moving into the main themes, I note two points:

(1) The weak ties Shining Path had with organized sectors and, in particular, the peasantry around 1980 were due to a series of reversals the party suffered during the 1970s within diverse social organizations where it had previously exercised influence, and to its incapacity to establish a significant presence in new organizations that were emerging during the second half of that decade (Degregori 1985b). However, these weak ties were also the consequence of an option that Sendero had been developing for several years, and which finally came together around 1977. In the early years of the decade (1970s), precisely when the other small parties that formed the Peruvian Left decided to "go to the masses," Shining Path withdrew to the University of Huamanga (Ayacucho), where its maximum leader, Abimael Guzmán, and the initial nucleus of Sendero were dedicated to the study of Marxism. They managed to elaborate an extremely orthodox party line, one that they proselytized among the university students. With these students they managed to form a small party, but one that was ideologically and organically very compact. Shining Path converted itself into a classic party that constructed itself from the top down, and from ideology to organization. It adhered to Stalin's maxim: "the party line decides everything, and when the party line is laid down and is *correct*, then the cadres decide everything." Therefore, social movements are of no interest. If, as one of Sendero's central mottos affirmed, *everything but power is an illusion*, then except for the party—which is the privileged instrument for taking power—everything is an illusion. Society is an illusion or, in any case, it is only of interest to the extent that the masses are molded in the image and likeness of the party. In that sense, they do not prioritize unions, communities, or federations, but rather they give precedence to the party's so-called generated organizations that constitute the tie between these organizations and the masses. Consequently, I will focus my analysis on the leadership and mid-level Senderista commanders, made up overwhelmingly of professors, university students, and teachers during the late 1970s, and particularly from 1980 onward.

(2) One must keep in mind, moreover, that the social base Shining Path constructed was in the Department of Ayacucho. Here the principal social movement during the 1960-'70s was not a peasant land invasion

Youth, Peasants, and Political Violence

movement, as in other parts of the Andes, but rather a movement composed of secondary school students demanding access to free education. It was this student movement that shook Ayacucho and Huanta in 1969 (Degregori 1990). Thus Sendero was expanding in a region with a low density of peasant organizing, at least of the sort that converged in the Confederación Campesina del Perú (CCP), composed of federations, unions, and other similar organizations.

The Nexus: Rural Youth

There have been few studies on the advances, and the limits, of Shining Path's insertion among the peasantry. Berg (1986) has emphasized how Sendero took advantage of the contradictions between communities and cooperatives in various zones in Andahuaylas; Isbell (1988) notes that for Sendero, the target of the revolution is the new stratum of merchants and intermediaries, which was strengthened by the agrarian reform; Manrique (1989) warns that the continued existence of rural bossism (*gamonalismo*), understood as the predominance of precapitalist commercial capital, provides fertile terrain for Sendero's advance in Junín.

Recognizing that the phenomenon requires a multifaceted approach, I am going to foreground the role of the young sons and daughters of *comuneros* (members of peasant communities). These sons and daughters are secondary school students (and even some youth in the final grades of primary school), and form a key link between Shining Path and the rural population. To illustrate this, I will use the testimony of a young man, "Nicario," from a community in Cangallo that I will call Rumi. The son of "middling peasants," with some family members on the coast (among them a brother), Nicario was a seventeen-year-old secondary school student when Sendero entered his community. For some two years, he was a member of Sendero's militia. As something of a "countertestimony," I will use the life history of "Arturo," another young man from Rumi who never joined SL. He was a militant in another group that, during this same period, formed the Izquierda Unida (United Left). (See testimony under the appendix heading at the end of this chapter.)

Nicario's testimony provides various points of entry. I highlight just a few aspects:

(1) In the zone there is a significant generation gap, and it is exacerbated by the incorporation of young people into Shining Path. Converted into the armed generation, these young people are going to subject/convince the adults. The relationship is ambiguous due to the familial and cultural ties

that bind generations; however, with the expansion of Sendero, suddenly these young people are "involved in something else."

(2) This is a politically and socially "available" youth. (a) In political terms: testimonies from other young people in the same community, from Arturo for example, reveal the tenuous presence of diverse Leftist tendencies at the same time Sendero's expansion begins. But in a short time, the young people joined Sendero, almost in their entirety. (b) In social terms: Nicario finds himself literally torn between two paths, and travels between them.[1] He could have joined the drug-trafficking trade, but served in Shining Path and ended up working in the informal sector in Lima.

What joins the two paths is the novelty and the hope of well-being; progress and/or "bettering oneself": by way of the market in one case; by way of the (new) state, that is to say power, on the other. Arturo, from the same community of Rumi, says something revealing about this:

> They said that Ayacucho was going to be a liberated zone by 1985. A famous illusion that they have created among the *muchachos* was, way back in 1981, that by '85 there would be an independent republic. Wouldn't you like to be a minister? Wouldn't you like to be a military leader? Be something, no? One *muchacho* told me that. In 1985 the revolution is going to triumph and then those of us in Sendero, those of us with more time as militants in Sendero, we're going to be ministers. It was a way of getting the young people's hopes up, no?

(3) The appearance of the university students who form the guerrilla columns reveals the seductive attributes of power: weapons, boots, and authority. Power appears in all its awesome splendor, and wins over the majority of young people who are assured they will be granted the same attributes. As Arturo recounts, "They were young people who studied in Cangallo. Adolescents who were desperate to learn about weapons, for example a machine gun. For them to use dynamite was a big deal. Only the brave did this—for them to grab a weapon was something from another level, more hierarchical." The young people squander this power. Their first actions are to paint walls and set off dynamite in the pueblo, thus disturbing the quiet of rural nights. According to Arturo, they "blew it up just for the sake of blowing it up. Nothing more."

(4) It is interesting to observe how, as one descends the pinnacle of the Shining Path pyramid toward the base, the motivations change, and the "Marxist-Leninist-Maoist science" is "contaminated" by the rural Andean context.

    (a) *Different motivations.* Elsewhere I have used the following simile: "Regarding the ideology, we could imagine the relationship between the old column of cadres, the new intermediate cadres, and the militants

        Youth, Peasants, and Political Violence

and sympathizers at the base who participate in the 'generated organizations' or in the 'popular guerrilla army,' as similar to that which exists among theologians, village priests and congregations" (Degregori 1989b, 24). I add, however, that in a hyperideologized, vertical party that is self-defined as a "war machine," those whom we might call "theologians" would continue to have the decisive weight. But in this text we are interested in the priests and their congregations. We could make the previous simile more precise with an illustration (see chart 1).

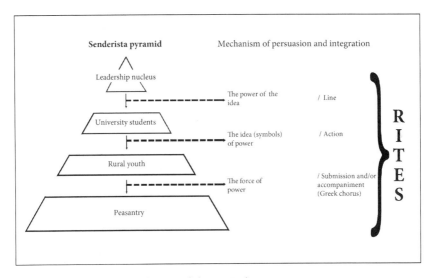

Chart 1 Structure and reproduction of Shining Path

Seduced by the absolutely coherent discourse of their professors, university students identify themselves with Shining Path, above all else through study of the party line. Rural secondary school students, seduced by the symbols of power with which the university students-converted-into-guerrillas are imbued, integrate themselves fundamentally via action. We recall the dynamite they detonated "just to blow it up." In both cases something we might call the "demonstration effect" plays a role. They join a prestigious organization that transforms them. Incorporation into Shining Path has many elements of a rite of passage or initiation into a religious sect: the armed sect.

To the peasantry, the new power demonstrates its coercive capacity, which already includes a certain measure of terror. Nicario tells us about executions in neighboring communities, when Sendero was already present in Rumi. However, Arturo relates a similar episode in a nearby community, *before* Sendero's arrival in Rumi:

There has been an experience where they assassinated a postal worker in the pueblo X, they cut off his testicle, cut out his tongue, accusing him of being an informer. So this generated, I don't know, like a wildfire it spread that they had executed him for being an informer and that this was how they were going to bury all the informers. It was a way of waging a war of nerves with the population.

Additionally, the appearance of Shining Path touches on several anthropological topics related to the "inversion of the world": they come from outside; they arrive at night, and in the region they are known as the *tuta puriq* (night walkers); they emerge in the light of day in the midst of a fiesta.

From the peasant masses they expect obedience and accompaniment. The image that comes to mind is that of a chorus that responds from the shadows to the slogans shouted by those who walk with Shining Path.

(b) *Contamination*: The official Marxist-Leninist discourse of Shining Path undergoes a transformation into a peasant utopia as it expands toward the peasantry and as the Shining Path project is shaped in Ayacucho.

Examples of this transformation are Sendero's ideas about a "strangled Lima" and the necessary return of the urban poor to the new rural republic;[2] the possibility of confronting the armed forces because of the massive desertions those forces would suffer; the vision of organization, which in other testimonies appears even more clearly; and the idea they have about street and other markets that appear only indirectly in Nicario's account—in the party demands that peasants not cultivate for the market.

When the armed forces enter in the region at the end of 1982, the "end of utopia" scenario reminds one of *La guerra del fin del mundo* by Mario Vargas Llosa. In Ayacucho the utopia sears the cadres' imaginations with flames but, in contrast with Antonio Conselheiro's vision, barely or briefly sparks the enthusiasm of the masses, as we shall see.

(5) Around 1982 the pure power to which Sendero aspires begins to construct a new state that in practice combines the party's monopoly on power, proper to Marxism-Leninism and Maoism, with older Andean forms of power and the state.[3] Corporal punishments, whippings, and hair cutting are a continuation of the old Andean lordly (*señorial*) society and the old *misti* power. The party's large-scale land cultivation resembled the massive projects conducted in the land of the Sun, the Inca, or the large landowner; the mobilization of large populations, both for planting crops as well as for the sort of *chaco* (hunting parties) that led to the seizure of Allpachaka, recalled the pre-Hispanic state or colonial *mitas*.[4]

Campesino Responses

However, the relationship between Shining Path and the peasantry in those years was far from harmonious. Steve J. Stern (1990) coined the term "resistant adaptation," which aptly captures the responses of the majority of the peasantry: those responses lie somewhere between acceptance and rebellion. Ayacuchan peasants are capable of adapting to the presence of Sendero because they share elements of an authoritarian *señorial* culture, in which Sendero appears as the new boss or patron (*patrón*), hard and inflexible, but "just" in displacing others who are, in general, unjust or abusive. The peasants resist when Sendero's ideology, political objectives, and methods collide with what we might call an Andean rationality, or in any case when Shining Path threatens the conditions for reproduction of the community (see chart 2).

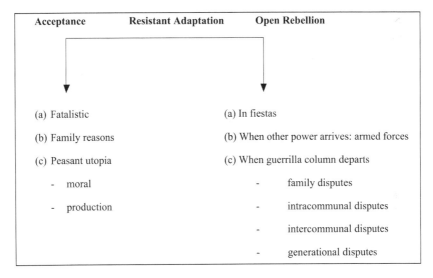

Chart 2 Peasant responses to Shining Path

Resistant Adaptation

The following testimony, from a community in the province of Sucre, succinctly sums up resistant adaptation:

> The lieutenant governor [state authority] continues to exercise [his position], but clandestinely. That is, when the *compañeros* [Shining Path]

come here, we tell them we don't have a lieutenant governor, that we haven't had one for some time, that they've taken away our official seals . . . and when the reactions come, well, they present themselves, that is, the authorities surface so that the pueblo doesn't have problems, but clandestinely. (Pedro, young adult peasant)

The following two testimonies, from the provinces of Huancasancos and Cangallo, respectively, refer to Shining Path's "people's trials" in which this attitude acquires harrowing characteristics:

So this woman, they punished her with fifty lashes because she had talked, complaining about the unfair distribution of the harvest. It was a poor family and she had been drinking. They cut her hair, shaved it off. And the other, they also gave him fifty lashes and cut an ear with scissors. His ear is still mutilated.
And what did people say?
Nothing. Well, punish but don't kill—just that. (Juvenal, adult peasant)

And the second testimony:

Now people are unhappy because [Shining Path] has done so many stupid things [cojudezas]. They've killed innocent people, saying they were informers. You know, I think, if someone has committed an error, they should be punished—just that. They should have whipped them, cut their hair . . . but not do what they did. They killed [the mayor] like he was a pig.
And what did people do?
Nothing. They were armed, what were we going to do? Nothing. That's why I say, they did so many stupid things. (Mariano, petty merchant)

The phrase "punish but do not kill" marks the limits of peasant acceptance. Death is the limit, at least in the ambit of the so-called people's trials. It is a limit that finally came to exasperate the Shining Path cadres, as we see in the following testimony. This testimony comes from a young man in a community in Cangallo who had participated in one of Sendero's "generated organizations":

So a person had collected money in the name of Sendero Luminoso and they had captured him. Such people were judged in the town plaza. That's when they asked people, "These men have done such and such"—saying that—"so what do you all say? Shall we kill them or punish them?"
That's when the community spoke: "Why are you going to kill them? Punish them," that's what the community said.

"Oh, you still have these archaic ideas of defending yourselves all the time. From now on we aren't going to ask. We already know that you are going to defend them. We need to cut off their heads because the bad weed must be totally exterminated. If we pardon the bad weed we are never going to triumph, never going to better ourselves." That's what they said. (Cesáreo, teacher)

In this case it is striking how the "archaic ideas" of the community stand in opposition to the anxiety of Shining Path cadres to "better ourselves." Although I have noted how Sendero becomes "contaminated" in the lower echelons by Andean elements, this contamination is insufficient because neither the ideology nor the political project emerged from peasant aspirations or imaginary. The Shining Path cadres, ideologized to the point of fundamentalism, are ready to kill and to die for their project, but they cannot succeed in winning over the "masses."[5] This is a utopia of cadres that cannot make itself a utopia of the masses. The cadres are vicars of a God who speaks, at times literally, Chinese.

Death, or rather the type of death that Shining Path imposed, constitutes one of the gaps that separates it from the peasantry (I have not included the heartbreaking and traumatic context in which these deaths are inflicted, and which appear in numerous testimonies). However, this is not only because the peasants have a "culture of life"; the image of peasants in Allpachaka embracing their cows and bulls to prevent their death is not simply romantic and telluric. These women are also shepherds, and for them the death of their cattle is equivalent to the destruction of a factory for its workers.

In the testimony I just cited, the dialogue continues:

But if they were delinquents, why did people insist they not kill them?
And their children? Who was going to take care of their families?

These are pragmatic concerns for a society in which the economic base is very precarious, that establishes intricate kinship ties and very complex reproduction strategies, and that has to maintain its labor force. Killing, eliminating a node in these networks, has repercussions beyond the nuclear family. A testimony from Allpachaka, gathered after its destruction, confirms this:

In Allpachaka there were a lot of cattle rustlers and they have killed them. So their families became anti-Senderistas and they have begun to denounce and point to innocent people as Senderistas. I think they shouldn't have killed them but rather punished them so they would correct their behavior. (Alejandro, university student, from a peasant family)

For Shining Path the peasant world appeared flat, without historical density or social complexity, divided only into rich, middling, and poor peasants, and into the good and the bad. When Sendero punishes a rich person who behaved badly—an abusive cattle rustler or someone immoral, an unfaithful spouse, or a drunk—they can win acceptance, because they are "correcting" the person, and they become functional members once again within the community. When they kill them, Sendero shreds the delicate social fabric and opens a Pandora's Box they are subsequently incapable of controlling.

Acceptance

When Shining Path is accepted, it is not so much for its project as for the possibility of obtaining some very concrete personal, family, or communal advantage. Berg (1986) has demonstrated this for Andahuaylas. A story from a community in La Mar explains the ways in which this dynamic unfolds:

> Maybe the worst thing Sendero could have done is having trusted very young people with little experience. I mean, those that came from other places [referring to the guerrilla columns] left sons and daughters of the same communities as their designated people in charge, and then they left. Those young people totally distorted the plans that Sendero had for governing. They opted for taking vengeful attitudes, acting on grudges. Maybe one father against another father because they had some sort of problem over boundaries in their *chacras*, over animals, theft, losses, fights between a man and a woman; because Sendero had given them responsibility for the locality, they began to take reprisals, revenge, and that is how the massacres happen. That's how people come to disagree with it. (José, teacher)

The speaker is a teacher, at the time a Shining Path sympathizer. The scenario he depicts is different. While the guerrilla column was in his locality—that is, while the university students were present—there were no problems. The problems begin when the column leaves, without knowing that in their wake they leave a hornet's nest of contradictions that could not be controlled later.

Open Rebellion

Generally, open rebellion occurs when the principal Shining Path column leaves, and more frequently when the armed forces arrive, representing another *patrón* who usually appears even more powerful than Sendero. It is, of course, Sendero's own errors that facilitate the formation of the "*rondas*," or community patrols, which depended on the armed forces in rural Ayacucho in later years.

I want to highlight two ways in which the logic of Shining Path is at odds with peasant logic, and how these contradictions can provoke open rebellion. One has to do with the entry of the armed forces. According to the laws of Maoist warfare, "when the enemy advances, we retreat." In effect, when the armed forces enter Ayacucho, Sendero falls back. In that moment, a contradiction emerges with the role of the traditional Andean *patrón*, whose place Sendero had come to occupy: the *patrón* protects. Thus, when Shining Path retreats, the sense of deception is great. The following statement from a community in Huanta resonates with slight variation across various testimonies: "They told us, 'It is necessary to be prepared for war, to destroy the enemy.' We believed them, but once they attacked Huanta and killed two *guardías*.[6] After the attack they escaped and they screwed us. They practically gave us up, sold us out. That's not a manly thing to do, *pues*" (Walter, peasant).

The other contradictory logic has to do with fiestas (celebrations). Shining Path tends to suppress traditional fiestas in various places. They allege that the celebrations are costly, but underlying this stance is the disdain cadres have for customs they label "archaic." However, there is more involved here; the party seems to be uncomfortable with the "inversion of the world" aspects of the fiestas. In the exercise of total power, such openings are not permitted. Their fears are not unfounded. In several places, such as Huancasancos and Huaychao, it is during fiestas that the population rebels against Shining Path. For example, in a community in Vilcashuamán, the Shining Path members suppress fiestas "because maybe when we are in the fiestas, they [the community] might betray us, there could be problems" (testimony of Pedro).

Young People between Two Worlds

Rural young people, who were key links in the chain of SL's expansion throughout the countryside, can become the weakest link. This is because they find themselves torn between two worlds (see chart 3). In Allpachaka, young people torn between party orders to eliminate the livestock and the weeping of the shepherds. In La Mar, torn between the governing logic of the party and familial loyalties, feuds, and vendettas. Torn between the party and the market as a possible route to "progress" and social mobility.

The army's entrance was a decisive moment. Nicario "breaks." Many others, however, opt to join the party and become the breeding ground that permits, in combination with other factors, the expansion of Shining Path

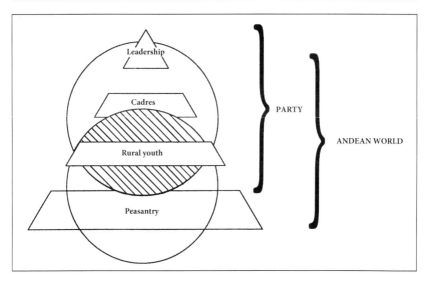

Chart 3 Relationship between the party and the "masses"

into different parts of the country. Others continue to be active in Ayacucho, but neither there nor in other parts of the country would there be a repetition of the Ayacuchan scenario from the beginning of the 1980s. Recourse to terror will have to increase as Sendero expands into other zones. In Ayacucho, Shining Path is largely converted into one actor among others: armed and powerful, but without the hegemony that characterized its first phase. It constitutes one faction within some communities, or it inserts itself in one or more communities at odds with others within a broader area. The party is immersed in contradictions that at times extend back to stages prior to the Spanish conquest (Degregori 1985a).

Sendero's strength in the years ahead comes, to a great extent, from the conduct of the armed forces. One of Shining Path's principal slogans states, "The party has a thousand eyes and a thousand ears." In other words, in general Sendero knows who to kill and, if the peasantry submits to their dictates, people can survive. Arturo speaks about Rumi: "With the threats to informers, the community opted not to say anything—just to remain quiet and live their lives. And if a Senderista asked for support, the people gave it, nothing more."

But while the party has a thousand eyes and ears, the armed forces are blind or, more specifically, color blind. They seem to see the world in black and white, and when they see dark skin they shoot without differentiating between terrorists and peasants. This pattern was particularly characteristic of the armed forces between 1983 and 1984.

Youth, Peasants, and Political Violence

In an admittedly schematic manner, one might say that beginning in 1983 in Ayacucho, a colonial army confronted a feudal counterpart. I want to finish with a testimony from La Mar, which reflects this cultural misunderstanding (*desencuentro*). The naval marines, the most coastal and racist of the three branches of the Peruvian armed forces, come to pursue the Senderistas who in turn seek cover in the highlands, beyond the reach of the marines:

> More or less a kilometer away from where the navy was, Shining Path members shouted in Quechua so the peasantry could understand everything. They shout, "Chay llapa chichuwarmi, chay llapa maricón, chay llapa miserable, llapa allqu, yanaumakuna, chaykuna qamuchun kaymanñoqankuwan tutaparakunankupaq, pilianankupaq." Because the marines did not understand Quechua, their guides translated for them: "This is how they're insulting you: 'pregnant women, faggots, scoundrels, dogs, black heads (referring to the black balaclavas they wore to ward off the cold), come meet up with us, fight with us.'" And they answered back: "Tell those motherfuckers, whores, terrorists full of shit, come down here and fight—if you're men, come down and fight here."

Appendix: Nicario's Testimony (Abbreviated)

The Jungle (Selva)

When we were still kids, we would go to the selva. We were growing, we needed to study, those kinds of things, and we already had to leave for the selva. For me, I liked it because there was a lot of fruit. So we were always going, to eat fruit—all types of fruit. There were mandarin oranges, bananas.

We would go anywhere where they needed workers. From Monday to Saturday we worked, from the early morning to the afternoon, and then we would rest.

With the *narcos*, it was no big deal, there were no problems. They looked for guys they could trust. For example, I had already gone about three times and according to them, they had seen that I was calm, quiet, that's why they said to me, "You know, you're going to work with us." So I went, helping. We worked from four in the morning to eleven at night, moving the liquid from the coca, getting the drug out with kerosene, drawing water out in a cylinder— that was the plan, all day long. I would have stayed with them, but I came back because at the time I was in love with a girl, in Rumi. They kept insisting, "Don't go, work with us, work just another year with us. . . . In Ayacucho, wherever you want, I'll buy you a house." I came back for her, but when I arrived in Rumi she was already with somebody else. So that's how I ended up there, so I just studied.

Sendero

In those times, Sendero still didn't exist, no? Sure, more or less I heard things, but only a little. They only painted walls, blocked the roads with rocks. So nobody took it seriously back then. The first were from the University of Huamanga—they started going out to organize in different communities. In the community of Mayu, quite a few of them arrived. But back then only three or four people attended the meetings, just a few people. Mostly they were young students; young women, married women didn't attend. That was 1981.

In my community there were three of four young students. But they were pretty reserved. Yes, we young people knew they were involved in that, but we didn't give it much importance. Instead, we insulted them, bothered them—opportunists, adventurers, no? So they didn't respond, they just looked at us, they laughed, that's how it was. We young people were independent, but we always lent them support. Like when there was a meeting in Cangallo, yes we participated in the meetings held by many of the Leftists groups—but fewer of those on the Right, no?

When I was in the second year of secondary school, I was the first of my contemporaries to attend their meetings. This guy from the University of San Cristóbal invited me. So I, well, I accepted easily . . . because at the time, it was '82, Sendero was quite active, with assaults, confrontations. So us young people started to talk about that. We already wanted to attend but nobody was talking to us, nobody said "Come on to the meeting, participate." But one time they invited me so I accepted. They chose me because we were friends. There was a military commander at the assembly, who was directing it. *Bueno*, he'd already been in it for a while, since '79, and because he had already been in Sendero for some time he had his position. So he came with his machine gun, and I was scared but approached him. He introduced himself in a deep voice: "Yes, *compañero*." Just like that, with his boots and everything. He greeted me and to the other guy, the one who invited me, he told him to come to a certain place—"We'll be waiting for you there."

There were twelve of us. From Rumi there were just two of us and the rest were from the community of Mayu, that's how the meeting was. The commander, more than anything, he explained Mao, how he had begun and had risen to power, and also how they [Shining Path] were carrying out actions and how many people were joining in those months, and what Comrade Gonzalo was thinking about the growth of Sendero.

Afterward, *bueno*, the assembly ended and they asked for everyone's opinion. Those who had attended before already knew how to express themselves, how to salute the Comrade, because the meetings primarily began by saluting Comrade Gonzalo, a combative salute, that was his trademark. But because I was attending for the first time, I didn't know anything. So I said, "*Compañeros*, excuse me. I come for the first time to the assembly and I am still not capable of presenting myself before you." "No," he told me, "you can speak. We only want your decision, to see if you can attend the other assemblies, or if you've only come to watch." That's what he said to me. So, because he said this to me like that, I said "No, I'm willing to attend." Others gave their decision that they were ready at any moment to go out with the *compañeros* to fight for our party. Everyone was saying that, and I also said that when it was my turn to speak. I said yes, I was also ready to go out. I said that because everyone says they were ready. So if I suddenly said that I wasn't ready yet, maybe they would start to criticize me because there was critique and auto-critique. That's how the assembly ended.

Bueno, from then on they began to pass me the word in the following weeks. So I began to spread the word to my friend, no? They gave us assignments in that first meeting, to everyone, in the second meeting or the following one, everyone had the obligation to bring one or two trusted friends, so that the group grew. So I brought my friend, my mother's godson.

The meetings were continuous, sometimes twice a week, in different communities. They gave us assignments. And about the party line, they talked to us about how there was so much bureaucracy in Peru and many delinquents, many thieves, rapists—and that the objective of Sendero was to make all of that disappear. And they were doing that, no? For example, there were thieves, there were abusive people, so with these people, when one attended the meetings they always brought their list. They know that in the communities we have men who are cattle rustlers, thieves; so with that person, first they warned them. The people who were in the [armed] group were in charge of that. We let them know, we lead them to the corner, no? They knocked on the door and talked with people. If they continued robbing or doing just any old thing, the next time they were going to kill them.

As I had already devoted myself to the party, I was already in Sendero, my first action was for the anniversary of the pueblo, in August. They took our oath, several of us, they named us leaders of groups in different communities. In my community, up until then there were somewhere around fifteen or sixteen of us. Almost all the young people were in it, we advanced rapidly, in about three months, almost all of us joined.

We reached the plaza exactly when they were serving breakfast. Yes, shouting, "Long live the guerrilla war!" And the women and the peasants were quiet when we entered and one of the *compañeros* began to speak. Some people, nervous women, were saying, "Maybe they're going to kill us." When we were already organized, right then some people were raising the flag in the park itself, and some were placing puppets with the words "We are going to kill the informers like this," with their throats slashed. Others were giving the peasants pamphlets that were called "Guerrilla War" and we only charged for the paper, cheap. *Bueno*, the person who spoke said they were defending the pueblo, the peasants. So the peasants, when they asked them, they all said they agreed. So, if they collaborated, yes, they could collaborate. Then they read a list of informers that had spoken against the party, so they would be careful, so they would not talk again.

Those of us from the pueblo, wore hoods. We were different from the [armed] group, we were defending the pueblo, as militia. And when there was any sort of action, they called us first. Those of us who were in charge in the community met with the military commander and the political commander, and after we met with all the militants, we set a date and scheduled an action. We were numerous, around 200 or more. For the most part, they were *muchachos* studying in the secondary school.

When they gave us an assignment, let's say, the leader of the group met with us and told us that for such a date you need to raise the flag, paint the walls in a community, place rocks in the highway, and set off dynamite. That night we not only carried out an action, it was all the communities and in all the provinces of Ayacucho. First, to start the action, the dynamite that was blown up was in the same province. Once it blew up in Cangallo, then the rest of us all already had a specific hour, no? In Cangallo it will blow up at seven o'clock sharp. But you, at seven o'clock sharp had to be in your place. So we, no sooner had the explosion gone off than we set the dynamite and everything was raised up.

Allpachaka

Everything was well organized. For example, they had carried out an assault on the cattle farm at Allpachaka, an experimental farm that belonged to the university. For that action, they had planned for something like two months. Some of the *compañeros* dedicated themselves to studying how many people were working, to see if there were police, and from what hour to what hour people worked. They investigated for something like a month and a half. Afterward the military and political commanders called all of us, and they posed the idea that they needed support from all the communities and participation from all the militants, and if possible those who were not militants. They said for them to attend the assault and not be afraid, there are no police, nothing. That is how they posed it, and we accepted.

Youth, Peasants, and Political Violence

Then, just a few days before the action they called a meeting with all of the militants. We met in X, far from the highway, at least 180 of us from throughout the province. We planned everything: where are we going to meet, what time we were going to leave, all of that. We concentrated ourselves in community A. In that zone the *compañeros* walked around freely with their weapons. In Rumi the *compañeros* were still a little scared, but not in A, not anymore. They arrived freely, walked about, it was practically a liberated zone, no? They came from everywhere, from the province of Víctor Fajardo, from Vilcashuamán, two or three communities participated but not more because they were far away. Each one of us carried our provisions—toasted corn, cheese, potatoes that we had gathered from all of the communities. That is, the peasants who were in agreement with what we asked prepared the lunch, and all the communities had collaborated with grains.

So in A there were about 500 or 600 of us, and that was just our group. From Chuschi, from other places they arrived at B, another community. Then we all went to B, and there were around 900 or more of us, and they kept arriving from other communities. They came from other communities and we must have had about 1,400 people. A lot. B is close to Allpachaka, about four or three hours on foot.

Bueno, we entered Allpachaka during the day. At five in the morning, all of us from the party rounded up the community of Allpachaka, so that nobody could leave. Other groups that were already appointed were beginning the action, taking all the peasants to the park, and in case they found someone in their house they were going to punish them, threatening them. So everyone came out to the park. When we entered the houses to search, we didn't find anyone, only dogs. And *bueno*, in the park the political commander from the zone of Cangallo and Huancapi was speaking. He took the floor. In those days, I didn't understand well what a deficit Peru had with the United States, how much we owed. When he said four hundred million dollars or something like that, that we had as a deficit, I didn't really understand what that would be, I said. And he spoke to us about how in Lima they maintained the big officials like a bull that produced nothing, like a little steer. In the sierra a steer has no value, a bull does have value, it works, but a steer no, lots of fat, no good for plowing, nothing. So like a steer they maintained the big officials in Lima, the big ministers, and the people who were working in ministries such as education, heath, a lot of people—the pueblo was maintaining them, there was lots of bureaucracy. To deal with that, Sendero was fighting and the goal was to seize power by means of a guerrilla war, from the country to the city, that was our goal: from the countryside to the city. Our goal was to stop selling the products that we cultivated in the communities, in that way the people in the capital, the people who do not work, they die of hunger they said, because we the peasants are the only ones who feed the big people, the millionaires, and at that times they were planning, for the next four years, five years, we will not let food enter Lima, everyone in Lima is going to die of hunger. And the poor? They said they are going to return, they must return to fight with us.

We took over the Allpachaka property because they wouldn't even let the workers taste the cheeses they were producing. The party found out about this—that those cheeses were not even eaten here in Peru. They exported them directly to Holland, I think. Something like that. We found out. Using the name of the university, they had created this cattle farm, and in reality the university didn't receive any benefits from Allpachaka. So the decision was made.

There were four bulls, really big bulls. So we killed those four bulls first. We killed them and began to carve them up. There were pots so we began to cook. We cooked potatoes with meat, we made soup, and we distributed it to people. To all the people, and to the women who were living there. We also gave them an assignment, that they bring their pots and cook in the big pots they had, and bring firewood for cooking. Absolutely all of us ate, and there was still food left over. And from other communities that had heard about what happened, the old women came and asked us to give them some meat, potatoes, whatever we had. It was two or three in the afternoon when they came, and we said fine, let them take whatever they can.

There in Allpachaka, there were beds, bed frames, tables, cheese, wines—everything. So we had to take everything out, give it away, and whatever was left over, whatever people couldn't take, we destroyed it. There was so much stored away. At least eight rooms, storage facilities. We went on a Saturday and they had planned to pick up the cheese on Monday, so we arrived at just the right time. And we burned the place they had stored the oats, we broke the doors, we broke down the walls. There were also pigs and guinea pigs, we let them loose.

With the cattle, we killed what we could. But when we were killing the cattle, the peasant women began to cry: "Poor little animals, why are you killing them like that? What guilt do they have?" How the women began to cry, "poor little ones," going on like that. So we left them. We left them, but we had already killed about a quarter of the cattle. About 70 or 80 cows. We intended to kill all of the livestock, but we couldn't because the peasant women started to cry.

We left there around five. When we had already entered the place, a man with his horse, he went straight to Ayacucho to let them know what was happening at Allpachaka. So the following day it was on the news, on Radio La Voz. At that moment, we were on the path, returning and some of the *compañeros* had small radios, so we listened and we were pleased, no?

The New Power

At that time Sendero appointed new authorities. We called an assembly to appoint our own authorities, the true authorities, from the community. The old ones didn't protest because the president's own son was in the party, definitely. His son had convinced him as well.

The new authorities administered justice. There were no executions in my communities, but there were in others. An execution was like, well, no? Take the person without them finding out, from one moment to the next, capture them in their house. If the person had been talking bad or for *a* or *b*, committing acts against the party, then right there they executed those people. For example, if someone gave the police in Cangallo a list of the *compañeros* who were active in the community, then that was already a crime against the party.

Obviously their family members felt pain, but they didn't know. Their family didn't know when there were these sorts of executions—it was from one moment to the next. They had various [executions] in C, D, E [communities left unnamed]. Straightaway one arrived in the park and we gathered the people together. The people watched, and were saying, "In case we find out about something, or if we see someone doing something for the party, it's better we stay silent. If the police come, our word needs to be 'we don't know, we don't know.'" They were saying that themselves. We also had to make that recommendation. Some people didn't agree, but they kept their mouths shut, they didn't say anything, they kept quiet, nothing more. Some peasants, peasant women, they cried. There was always fear and sadness when they killed someone in front of people.

So there were now new authorities and the new authorities called everyone for communal work, where they planted crops for the party—like barley, wheat, potatoes, and corn. The communities always have their land, and we were planting there. It was not for the community but for provisioning the *compañeros* who were in the countryside. That way for whatever happened, to work, or when people had nothing to eat. Some people have only a small plot of land, so it could help those people. So it was sort of a communal task, with planting, and in each of the four corners of the plots was a flag. The best reception was in Chuschi. The community had four or five hectares—oh more, like eight hectares of land. So they plowed the land, using about sixty bulls with yokes, never before had they used so many at once. The yokes were from Chuschi and all the surrounding communities, they also came from F, some from A. They planted from seven in the morning until 6:30 at night with sixty yokes. At the beginning, twelve sticks of dynamite were blown up; then at midnight, six sticks of dynamite; then in the afternoon twelve. The work was successful, and it was the first time they did this in Chuschi. But the party wasn't able to harvest the crops because the army came in.

The Army

When the army arrived, the women were so afraid. The peasant women started to gather together and discuss things, to cry, no? "What have we gotten ourselves into?" they said. What they said was: "Certainly they are going to kill all of us, now the army has already come," they were saying. Above the community are curves and more curves. From up there about fifty army trucks started to come down. It was around eight in the morning. I was watching from the steps of my house, and I went outside. The women had gathered in the corner and everyone, everyone was crying. "Now it's certain they are going to kill everyone," that's what they were saying. The women were crying, all around, everyone crying. But the trucks passed by, onto Cangallo itself.

Our thought was that we were going to have even more support with the army because everyone in the army was the child of poor people, hungry and really poor, no? That was what the *muchachos* in the party thought, and that how we talked in meetings. "It's to our advantage that the army comes out." That's what the commanders were saying, that we were going to have more support and that they (the soldiers) were going to join the party. Those soldiers were children of peasants.

We sought to gather all the peasants together, but the peasants were worried about leaving their communities. In those days some peasant women, some men took their clothes, their belongings and were leaving for Ayacucho. Helicopters started coming, war planes, the peasants were already frightened, they already didn't want to participate. They were saying, "Suddenly they find us in a meeting and how will we defend ourselves? We don't have enough weapons for everyone." We were saying, "Don't worry, we're going to defend you." But there was already no support, that's where the support for Sendero was lost.

The commanders were saying, "If they confront us, we will fight back and we will succeed." But we didn't have enough weapons, only some grenades, sticks of dynamites—we didn't have anything else. Machine guns, revolvers, FAL [automatic weapons], we didn't have those. So there was a clash with a group from the army, and four *compañeros* and four weapons fell. In that moment, we met with all the militants and all the guerrillas from throughout Cangallo. After three days, right there we met. Quickly, that's all. We even thought we might still battle the army on the highway, but it was not possible. The guerrillas were ready, but the militias from the communities were terrified.

Later, in G there was a battle, from six in the morning until four in the afternoon, all day. From Sendero twelve people fell, more than anything key people. From the army, five or six fell. It wasn't like a confrontation with the police, who were easier. But now it was a little difficult. So in different communities we held meetings, continuously, day and night, practically no one rested anymore. They told the peasants not to be afraid, that we were always going to be operating in the zone, we were going to take care of them, whenever there was something we would be there. That's how we left it with them. Afterward, about ten days later, an assembly was called for the entire province of Cangallo. Commissions also arrived from Vilcashuamán, Huancapi, Huanta, and San Miguel. They told me, because I couldn't attend, that they had decided to divide up all the departments, and for each group there would be four guerrillas and a political commander. The rest remained in Ayacucho [referring to the capital city, Huamanga], continuing the meetings with peasants, carrying out actions. But it wasn't like before, there were so few people. It's that the army had already started to patrol the communities, to commit massacres and abuses, including they grabbed livestock like bulls, pigs, they carried them off to eat, they began to break down doors, knock down houses, beat peasants and peasant women, carry them off as prisoners to the provinces and disappear them. So the peasants were already afraid.

I was not affected because I had my hiding place where I slept. It was just below my house, in a ravine, nothing ever happened to me. My mission was to keep working with people in the pueblo, but people in the pueblo no longer wanted to attend the meetings; only us militants keep holding the meetings. The militants, we were also participating as guerrillas day and night, from the moment the army arrived, day and night. And finally the moment came when we had to decide, no? "Who is going with the party and who stays here to continue with the community?" The party needed thirty-four committed people. They had been something like fifty or more. As the party never rejects committed people, everyone went, to other departments, other work groups. I stayed working, but there were only four or five of us. No more. We had contact with the guerrillas. They were mostly in the highland areas. When they passed by, we gave them food. They kept telling us to not be afraid, that the army was going to retreat.

By this time I was also, well practically discouraged. That's why I came to Lima. I couldn't continue—it was very difficult.

The Other Path

To the community, *bueno*, I cannot return because the police are looking for me. Sendero, I don't know what they would say to me; certainly they would tell me I am a reactionary spy. I came [to Lima] without permission. Later, after I left, they discussed my case in an assembly. They were saying, "Certainly he must not be in agreement with the struggle, that's why he left without telling us." But they haven't bothered me. When I arrived here, someone who lives in X called me for a meeting. He knew I had participated there and he wanted to make a time to meet. I told him, "Ok, I'll go at seven." I told him that but I didn't go. Two or three months later, they sent me a card from the community, the *compañeros* who were in the countryside, they sent an address so I could contact them, but I did not do it, everything could suddenly fall apart. After that I had no more contact. But if they grow in Lima, then I will have to join.

I don't know if they can win, *bueno*, they can win but I know it will take longer. The *compañeros* made a mistake. They said that in 1990 there was going to be the New Democratic Republic. I think it will be around '95, maybe by 2000.

Harvesting Storms

Peasant Rondas *and the Defeat of Shining Path in Ayacucho*

Can a spark rebel against a bonfire? . . . How can grains detain the grinding of the mill? They will be ground into dust.

Abimael Guzmán, "Por la Nueva Bandera"

When the war began in May 1980, Shining Path was a party consisting mainly of teachers and university professors and students with little influence among the regional peasantry. Nonetheless, by the end of 1982, when the armed forces assumed military and political control of Ayacucho, Shining Path had easily displaced the police forces from broad rural zones of the region's northern provinces, and it was preparing to lay siege to the departmental capital.[1]

Rural Youth and the Peasantry

The key to this vertiginous expansion was the significant number of rural youth with secondary-school education, or in some instances no more than a primary-school education, who swelled the party ranks and constituted the most active sector of Shining Path's rural "generated organizations." Subsequently, they were incorporated into the apparatus of the "new state" that Shining Path was constructing. Shining Path clearly *needed* this sector. Where it did not exist, Shining Path found it very difficult to establish solid links with the peasantry.[2]

These were the politically and socially "available" youth who, in their secondary schools, had been exposed either to Shining Path discourse, or at least to what Portocarrero and Oliart (1989) refer to as the "critical idea of Peru": thought critical of the social order in a confrontational yet authoritarian manner. The presence of other parties of the Left in some parts of the region, however tenuous, also encouraged youthful radicalism. In addition these were youth in search of an identity; their parents' "traditional" Andean identity seemed remote after exposure to the "myth of progress" (Degregori 1986b). This myth was disseminated in the schools and mass media, and was even promoted by their own parents. These were youth, finally, who had little hope of achieving such progress by way of the market, migration, or more education. Suddenly, they were presented with the concrete possibility of social ascent through the new Senderista state.[3] Shining Path militancy may thus be seen, in part, as a path for social mobility. Arturo, a youth from the community of Rumi, recalls: "They said that Ayacucho was going to be a liberated zone by 1985. A famous illusion that they created among the *muchachos* was, way back in 1981, that by '85 there would be an independent republic. Wouldn't you like to be a minister? Wouldn't you like to be a military leader? Be something, no?"

Power seduced these secondary students, who were also captivated by the examples presented by other youth, the university students-cum-guerillas, who made up the majority of the Shining Path columns. Nicario, also of Rumi, recalled his encounter with one of them:

> This guy from the University of San Cristóbal invited me. So I, well, I accepted easily . . . because at the time, it was '82, Sendero was quite active, with assaults, confrontations. . . . There was a military commander [*mando*] at the assembly, who was directing it. . . . So he came with his machine gun, and I was scared but approached him. He introduced himself in a deep voice: "Yes, *compañero*." Just like that, with his boots and everything.

Power appeared in all its fearful splendor, and gained the adherence of most youth in Rumi, whom it promised to invest with the same attributes. The young people were intoxicated with this power. Their first actions were to paint walls and set off dynamite in the town, breaking the silence of rural nights. According to Arturo, "We blew it up just for the sake of blowing it up. Nothing more."

For the university students who constituted the Senderista hard core, the party was a "total identity." A sector of rural youth also came to internalize

Shining Path militancy to this extent.[4] For many young people, however, what was important was not merely social mobility, but the concrete exercise of power in their own localities, along with a touch of youthful adventure. This was especially the case during the early years, when the violence had not yet spun out of control and everything still seemed relatively easy.

Another important factor was something that we might call the demonstration effect. Youth were inspired to join an organization that was on the rise, prestigious, with a demonstrated effectiveness. Such an organization would empower and transform them. Joining Shining Path had elements of a rite of passage or of initiation into a religious sect: the armed sect.

This beachhead among rural youth enabled Shining Path to spread among the peasantry. It was most successful where there existed a significant generational gap in educational levels. Once converted into an armed generation, in many outlying hamlets (*pagos*) and communities, the youth then proceeded to seduce, convince, or pressure their parents, who had sent their children to school so that, rather than grope their way "blindly" through the world, they could encounter paths of mobility in a complex and discriminatory society. Many adults believed that if educated youth said something, it had to have some truth to it. The young people were the "ones with eyes" (*ñawiyoq*), who "saw" things that their "ignorant" parents had perhaps not noticed.[5] Even when, internally, they disagreed with the youth's discourse, the reaction of the adults was ambiguous because of the familial and cultural ties that bound the generations together.

In addition to taking advantage of kinship ties, Shining Path made a show of displaying its coercive capabilities to the peasantry. From the beginning, Senderistas included a measure of terror. Shining Path thus occupied the place of the traditional Andean boss or patron (*patrón*). As a "new" patron, Shining Path was hard and inflexible yet "just," and displaced the generally incompetent and abusive authorities. From this position, Shining Path tried to obtain concrete benefits for the peasantry and located itself at the crux of local conflicts. Berg (1992) has emphasized how Shining Path took advantage of conflicts between communities and cooperatives in some of the zones of Andahuaylas. Isbell (1992) has noted how in Chuschi, Shining Path made some livestock thieves the target of its attacks. Manrique (1989) has referred to how Shining Path worked on the basis of the conflicts between the peasantry and the Cahuide Agricultural Society (one of the SAIS, or Agricultural Societies of Social Interest, large productive enterprises created by Velasco's land reform program) in the high zones of Junín. In addition, the party implanted a very strict moral order.

Ayacucho provided Shining Path with a favorable scenario. In Ayacucho, among the ruins of rural bossism (*gamonalismo*), there still existed small local fiefdoms of abusive *mistis*. The region had relatively few peasant organizations and relatively many students. Education enjoyed a special prestige, to the point that the principal social movement of previous decades had been organized not around demands for land but rather around demands for free education (Degregori 1990). Under these circumstances, the peasantry was relatively disposed to accept Shining Path as a new *patrón*, one that appeared more powerful, moreover, than the former local authorities or the state-as-*patrón*. Shining Path swept out the state's repressive apparatus, the police forces. The peasants' acceptance was basically pragmatic, provided in exchange for concrete gains on a personal, familial, or communal level, as Berg (1992) has demonstrated for Andahuaylas. But, this tactical acceptance opened the door to the possibility, over the long term, of a more strategic identification with the Senderista project.

Indeed, Shining Path seemed to be on the verge of gaining deeper peasant support during the second half of 1982, a crucial moment for the region. For Shining Path, this was a moment of euphoria. The party had celebrated its Second National Conference and had begun to develop the last stage of its plan "to unleash the Guerrilla War," which consisted in "hammering away [*batir*] to advance toward the Bases of Support" (Gorriti Ellenbogen 1990, chap. 15). The influence of the party spread like wildfire in the rural zones and also grew in the departmental capital. There, in March, Sendero successfully attacked the jail and liberated dozens of imprisoned cadres; and in September, the funeral of the young Senderista leader Edith Lagos drew more than 10,000 people.

But as often occurs, the factors that would contribute to its failure were already emerging, unnoticed, in the midst of all this success. To begin, neither the youth nor the cadres seemed to have a clear medium-range vision. They lived in a present of triumph and they dreamed of a future with marks of a peasantist utopia: the armed forces would suffer massive desertions and their helicopters would be shot down with slings (*huaracas*); Lima would be strangled, and the urban poor would return once again to the new rural republic.[6] Toward October, in various places, the party prepared for the first agricultural campaign of the new state-in-construction, where soon there would be no more hunger.

First Points of Rupture

This utopia caught fire in the imagination of the cadres, but it struck fewer sparks among the masses, for whom enthusiasm was ephemeral at best. Shining Path was successful in "hammering the countryside" (Gorriti Ellenbogen 1990). Its problems began when, having cleared the terrain, it began to construct its "new power." At various levels, fault lines began to appear that would harm the Senderista project. Let us consider four points of rupture: the organization of production, the organization of political power, the role of violence in the new order, and the physical security of the peasant population.

The Organization of Production

Shining Path privileged collective forms of organizing production. During the planting season, toward the end of 1982, Shining Path did not seem to encounter great resistance. Resistance became more evident in some places during the harvest, at which point the peasants found out that collectively produced crops were destined for the party.[7]

In other places, finally, problems related to production emerged when Shining Path demanded that the peasants plant only for the party and for self-subsistence, and then proceeded to close off peasant fairs and markets. This strategy of conquering and then closing off territories, in order to block the flow of agricultural produce and thus asphyxiate cities, clashed with peasant families' own strategies of reproduction. The families' survival strategies transcended the limits of the hamlet or pueblo, and were based on networks of kinship and community origin that established links in different areas of the countryside and in cities (Golte and Adams 1985; Steinhauf 1991). The cities, on the other hand, were not supplied only or even mostly by their immediate rural hinterlands.[8] Elsewhere I have discussed the difficulties that Shining Path encountered toward the end of 1982 upon closing the market at Lirio in the heights of Huanta, where the supposedly isolated Iquichano peasants supplied themselves with a variety of manufactured products (Degregori 1985a). Fissures related to production, although present from the early 1980s, would not deepen to the point of irrevocability until the late 1980s.

The New Power

It was in the construction of a new political power that Shining Path would encounter greater difficulties from the start. In the second semester of 1982, and as a part of its plan to "hammer the countryside," Sendero decided to replace communal authorities with commissaries representing the new power.

According to the Maoist script, in order to wage a more successful people's war, the party had to rely on the impoverished stratum among peasants. These peasants, rather than the middling or rich ones, were "those most disposed to accept the leadership of the Communist Party" (Mao Zedong 1971a). Shining

Path was surprised to encounter, however, its greatest problems in the poorest zones, which were at the same time the most "Indian" and "traditional." Coronel describes what occurred in the Iquichano communities that were still governed by the *vara* system, a hierarchical and ritualized structure of authority at the pinnacle of which sat the *varayocc* or *alcalde vara* ("keeper of the staff") who personified the community and who assumed that post at an advanced age, having ascended via a community ladder of civic-religious posts or *cargos* (see Vergara et al. 1985). The replacement of these authorities by young Senderista cadres was an affront not only to communal organization but to the community's whole cosmovision. For Shining Path, the peasant world appeared one-dimensional, without historical density or social complexity, divided simply into poor, middling, and rich peasants. Indeed, by proceeding in this manner, Shining Path would often end up depending on the youth of the middle and upper strata, neutralizing or winning over the adults of these same strata, and imposing itself on, repressing, and finally massacring the poorer peasants.

Above all, it was when Shining Path refused to recognize community authorities that the first overt rebellions occurred. But even in those communities that no longer elected *varayocc* officials but organized communal government according to national legislation, the installation of new authorities tended to cause problems. In some, the family connections between "the old and new power," to employ Shining Path terminology, initially neutralized resistance. In Rumi, "the old [authorities] didn't protest because the president's own son was in the party, definitely. His son had convinced him as well" (Nicario). But in many other places, the youthfulness of the Shining Path authorities was upsetting. Not only did it break generational hierarchies. In addition, "Gonzalo Thought" had not managed to disengage the rural youth from the tightly woven networks of kinship and community relations, with their own dynamic of reciprocities, grudges, hatreds, and preferences, in which they had been long immersed. As a result, the youthful representatives of the new power were frequently dragged into inter- and intra-communal disputes.

An account from the community of Tambo-La Mar explains one of the ways that this dynamic played itself out:

> Maybe the worst thing Sendero could have done is having trusted very young people with little experience. . . . Those young people totally distorted the plans that Sendero had for governing. They opted for taking vengeful attitudes, acting on grudges. Maybe one father against another father because they had some sort of problem over boundaries in their *chacras*, over animals, theft, losses, fights between a man and a woman; because Sendero had given them responsibility for the locality, they began

to take reprisals, revenge, and that is how the massacres happen. That's how people come to disagree with it. (José, teacher)

The guerrilla column would leave, without realizing it had left behind a hornet's nest of contradictions that could not be solved.[9] Even if in these cases no overt rebellion took place, the imposition of the new authorities generated initial resentments and the first peasant allies of the armed forces, "informers" (*soplones*) in the Senderista terminology.

Violence in the New Order

The role of violence in the new order also produced ruptures. By 1980, the grand "semifeudal" scenario against which Sendero had imagined waging its epic battles was actually in ruins, already destroyed by the combined forces of the market, the state, peasant pressure, the great rural-to-urban migrations, and the agrarian reform. Inspired by Mao Zedong, Shining Path programmed for 1980–81 "harvest uprisings" and land invasions. The results were meager, as they only took some surviving haciendas (Gorriti Ellenbogen 1990; Tapia 1995). The only action that compared with the massive land mobilizations of the 1960s, although carried out under a radically distinct banner, occurred in 1982, when Shining Path demolished Allpachaka, a university-sponsored experimental farm. The Senderistas also took some cooperatives that had been created in the agrarian reform (Coronel 1996). But apart from the police, whom Shining Path placed on the run during the early years by dynamiting their rural posts, the most important targets were abusive merchants, cattle thieves, corrupt judges, and drunk husbands.

Without a doubt, all of these people constituted real problems for the peasantry. Nonetheless, to confront them did not require constructing a "war machine," much less the colossal campaign of horror that bloodied the region. The considerable success of the peasant patrols (*rondas*) in the northern reaches of Piura and Cajamarca had illustrated that peasants could deal with such problems with very little violence (Starn 1991b; Huber 1995).

But Shining Path had three features that made it different from the northern *rondas*: an ideology that made violence an absolute value rather than a relative or proportionate instrument, a "molecular" strategy for constructing its "counterpower," and a totalitarian political project. Sendero's ideology took violence beyond the classic Maoist confines of the people's war. For Shining Path violence was, in addition, a purifying force that extirpated the old (the bad) at its roots. The militants' ideological zeal was fed constantly by the leadership, particularly by the supreme leader Abimael Guzmán, who tended to exalt violent purification.[10] Due to the absence of important regional targets, such as large landowners, Shining Path ended up concentrating all of this purifying zeal on the dynamics of micropower, in daily life, and "social cleansing."[11] In addition, the strategy of Shining Path was to "hammer the countryside" and liberate zones in which Sendero would not only construct a new state but a new society, controlled by the party even in its most minute details.

Ideological zeal, military strategy, and the totalitarian political project came together in the Fourth Plenary of the Central Committee, celebrated in May 1981. There Guzmán propagated the idea of "the blood quota" (*la cuota*) that would be necessary for the triumph of the revolution, and warned of the necessity of preparing for an inevitable "blood bath." The militants had to be ready to ford "the river of blood" of the revolution while "carrying their lives in their fingertips." The Fourth Plenary session agreed "to intensify radically the violence," and justified the escalation in the following terms: "They [the reaction] form lakes [of blood], we saturate handkerchiefs" (Gorriti Ellenbogen 1990, chap. 10).

It is against this background that we must locate the meaning of the 1982 decision to "hammer the countryside." "In Hammering, the key is to demolish [*arrasar*], and demolish means not to leave anything." It was necessary to "dislocate the power of the bosses [*gamonales*], disarrange the power of the authorities and hit the live forces of the enemy . . . clean out the zone, leave an empty plain [*dejar pampa*]."[12]

The following two testimonies, from the provinces of Huancasancos and Cangallo, respectively, refer to Shining Path's "people's tribunals," in which the strategy of "hammering" materialized with heartrending consequences.

> So this woman, they punished her with fifty lashes because she had talked, complaining about the unfair distribution of the harvest. It was a poor family and she had been drinking. They cut her hair, shaved it off. And the other, they also gave him fifty lashes and cut an ear with scissors, so now he is *qoro rinri* [mutilated ear]. His ear is still mutilated.
> And what did people say?
> Nothing. Well, punish but don't kill—just that. (Juvenal, adult peasant)

Or, consider a second testimony:

> Now people are unhappy because [Shining Path] has done so many stupid things [*cojudezas*]. They've killed innocent people, saying they were informers [*soplones*]. You know, I think, if someone has committed an error, they should be punished—just that. They should have whipped them, cut their hair . . . but not do what they did. They killed [the mayor] like he was a pig.

And what did people do?

Nothing. They were armed, what were we going to do? Nothing. That's why I say, they did so many stupid things. (Mariano, petty merchant)

The phrase "punish but don't kill" marks the limits of peasant acceptance, at least in the ambit of the so-called people's tribunals. It was a limit that came to exasperate the Senderista cadres, as can be seen in the following testimonial from a community in Cangallo, by a young teacher who at that time participated in a Shining Path "generated organization":

So a person had collected money in the name of Sendero Luminoso and they had captured him. Such people were judged in the town plaza. That's when they asked people, "These men have done such and such"—saying that—"so what do you all say? Shall we kill them or punish them?"

That's when the community spoke: "Why are you going to kill them? Punish them," that's what the community said.

"Oh, you still have these archaic ideas of defending yourselves all the time. From now on we aren't going to ask. We already know that you are going to defend them. We need to cut off their heads because the bad weed must be totally exterminated. If we pardon the bad weed we are never going to triumph, never going to better ourselves [*superarnos*]." That's what they said. (Cesáreo, teacher)

This account illustrates the tragic disjunctures of those years, between the anxiousness of the youthful cadres to "better ourselves" and what they considered the "archaic ideas" of the community, that is, between the Senderista project and "Andean rationality." The Shining Path cadres, ideologized to the point of fundamentalism, ready to kill and to die for their project, did not know or respect the peasant codes. Their vision was a utopia of cadres that could not become a code of masses. They were priests for a god that spoke (sometimes literally) Chinese.[13]

Let us explain further. In an environment where rural *gamonalismo*, although in shambles, still provided codes of domination and subordination, in a region without a strong network of new peasant organizations and with a weakly developed market, in an area that did not have the opportunity to explore the democratic spaces that opened up in other parts of the country after the 1980 municipal elections, the peasants seemed disposed to accept a new patron and even accept his punishment. Structural and political violence were not new to them. Corporal punishments, including lashings and haircuts, represented continuities from landed society and the old *misti* power; the peasants knew how to survive such violence and how to ridicule and combat it. But the hyperideological violence of Shining Path was alien to them; this violence did not play itself out according to the traditional codes. In the testimonial just cited, the dialogue with Cesáreo continued as follows:

> But if they were delinquents, why did people insist they not kill them? And their children? Who was going to take care of their families?

In other words, death surpassed the limit of the tolerable, but not simply because the peasants may have a "culture of life." Rather, their reasons were pragmatic. In a society with a precarious economy that establishes intricate networks of kinship and complex strategies of reproduction, one had to take great care to protect the labor force. To kill, to eliminate a link in one of these networks, had repercussions beyond the nuclear family of the condemned. I noted earlier that when Shining Path initiated the war, the landowners had practically disappeared from Ayacucho. Therefore, in many cases the "targets of the revolution" were small local exploiters, arrogant and in many cases abusive, but also linked by connection of kinship, social origin, and daily life to the communities, or at least to sectors of *comuneros*. A commentary regarding the Allpachaka estate, collected after its destruction, provides evidence of this point: "In Allpachaka there were a lot of cattle rustlers and they have killed them. So their families became anti-Senderistas and they have begun to denounce and point to innocent people as Senderistas. I think they shouldn't have killed them but rather punished them so they would correct their behavior" (Alejandro, university student, from a peasant family).

To punish so that they behave is one of the fundamental powers of legitimate authority, be it *comunal* or *misti*. By killing, Sendero tears up a delicate social fabric and opens a Pandora's Box that it proves unable to control.

To utilize jargon that presently enjoys a certain prestige, we may say that as far as the economy of violence was concerned, Shining Path's macroeconomic assumptions were not in accord with the microeconomic conduct of the agents. The point of departure for the macroeconomic analysis of Shining Path violence was the idea that everyday structural violence was more lethal. Criticizing the speech of Monsignor Dammert during the inauguration of the Consejo por la Paz, Guzmán (1992, 17) observes:

> He preaches peace to those who are dying of hunger. . . . In Peru, because of the iniquitous dominant system 60,000 children under one year of age die each year, according to figures from 1990. Compare this to the figures on officially recognized deaths . . . over the course of ten years of popular war. The total death count comes to one third the number of children under the age of one who have died in a single year. Who kills children in the cradle? Fujimori and the reactionary state.

Shining Path argued that its model was more expeditious and, in the medium term, less costly in human lives, because the revolution would eliminate poverty, hunger, and structural violence in general.[14] From the point of view of the peasant agents, however, political violence was added to structural violence. The latter was already more than enough to bear, and the two together would prove unbearable in the short term. To paraphrase Keynes, in the long term—in this case, the long term envisioned by the Shining Path utopia—we will all be dead.

In juridical terms, the punishments that Shining Path imposed were increasingly out of proportion with the magnitude of the supposed crimes, which, of course, Shining Path categorized according to a totally alien notion of law, distant from everyday common law as well as national jurisprudence. According to Gálvez (1987), in what he called (for descriptive purposes only) "peasant law," punishments often included physical exaction but very rarely included death. Capital punishment was contemplated only when the security of the group as a whole was believed to be threatened, especially in cases of animal thievery, and only after exhausting all other possibilities. The fundamental tenet of the so-called Andean common law is persuasion, aimed at restoring group unity.[15] Therefore, when naming communal authorities and justices of the peace (who are nominated by the community and ratified by the state), the communal assembly takes into consideration mainly who is considered "fair" and "upright" in the eyes of the group. The authorities are individuals who know the people and the customs of the community.

This model is obviously an idealization, in practice eroded by conflicts derived from the expansion of the market, peasant differentiation, the increasing prioritization of family over communal interests, and the consolidation of power cliques within the community (Gálvez 1987). But, these problems were not so great as to nullify the general principles previously outlined. In addition, Shining Path proved so oblivious to reality that, instead of taking advantage of these contradictions, it stumbled into them and found itself trapped in intracommunal and intercommunal conflicts.

Beyond economic factors, there certainly existed other reasons, of equal or more importance, for peasant rejection of Shining Path. Nicario narrated an episode during the destruction of Allpachaka that reveals the complexity of motivations: "With the cattle, we killed what we could. But when we were killing the cattle, the peasant women began to cry: "Poor little animals, why are you killing them like that? What guilt do they have?' How the women began to cry, 'poor little ones,' going on like that. So we left them. . . . We intended to kill all of the livestock, but we couldn't because the peasant women started to cry."

The image of the peasants hugging cows and bulls to avoid their death is not simply romantic and earthy. The women are herders, and the death of their cattle is for them the equivalent of the destruction of a factory for its workers. But if it is true that the herders were *not only* telluric and lovers of life, it is *also* true that they were people who appreciated the lives of their animals.

In Umaro and in Purus (Huanta Province), I have seen mature men, elders and former authorities, cry inconsolably when they recalled the mutilating and unbearable *form* in which Shining Path killed. As if slaughtering a hog, the cadres made the victim kneel and proceeded to cut the throat, allow the blood to run, and sometimes crush the victim's head with a stone. In Senderista language, the point was "to smash with a stone as if [destroying] a frog." They did this with the deluded economicist pretext of "saving ammunition." And afterward, they often refused to allow the burial of the victims, the universal rite of mourning. If we take into consideration the violence exercised by the armed forces, which in the period 1983 to 1985 and in many zones even until 1988 far outstripped Shining Path violence, we can begin to get an idea of the inferno through which the region lived.[16] One must recall that if all of Peru had suffered the same level of violence as Ayacucho, the national death toll would have been some 450,000, not 25,000. (Editor's note: This essay was written before the Peruvian truth commission established an estimate of some 69,000 dead.)

Ponciano del Pino Huamán describes the most surprising case of peasant repudiation of Shining Path for reasons that transcend mere "rational choice." Evangelical Pentecostals along the Apurímac River resisted Shining Path on the basis of another "total identity." The result was a not-so-holy war that concluded with the triumph of the Evangelicals and, inadvertently, resulted in a victory for drug traffickers as well.

The frequency of death, the social proximity of the victims, and the traumatic context in which the killings took place also affected the rural youth. They were torn between party ideology on the one hand, and their family ties, communal connections, and common sense on the other.

> Obviously their family members felt pain, but they didn't know . . . when there were these sorts of executions—it was from one moment to the next. . . . The people watched, and were saying, "In case we find out about something, or if we see someone doing something for the party, it's better we stay silent. If the police come, our word needs to be 'we don't know, we don't know.'" . . . We also had to make that recommendation. Some people didn't agree, but they kept their mouths shut, they didn't say any-thing, they kept quiet, nothing more. Some peasants, peasant women,

they cried. There was always fear and sadness when they killed someone in front of people. (Nicario)

The pain and the grief were two of the various loose threads that, over succeeding years, the extended family and subsequently the *rondas* began to pull, until they began to untangle the Senderista knot.[17]

The Physical Security of the Population

The military occupation revealed a fourth fissure, the product of a discrepancy between traditional strategies of Andean domination and the strategy of "people's war." According to Maoist guerrilla precepts, *when the enemy advances, we retreat.* When the armed forces entered Ayacucho, Shining Path retreated in order to protect its own cadres. But in doing so, Sendero clashed with the role of the traditional Andean *patrón* who *protects* his clients.[18] Thus, Shining Path's retreat left many sectors of the population feeling that they had been greatly deceived. The following account relates what occurred in a hamlet in the valley of Huanta. Similar accounts, with minor variations, were repeated in various other testimonials. "They told us, 'It is necessary to be prepared for war, to destroy the enemy.' We believed them, but once they attacked Huanta and killed two *guardías* [police]. After the attack they escaped and they screwed us. They practically gave us up, sold us out. That's not a manly thing to do, *pues* [*eso no es de hombres, pues*]" (Walter, peasant).

For sectors of the population that Shining Path was not capable of protecting, the armed forces became a "lesser evil," or, in any case, an even more powerful *patrón* than Shining Path, with which it was necessary to retain good relations. This was, moreover, one of the objectives of the genocidal offensive of 1983–84: to dry up the water in which the Senderista fish swam by terrorizing the peasantry and preventing support for Shining Path. What is surprising is that, despite its severity, in many places this strategy did not function perfectly.

Blockage of the First Ruptures

In reality, while it did make already-existing fissures more visible, the overriding consequence of the armed forces' strategy in those years was to block the development of contradictions between the peasants and Shining Path. Shining Path was capable of resealing these first points of rupture because, upon unleashing a genocidal violence, the armed forces converted the countryside of Ayacucho into an Armageddon. In many instances, this made

Shining Path appear as the "lesser evil." Such was the case in the valley of Huanta, according to Coronel (1996). In the words of Shining Path: they burned the prairie and "the reaction fanned the fire."

Resistant Adaptation

But the "lesser evil" was an external force. The peasants did not internalize Shining Path ideology. Rather, they displayed what Stern (1990) has called "resistant adaptation." The peasants' pragmatic acceptance of the early years did not grow into long-term identification with the Shining Path project. Except in a few pockets, the relationship settled into one of resistant adaptation, located somewhere between acceptance and open rebellion. The following testimonial, from a community of the province of Sucre, clearly illustrates what we mean by resistant adaptation.

> The lieutenant governor [of the community] continues to exercise [his authority], but clandestinely. That is, when the *compañeros* [Shining Path] come here, we tell them we don't have a lieutenant governor, that we haven't had one for some time, that they've taken away our official seals . . . and when the reactions come, well, they present themselves, that is, the authorities surface so that the pueblo doesn't have problems, but clandestinely. (Pedro, young adult peasant)

The concept is somewhat similar to that which Scott (1985) calls "the weapons of the weak," which given the extreme situation of that time were the only weapons available for the peasantry. In the following account by a sixty-one-year-old peasant woman from Acos-Vinchos, recorded by Celina Salcedo, the astuteness of resistant adaptation acquires aspects of the picaresque.

> When they had come the *tuta puriq* [night walkers] have told us: "Tomorrow in the afternoon you are going to form up and there we will see," they told us, and we were all afraid, thinking: What are they going to do with us? Surely they are going to kill us. When they had gone, everyone got together, men and women, big and small; don Constantino, Jesús, and don Teodosio have learned and they told us: "We are going to form up like they said then we'll say we are going to stand watch, and afterwards, when they are all here, we will shout, 'The soldiers [*cabitos*] are coming'; and we will come in running.[19] And then they will leave." That's how they told us. [The next day] just as we had agreed, those who had been standing watch started shouting and running and saying "The *cabitos* are coming! The *cabitos* are coming!" Then the *tuta puriq* started to run and escape like crazy. Since then they haven't come back.

Externalization

One shattering episode symbolizes how Shining Path regressed once again into an external actor: the massacre of more than eighty peasants in the community of Lucanamarca (Víctor Fajardo Province) in April 1983. Abimael Guzmán himself justified the massacre:

> Confronted with the use of armed bands and reactionary military action, we responded decisively with one action: Lucanamarca. Neither they nor we will forget it, of course, because there they saw a response that had not been imagined. There more than 80 were annihilated, this is the reality, and we say it, here there was excess. . . . [But] our problem was to give a bruising blow to restrain them, to make them understand that the thing was not so easy. In some occasions, such as this, it was the Central Leadership itself that planned the actions and ordered everything, that is how it was. . . . I reiterate, the principal thing was to make them understand that we were a hard bone to chew, and that we were ready to do anything, anything. (Guzmán 1988, 19–20)

Shining Path decided to compete blow-for-blow with the state in the exercise of violence against the population and to beat the state on this terrain as well. Several years later, Guzmán would continue to proclaim that "the triumph of the revolution will cost a million deaths."[20]

Thus, beginning in 1983, most of the region, with few exceptions, was besieged by two objectively external armies. Each entered the battlefield from opposite extremes. One of the principal slogans of Shining Path was "the party has a thousand eyes and a thousand ears." To put it brutally, in these times Shining Path knew those they killed, even in Lucanamarca; the peasants who submitted to Sendero's dictates would survive. But while the party had a thousand eyes and a thousand ears, the armed forces were blind, or, rather, color-blind. They saw only black and white. Recent arrivals in the region, they tried to reproduce in the Andes the same repressive strategies that had proved successful in the Southern Cone. They did not perceive nuances; when they saw dark skin, they fired.

As for the rural youth, their trajectory during the years following the military intervention may serve as a guide to the overall trajectory of Shining Path. These youth, a critical link for Shining Path's expansion in the countryside, remained torn between two logics and two worlds. Torn in Allpachaka between the party orders to kill the cattle and the weeping of the shepherdesses; torn in La Mar between the party's governing logic, on the one hand, and local loyalties, grudges, and family vendettas, on the other; and torn between the party and the market as potential avenues to achieve "progress" and social mobility. The arrival of the military increased such tensions. When Shining Path decided to respond in kind against the state, thus mirroring the latter's violence against the population, a decisive disenchantment emerged among young people.

What happened among the youth of Rumi encapsulates such disenchantment. Nicario's political loyalty to the party broke, while others, including a brother, opted to join the party and become the seedbed that nursed, along with other factors, the growth of Shining Path in various regions of the country. While it lost peasants, it gained support from youth. Once again it converted social failure into political victory.[21] But in no other region would the scenario of Ayacucho's rapid growth in the early 1980s be repeated. In the following years, as it expanded into other zones, Shining Path's reliance on terror, and its character as an antisocial movement, would become even more marked.

In Ayacucho, Shining Path remained in many areas on the social frontier, in limbo, neither inside nor completely outside of the peasant society that adapted or resisted. Converted into one actor among others, armed and thus powerful, but without the kind of hegemony that it enjoyed in the first stage, Shining Path became either a faction within communities; or an implant within some communities caught up in confrontation with neighboring communities, acting out intercommunal conflicts that sometimes dated back even to pre-Hispanic times (Degregori 1985a); or a conqueror of populations that provided "support bases" (*bases de apoyo*) that would prove increasingly coerced over the medium run.

Second Points of Rupture

With ups and downs for Shining Path, this situation lasted in the region for a half decade. For large sectors of the population, such a situation was an agonizing quagmire. For Shining Path, this interim represented the normal development of the strategy of protracted war (*guerra prolongada*):

> '83 and '84 are the years of struggle around reestablishment versus counter-reestablishment, that is, the counterrevolutionary war to squash the new power and reestablish the Old and the popular war to defend, develop, and construct the recently emerged Popular Power . . . from '85 until today [we fight for] the continuation of the defense, development and construction that maintains the support bases [*bases de apoyo*] and

[for] the expansion of the people's war to the whole ambit of our mountains from North to South. (PCP-SL 1989c, 220)

The 1986 pamphlet "To Develop the People's War in Service of the World Revolution," from which this quote is taken, recounts six years of violence in a manner that erases the contradictions and fissures previously discussed. For Sendero, such complications seemed less important. Indeed, Shining Path did continue to challenge the armed forces for control over various parts of the Ayacucho region. Even more important, it did indeed manage to "break the siege" and expand into other zones of the country, especially Junín and the Huallaga Valley, the principal coca-leaf producing region in the world, and Lima.

Soon after the party's 1988 Congress, the leadership considered that the moment had arrived to attain "strategic equilibrium." According to Mao Zedong (1971b), the "protracted struggle" develops through three strategic phases: defense, equilibrium, and offense. Shining Path decided in 1989 that the moment for moving from the first stage to the second had arrived.[22] To achieve such equilibrium at the military level required more combatants, which Sendero could obtain from the youth wing that had always constituted its seedbed, or through forced recruitment in the rural zones where Sendero had established a presence. Shining Path needed more and better arms, which it could acquire based on its stronghold in the Huallaga Valley and its connection with drug traffickers. But if, as Mao said, the guerrilla army had to move among the masses like a "fish in water," then Shining Path needed not simply the peasants' neutrality or passive assent (the "resistant adaptation" discussed earlier) but their more active support. And it was precisely on this point that Sendero's problems increased. Shining Path's demands increased and they battered the fragile equilibrium of "resistant adaptation" that had prevailed in many places. More young recruits, more supplies, more participation of the population as an exposed "mass" (*masa*) in military actions, an intensified Senderista discipline prone to the rapid and summary application of the death penalty: all of these pressures undermined adaptation and pushed for resistance. Repudiation became even more blatant in 1989–90, as a national economic crisis coincided with a prolonged drought.[23]

Shining Path reacted by increasing violence against the peasantry. But, all this achieved was the proliferation of *rondas*, to the point that, by 1990, Sendero had become trapped in a kind of trench warfare against the Self-Defense Committees. This constituted the first strategic victory for the armed forces and the first real defeat of Shining Path since the war had started. This defeat was offset, however, by Shining Path's advances in the Amazon Basin, especially coca-growing zones, and in the cities, especially Lima.

Why this defeat of Shining Path? If we look from the perspective of peasant society, Shining Path and the armed forces followed opposite trajectories. While the former became more distant, the latter forged closer ties. As Shining Path grew more "external" to peasant society, the armed forces became more "internal" to the population.

In 1983, the armed forces entered an unknown territory in which they exercised indiscriminate repression; anyone was a potential enemy. The marines—from the navy, the most racist branch of the military and the branch whose recruits were heavily drawn from Lima and the rest of the coast—played the key role in the provinces of Huanta and La Mar. Beginning in 1985, however, the army—whose soldiers were more largely drawn from the sierra folk (*serranos*)—replaced the marines. Toward the end of the decade, when the armed forces passed from indiscriminate to selective repression, one might say that they installed themselves at the frontiers of peasant society and began to penetrate it, first through the actions of veteran soldiers who had graduated from their obligatory military service (*licenciados*) and increasingly in the 1990s, through aid-oriented policies (*políticas asistencialistas*) and infrastructural projects. Thus the military came to represent a state that, despite its extreme crisis, still had more cards up its sleeve than Shining Path, which could only offer more hardship. Finally, by recruiting youth who were allowed to do their obligatory military service in their own communities, and by distributing weapons to the *rondas*—even though these arms were merely shotguns—the armed forces, and the state that they represented, demonstrated that they had obtained hegemony in the zones.[24]

It is worth mentioning an important element of this reconquest: the armed forces did not seek total control of everyday life, as Shining Path did. To be sure, the obligatory weekly visits of the peasant "commands" to the barracks, the marches, and the attentions paid to the visiting army patrols could be inconvenient. But the armed forces did not otherwise interfere greatly in the daily life of the population, worn down by Senderista zeal.

By contrast, Shining Path grew more distant from the peasantry, which had passed from pragmatic acceptance, to resistant adaptation, and finally to overt rebellion against the party. In the initial years, the Senderista cadres were natives of the region or had lived there for a long time, and the new recruits were local rural youth who enabled Shining Path to become a force within communities. From this privileged social location Shining Path began to retreat toward the frontiers of community identity, beginning in 1983. Along the frontiers it experienced the peasants' resistant adaptation, and from the frontiers it was eventually expelled by the *rondas* that closed off, often literally, an ever-expanding territory.

Thus, while during the initial years the war made sadly famous the names of various communities demolished by the military—including Secce, Pucayacu, Accomarca, Umaro, Bellavista, Ccayara—by around 1988, it was Shining Path's massacres that populated the map of regional death. In little more than four years, between December 1987 and February 1992, an incomplete count provides us with a total of sixteen Senderista massacres of twelve or more persons (see IDL 1992). While the armed forces moved toward a policy of more selective repression,[25] Shining Path moved from "selective annihilations," which it justified as actions "accomplished without any cruelty, as simple and expeditious justice" (PCP-SL 1989c), to great massacres. In many places, therefore, decisive sectors of the peasantry would opt for a pragmatic alliance with the armed forces (for further analysis, see Coronel 1996 and del Pino Huamán 1992).

Two anecdotes illustrate this evolution. In the early years of military intervention a whole mythology emerged around the marines. It was said that they included Argentine mercenaries. Even peasants who had long experienced discrimination could perhaps not imagine that actual Peruvians could treat their national compatriots in such a manner. In April 1994, in a truck that went toward the market of Chaca, in the heights of Huanta, I conversed with a leader of Chaca, who had lived in the Apurímac River zone in the worst years of the violence. He recalled the panic aroused by these supposed mercenaries:

> They lowered the helicopter shooting off their rounds. It could be a leaf that fell off a tree and right away they'd be shooting rounds. They didn't know how to walk, they didn't know the terrain, they were leftovers from the Malvinas War who had been asked to advise. They ended up castaways idling their time listening to strange music.
>
> They also had the Killers [*Matadores*]. In a cage no more they stood, they did not go out. Through a little window they got food. They were male but they had hair down to here [*he pointed to his waist*]. Once they stuck a terrorist in the cage and they opened his heart and sucked and sucked on the blood that came out, saying, "How delicious."[26]

Upon arriving in Chaca, however, we found a lone official of the army passing among hundreds of fair-goers, peasants, and merchants, like a fish in water, with only a pistol and two *piñitas* (a slang word for grenades, literally "little pineapples") hanging from his belt, "just in case." A lot of water had run under the bridges. In San José de Secce, the district seat, the conscripts doing their obligatory military service were Quechua-speaking locals.

By contrast, Shining Path ended up identified with the devil, the anti-Christ, or with the terrible Andean *ñakaq* or *pishtacu*.[27] But as much or more than the massacres of *comuneros*, the event that best exemplifies the externalization of Shining Path in the region was the random death initiated in 1990 against the truck drivers on the Ayacucho–San Francisco route. In one of Shining Path's frequent blockades to demand quota payments (*cupos*) and settle "accounts in blood" (*cuentas de sangre*), one of the drivers escaped and notified a military detachment, which attacked and killed some Senderistas. Shining Path retaliated by initiating an indiscriminate massacre of drivers, chosen practically at random.[28] This was the kind of reflex that had been typical of the armed forces in 1983 and 1984.

Shining Path's Blind Spots and Defeat

It is strange that Shining Path seemed to miss the significance of the proliferating *rondas* and the new relationship between the peasantry and the armed forces. Sendero did not consider this development to be an important setback. On the contrary, in 1991, Shining Path proclaimed it was at last gaining "strategic equilibrium."

Until 1991, Shining Path documents did not include an in-depth analysis of the proliferating *rondas*. That year a Shining Path document, titled "Let the strategic equilibrium shake the country more!" defined the *rondas* as mechanisms of counterrevolutionary "low intensity warfare" employed by Fujimori, the military, and Yankee imperialism (PCP-SL 1991, 52). The document went on to provide a cumbersome *legal* analysis of legislation then under debate to legalize the Self-Defense Committees.[29] Near the end of 1991, *El Diario*, the mouthpiece of Shining Path, went beyond definitions and offered an analysis radically estranged from reality. It affirmed that the *rondas*, or "armed goons" (*mesnadas*) in Senderista slang, had "hit bottom," since "only five percent maintained themselves continuously since they were created by the marines or the army. The rest have been recomposed many times and lately dozens have been vacillating without direction, between dissolving and lining up against their mentors" (*El Diario* 1991b, 3).

Only in 1992 did the Senderistas seem to take notice of what was going on. The Plenary of the Central Committee affirmed:

> The problem is that they express an inflection; this is the problem. . . . They have occupied some points and displaced us. So they have subjected the masses . . . with threats even of death, and now they are masses pressured by the enemy. So our problem here, what is it? It is that we are restricted in our infiltration work among the *mesnadas* and this we must

correct in order to penetrate them, unmask them, undermine them, until we make them explode. (PCP-SL 1992b)

But the new directive, which included a greater emphasis on persuasion, arrived too late.

Shining Path's total disorientation reflected the various blind spots of the party or, if one prefers, of "Gonzalo Thought." The party's vision included an "optimistic fatalism," derived from a teleological view of history; a concept of social and political actors as "essences in action," as carriers of structures that inexorably determined their trajectory; a perception of the peasantry as incapable of initiative; a strategy of *prolonged* war through the construction of support bases and liberated zones; and finally, a disdain for Andean culture. These blind spots meant that Sendero's reading of the Peruvian and global situations did not fit well with real dynamics of Peru and the world.[30]

Essences in Action

I have already referred to the themes of violence and the discordance between the logic of the party and social dynamics. It only remains to add that, in 1982, the decision of the party to increase the violence and the subsequent initiation of executions (*ajusticiamientos*) contributed to deepen the divisions between Shining Path and the population. And in the late 1980s, the increase in violence against the *rondas* reaffirmed those who were already convinced, convinced the unconvinced, and impelled entire communities into an alliance with the armed forces. For Shining Path, violence was not merely the midwife but rather the mother and motor of history. According to their documents, this history did not advance in a straight line but rather with zigzags and retreats. But such setbacks occur strictly within the limits of a predetermined general trajectory; more than a script, history fulfills its destiny.

The armed forces, for example, were tagged in the Shining Path documents now and again as "specialists in defeat." Their essential character could not really change. The military could only go on fatally revealing its genocidal essence and its dependence on imperialism. In reality, however, in the 1990s the armed forces left Shining Path "off-side" (to use a soccer metaphor) by not fulfilling their preordained "destiny" of increasing massively their indiscriminate repression.[31]

The peasants, for their part, were for Sendero the "arena of contention between revolution and counterrevolution" (PCP-SL 1991, 4). Passive actors, of zero worth, they only obtained value when added to one or another band. Shining Path, for its part, was the depository of Truth, with a leader who was a "guarantor of victory"—through his capacity to interpret the laws of history.

The peasants were "condemned to triumph." Sooner or later through the development of the protracted popular struggle, the peasants finally would follow their destiny and gravitate toward Shining Path like butterflies to a light. Why?

> Objectively, [the counterrevolution] does not represent the interest of the people, we do, they cannot win over the masses, they have to force them, repress them so that the masses will follow them and this leads to resistance; in our case we can get them to follow us because we can make them see what is objective, that we represent their interests. (PCP-SL 1991, 4)

So there was no problem, at least no grave problem. According to Shining Path, the establishment of the "new power" in a zone could be followed by the reestablishment of the old power for a period and later the counter-reestablishment of the new power, and so on, until the consolidation of the liberated zones was achieved and the new republic emerged. The proliferation of the *rondas* was seen as one more episode of "reestablishment."

Perceptions of Time and Space

The Senderistas did not notice that the prolonged character of the war and their strategies of constructing support bases clashed with the peasants' conception of time and space. Such considerations did not matter much, if at all, to Sendero. The outcome of the story of Nicario is in a sense paradigmatic of a peasantry whose reproduction takes place substantially, despite poverty, through the market. The peasants, in particular youth, also had aspirations of social mobility that they learned in school and from mass media. The periods in which families made their plans were measured in the cycles of life (human, agricultural, and animal) and in the time that it took for their children to mature. Such time markers were not those of the protracted people's war that, by the end of the 1980s, seemed to stretch out in unending cycles of establishment, reestablishment, and counter-reestablishment . . . ad infinitum. When Shining Path tried to impose an even tougher rhythm of war, precisely in the years when the peasants were suffering drought and economic crisis, the threads of adaptation finally snapped.

On the other hand, the physical spaces in which the peasantry operated to sustain and reproduce life were vast. Networks of kinship and ethnic origin encompassed both the countryside and the city, and could reach as far as mines in the high tablelands (*punas*) and coca fields in the jungle (*selva*). Such spatially dispersed networks clashed with Shining Path's strategy of taking over bounded territorial spaces and converting them into support bases that tended toward isolation. After the initial years, and especially when the armed forces arrived and the peasants found themselves caught between two fires, large numbers of those who could leave joined the flood of refugees to Ayacucho city and to Lima. In many places, Shining Path ended up ruling over half-empty spaces, in which only the weakest remained trapped; that is, the poor, monolingual peasants who lacked urban connections and the native Asháninkas of the jungle zones were those most subject to Shining Path's "total domination."

Andean Culture

Shining Path's clash with peasants' notions of time and space was part of a wider collision with Andean culture. I do not refer to notions such as the myth of the hero-redeemer Inkarrí, or the inversion of the world through a *pachacuti* (cataclysm), but rather to the ensemble of the institutions important for the Ayacuchan Quechua peasantry. This ensemble included the extended family, the community, principles of reciprocity, generational age hierarchy, and rituals, fiestas, and religion in general.

The religious clash merits particular comment. According to del Pino Huamán, the Senderistas were exasperated by the militant zeal of the Protestant Evangelicals (who won considerable converts in the countryside) and their refusal "to serve two masters." As for Andean religion and popular Catholicism, Shining Path considered such beliefs archaic and disgusting, and actively tried to suppress community rituals and fiestas.

In addition to the fiestas' economic costs, viewed through a utilitarian lens, the party seemed discomforted by the "inversion of the world" that marked the ambience of fiestas. "Total power" did not permit such openings. Senderista fears were not unfounded. In several places, including Huancasancos and Huaychao, it was during such celebrations that the population rebelled. In a community in Vilcashuamán, the Senderistas suppressed the fiesta "because maybe when we are in the fiestas, they [the community] might betray us, there could be problems" (testimony of Pedro).

Shining Path's disdain for the cultural manifestation of the Quechua-speaking peasantry was based in a particular theory. "Maoism teaches us that a given culture is a reflection, on the ideological plane, of the politics and the economy of a given society" (*El Diario*, 13 September 1989). If this were true, then Andean art and culture were mere remnants of the past, "a reflection of the existence of man under landlord oppression, which reflects the technological and scientific backwardness of the countryside, which reflects the customs, beliefs, superstitions, feudal and anti-scientific ideas of the peasantry, product of centuries of oppression and exploitation that have subsumed it in igno-rance. . . . This is the character of what is called 'folklore'" (Márquez 1989).

Parting from this theory and practice, I believe it is valid to characterize the Senderistas as the new *mistis*, influenced by schooling and by Marxism.[32] Elsewhere (see chapter 7), I have likened the Senderistas with a third brother of the Aragón de Peralta family, protagonists of José María Arguedas's *Todas las sangres* (1964). If we take as an example another novel by Arguedas, *Yawar Fiesta* (1941), it is easy to identify Don Bruno with the traditional *mistis* (Julián Aranguena, for example) who were in favor of the "Indian-style bullfight," and Don Fermín with the national authorities and the "progressive" *mistis* who opposed the "Indian bullfight" and tried to "civilize" it by bringing in a Spanish bullfighter to Puquio. This group would include the university *chalos* (bilingual youth who have been educated and urbanized) who seek "the progress of the town" and help to contract the bullfighter. But Indians of the Qayau ayllu manage to capture the ferocious bull Misitu; the university students succumb to the will of the *comuneros*, and as they are overcome with happiness and pride, they put aside for the moment their "desires for progress." The Spaniard fails in the bullfight and it is the Indians who jump in the ring, to the joy of the progressive *mistis*. In the last line of the novel, the mayor turns to the subprefect: "See, Señor Subprefect? These are our bullfights. The true *Yawar Fiesta!*"

The ending would have been different if the third brother had been there, who might easily be identified with hypothetical Senderista students or professors who would not have succumbed to the strength of the Indians of Qayau. If Shining Path had been present, it might have killed Misitu or prohibited the fiesta. If the fiesta had been permitted, the party would have framed the matter as a strictly tactical concession and perhaps managed to suppress the pride that overcame the Puquiano students.

It is impressive to observe that, in the 1980s, in the Peruvian sierra, the conflict between *mistis* and Indians portrayed forty years earlier in *Yawar Fiesta* was partially replicated, and that, once again, the *mistis*, converted into "revolutionaries," ended up defeated by the "Indians," transformed into *ronderos*.

7

How Difficult It Is
to Be God

Ideology and Political Violence
in Shining Path

The Partido Comunista del Perú–Sendero Luminoso
(PCP-SL), or Shining Path, emerged from the encounter,
which took place during the 1960s and 1970s in Ayacucho, of a *mestizo* intellectual elite "de provincia" and university students who were also Andean and
mestizo highlanders (Degregori 1985a). Why did the political party born from
this encounter prove capable of such violence? What factors in the history of
Peru, and in the culture of the two social groups that constitute Sendero, made
that violence possible? And why did these actors "communicate" with other
political and social forces only in terms of absolute confrontation?

While the old guard of Senderista intellectuals clearly left their mark on
Shining Path, it was young provincial *mestizos* with a higher-than-average
education who constituted the backbone of the organization (Chávez de Paz
1989). In this chapter I discuss both groups. But first, it is necessary to emphasize
that those who joined Shining Path were a *minority* of young people and intellectuals in the provinces. In spite of the crisis in Peru and the lack of political
alternatives, the immense majority channeled their radicalism through more
flexible and constructive conduits.

Youth: The Children of the Deceived Search for the Sword of Truth to Avenge Their Deception

As happens frequently in our country, in order to understand we have to go back to the beginning. One could go back to the birth of Peru and see the triumph of the *conquistadores* as a product, among other things, of the manipulation of communication. We should remember that in the meeting—or rather the ambush—in Cajamarca that gave birth to Peru in 1532, Father Valverde came forward with a book in his hands—the Bible—and said to Juan Santos Atahualpa: "This is the word of God." The Inca, unfamiliar with the written word, lifted the book to his ear, heard not a word, threw the Bible to the ground, and, with this gesture, "justified" the conquest.

From the beginning, then, mastery of the Spanish language, reading and writing, were instruments of domination. Max Hernández tells Ricardo Palma's story about a *conquistador* who grew melons in Pachacámac; when they ripened he sent some as a gift to a friend in Lima. He gave the Indian bearers a letter and warned them not to eat a single melon because the letter would betray them. In mid-journey, tempted by hunger and the aroma of the fresh fruit, the Indians carefully hid the sheet of paper and ate some melons, confident that the letter could not have seen them. The tale ends with the astonishment of the Indians before the power of the written word when the recipient of the melons tells them precisely how many melons they have eaten.

Thus there emerged a society based on deceit, one that was made possible by, among other factors, the monopoly exercised by the rulers over the Spanish language. Since then, the conquered populations have swung between resignation and rebellion. These are, of course, idealized extremes that in reality are closely interrelated, and even blended together in contradictory ways. The concept "resistant adaptation" (Stern 1990) expresses much of what characterizes these intermediary positions.

Resignation is internalized even in myths. One of the variants of the myth of Inkarrí (Marzal 1979, 12) says that the *mistis* are the *chanas* of creation, the youngest children of God, and consequently the most indulged. God gave them the gift of speaking Spanish, and this is why "they do as they please." Their dominance is arbitrary; in the words of Gonzalo Portocarrero (1984), it is a "total domination."

The other attitude is rebellion, which in turn swings between two idealized extremes: on the one hand, Andean culture turns in on itself, rejecting "the West," and on the other, the conquerors' instruments of domination are

How Difficult It Is to Be God

appropriated. Both variants can be traced back to the sixteenth century. The Taqi Onqoy movement in the mid-sixteenth century is an example of the turning inward, as is the rebellion of Juan Santos Atahualpa in the middle of the eighteenth century. At the opposite pole is Manco Inca II trying to form a cavalry and using firearms in order to oppose the Spanish. Túpac Amaru II would be closer to this second pole; Túpac Katari closer to the first. What merits emphasis, however, is that in the twentieth century, the second pole of rebellion predominates: that which seeks to appropriate for itself the instruments of power of the dominant. And among these the key instrument is education. To wrest from the *mistis* their monopoly of knowledge is equivalent to the gesture of Prometheus in stealing fire from the gods. Here, the Andean populations take away the monopoly of Spanish language from the *mistis*, who behaved like gods while they were still able to exercise their "total domination."

As the twentieth century advanced, the eagerness of the Andean populations to acquire education proved quite exceptional. According to statistics of CEPAL (1985) on educational coverage in Latin American countries, Peru passed from fourteenth place in 1960 to fourth place in 1980. Among the roughly seventy nations the United Nations designates as "countries with medium levels of development," the percentage increase in young people eighteen to twenty-five years old who pursued secondary education is as follows: Overall in these seventy countries the proportion rose from 17 percent in 1960 to 52 percent in 1980. During the same period, the percentage of eighteen- to twenty-five-year-olds in Peru pursuing secondary education rose from 19 to 76 percent. The educational ambitions of students were not matched by the state's provision of resources, and in fact the push for education advanced against a current of state withdrawal. From the 1960s onward, state investment in education exhibits a steady decline in relative terms (Degregori 1989a).

My hypothesis would be that the impulse for education was stronger among the Andean populations than among the *criollos*. But what do Andean populations seek from education?[1] They seek, in effect, highly pragmatic tools for their democratic struggle against the *mistis* and local power-holders and to make a place for themselves in "national society." They seek to learn reading, writing, and arithmetic. But in addition, they also seek *the truth*. Various testimonies collected in Ayacucho, where Shining Path originated during a time most relevant to my argument, may illustrate this. In 1969, an important movement developed in Ayacucho and Huanta, requesting the restoration of free education that had been suspended by the government of General Velasco. Young secondary students were the catalyzing element, but at its climax, peasants took the city of Huanta and the urban-popular sectors rose up en masse in Ayacucho. Shortly afterward, when he was collecting data for his thesis on the movement, Aracelio Castillo asked a peasant leader from Huanta how he saw the situation of the peasants. The leader replied, "As compared to the abuses of former times, clearly it is a little better now. But they need someone to teach them, someone to give them guidance; there should be courses . . . to see if in this way they can progress and free themselves from slavery, from deception—if not, they will remain poor and exploited" (Castillo 1972, 272).

To be educated, then, is equivalent to "freeing oneself from deception," a point of departure from which education may take on explosive implications. A neighborhood leader from Ayacucho told Castillo shortly after the movement of 1969: "There have been demonstrations when they wanted to close our University San Cristóbal de Huamanga, which others criticize for corrupting good Christian souls . . . instead of recognizing that the University was awakening us, that we were learning something new, something objective, this is what they don't like, it doesn't please these people at all because they want us to continue being deceived" (Castillo 1972, 280).

To this deception, which goes back to the moment of the Conquest, is contrasted the "objective truth" that one achieves through education. At the height of the movement for free education, a statement from the Front for the Defense of the People of Ayacucho (Frente de Defensa del Pueblo de Ayacucho) declared that "the Military Junta has abolished free education because they know perfectly well that when the children of workers and peasants open their eyes it endangers their own power and wealth" (Castillo 1972, 205).

Traditional power, based not only on the monopoly of the means of production but also on the monopoly of knowledge and its manipulation through deception, crumbles as soon as the dominated break both monopolies. For this reason, education is seen as a victory over deception and, consequently, as rebellion against and "danger" for the dominant groups.

But although the struggle for education has clear democratizing effects at the social level, it does not necessarily imply qualitative democratic progress in all political and cultural spheres. If we go back to the testimony of the leader from Huanta, for example, we see that according to him, the peasants "need someone to teach them," someone—implicitly from outside—to give them guidance. The traditional hierarchy is thus produced in the relationship between teacher (*mestizo*/urban) and student (*campesino*/indigenous). Mass education can develop, then, without substantially breaking the conceptions of traditional society. In this case we have education that is not liberating but authoritarian and ethnocidal.

When Castillo asked the same leader what aspirations he would wish for the *campesinos* of Huanta, the complexity of the *campesino* proposal appears even more evident: "The greatest aspiration is progress for the people in the countryside; it would be that their helpers—or, better said, their guides—orient them on how to achieve progress, to avoid the vices of the *campesinos*, the vices of drink, coca and cigarettes. If they carry on with these vices, we shall never find a better life" (Castillo 1972, 272).

We used to think of the association between ignorance and vice as the province of oligarchic ideology, but we see here that it can also form part of the *campesino* outlook, where anxiety for progress is mixed with the demand for a conservative moral order (rejecting alcohol, coca, and cigarettes), and with the need for a guide who would lead them to desired objectives.[2] Perhaps it is the context of being interviewed by a distinguished university professor such as Castillo that influences the *campesino* leader to ask for guidance from the outside. We cannot be certain, but what does seem apparent is that his aspirations can equally be satisfied by various evangelical Christian sects or by Shining Path.

Indeed, if we start from the need for an external guide, the appearance of a caudillo-teacher like Shining Path's university professor leader should not come as a surprise. This account also makes more understandable Sendero's moralizing aspect, as exemplified by their punishments for adulterers and drunkards. And it explains why Marxism manuals were so popular in Peruvian universities in the 1970s.[3] Students were pouring into the universities at that time—young Andeans from the provinces who were the children of those same deceived *campesinos*. There they were presented with a simplified and therefore more accessible version of a theory—Marxism-Leninism—which claimed to be the only "scientific truth," legitimated by references to the classics of Marxism, its source of authority. This science proclaimed a new but strictly hierarchical order in which they, on joining the party and its truth, could pass from the bottom to the pinnacle of the social pyramid—and to the top of the pyramid of knowledge. We must not forget that they were university students.

It is worth asking whether it is in this great need for order and progress, in a context where elements of traditional hierarchy still prevailed, that we can find one of the roots of the quasi-religious scientism of Shining Path, for which "the ideology of the proletariat is scientific, exact, all-powerful" (*El Diario* 1989), or, as their own documents put it, "all-powerful because it is the truth" (PCP-SL 1988c, 2). Can we not also find here one of the sources of the personality cult and the sanctification of "Gonzalo Thought"? The caudillo-teacher is the embodiment of education and thus also the incarnation of the guide, the truth, and virtue. Because according to Sendero thinking, proletarian ideology has almost divine status. What we are dealing with is a new deity, capable of defeating the old *Wiracochas*, the gods who for centuries subjected the populace to "total domination."

If in general gaining access to basic education involves breaking with deception, those who get to the university have to go further and seek out unfailingly something beyond truth, namely *coherence*. Why? A partial reply can be found by elaborating on ideas suggested in an article by Umberto Eco (1986) on the topic of "cargo cults." For the Andean *campesinos* who set out to conquer "progress," school constitutes a first stage, a kind of "cargo cult;" for those of their children who reach university, modernity would be to some extent like a *pidgin*, a bridging device. Let me explain.

Anthropologists are familiar with the concept of "cargo cults," a term that arose as a result of World War II when the Allies established military bases in the territories of the indigenous peoples of Papua New Guinea and constructed runways where cargo planes would land in secret. At night, the beacons on the sides of the runway formed two lines of light between which the cargo plane came down from the skies, and the Papuans who helped the Allies saw how the goods of modernity came out from the belly of the planes. Some of these goods were then given to them in return for their loyalty. When the war ended, the Allies withdrew and closed the airports, but the Papuans kept waiting for the planes to return. They established a cult to the cargo planes. At certain times they would go to the runway, construct a plane of bamboo, light all the beacons and wait for the return of the cargo to bring them the goods of modernity.[4]

Schooling in Peru has something in common with the manufactured goods of modernity in the cargo cults, to some extent for all Peruvians, but perhaps especially for the *campesinos*. A book by Juan Ansión (1989a) shows that schools in the Andean communities are somewhat like a "black box," a technological package that is imported from the outside with unknown contents. It is not really clear what is inside, or how the box works; it is a kind of capsule of modernity that is placed in the main square where the children will learn the secret mechanisms that allow one to get on in today's world, especially the urban world. There develops then an almost super-human expectation in the power of education.

But the children or grandchildren who reach the university also feel that modernity comes to them in loose threads, in snippets, in fragments. Modernity for them is experienced as a kind of pidgin, one of those intermediary languages spoken in parts of Oceania where several languages are mixed together in somewhat indeterminate ways. That is how modernity reaches all of us in Peru and Latin America. Mario Vargas Llosa's own proposal to convert us into a "European country" contains much of a cargo cult and a desire to get beyond the level of pidgin.[5] But this perception of a fragmented world would seem to be especially acute among young provincial and *mestizo* university students in a region such as Ayacucho, where the modernizing agent has not been economic—mines, industry, or commercial agriculture—but rather fundamentally ideological—the university. With a bit of exaggeration, admittedly, we could say that in Ayacucho it is not economic change that leads to social and cultural change, but the reverse: what arrives first of all is an *idea*.

Without any foundation in material changes, the pidgin sensation intensifies and becomes unbearable. Young people find themselves in a no-man's land between two worlds: on the one hand, the traditional Andean world of their parents whose myths, rites, and customs they no longer fully share and, on the other hand, the Western world, or more precisely the urban, *criollo* one, a world that rejects them as provincials, *mestizos*, speakers of Quechua. The students demand a sense of *coherence*, a "world view" able to substitute for the traditional Andean one that is no longer theirs, and that is more accessible to them than the many different and complicated theories offered by the social sciences and philosophy. And they believe they have found what they are looking for in this rigid ideology that claims to be the sole truth and gives them the illusion of absolute coherence, namely Marxism-Leninism-Maoism.

This feeling would appear to be common to large numbers of young people in different regions, but in Ayacucho it is especially acute. Moreover, while in most universities students find books or professors who merely convey Marxist-Leninist ideas and try without success to forge an effective political organization, in the University of Huamanga there is a Maoist intellectual nucleus that has come together as a political party. So, there one encounters not only the books that teach this quasi-secret truth but also real people and an organization that offers a new identity to those for whom the traditional Andean identity of their parents no longer seems sufficient. The students gain the possibility of being a part of this new, all-powerful entity, the party "guided by the ideology of the Marxist-Leninist proletariat."

Here it must be recalled that according to Shining Path theory, it is not necessary that the proletariat actually exist in some place; it is enough that the proletarian *idea* has reached them. In the University of Ayacucho it was embodied in the caudillo-professor, Abimael Guzmán. In Sendero's posters, a central space is occupied by Guzmán wearing his suit and spectacles and with a book in his hand. There is not any other leader in the Marxist tradition whose intellectual character is emphasized so strongly when he is depicted surrounded by guns and flags with the red sun in the background. In contrast to the warm quality of other leaders on the Peruvian political scene—such as Belaúnde, García, or Barrantes—the caudillo-professor is cold, although he is still able to burn, like dry-ice.

Such, then, are the young people who follow Shining Path, seeking truth and coherence. When they think they have found it, they are capable of extremes of violence in imposing and defending it.

Intellectuals: The Lost Brother of the Aragón de Peralta Family Wishes to Modernize His Indians through the Socialist Path

As is well known, the principal characters of Jose María Arguedas's *Todas las sangres* are two landowner brothers: Don Bruno and Don Fermín Aragón de Peralta.[6] Don Bruno was a traditionalist. In his own way he loved "his" Indians and wished to protect them from the impact of modernization. Don Fermín, by contrast, wanted to modernize them through the path of capitalism. Arguedas puts in the mouth of Don Fermín the following phrase: "With our Indians I shall overcome the wall that the capitalists of Lima have put around me" ([1964] 1980, 20).

Let us imagine a lost son of the Aragón de Peralta who did not appear in *Todas las sangres*, perhaps because he was an illegitimate child. In any case, he is poor and not light-skinned and fair-haired like his brothers, but dark. He too wants to modernize the Indians over whom he considers himself to have as great a claim—if not greater—than that of his two brothers. After all, he is closer to the Indians in origin and perhaps also in his lived experience. Besides, material wealth doesn't matter so much to this third son since he is an intellectual. I am referring to the provincial, *mestizo*, petit-bourgeois intellectual who constitutes the original core of Shining Path. If Fermín relies on the economy and his capital, this third brother relies on a weapon that he considers to be much more powerful: a new ideology that is Marxism-Leninism-Maoism.

I disagree with some interpretations that view Shining Path as a messianic or millenarian movement rooted in pre-Hispanic Andean tradition. I believe that Sendero arrives at messianism, or a kind of religious vision, but that it does so through what we could call an "excess of reason." They are the last children of the Age of Enlightenment who, two hundred years down the road, lost in the Andes, have converted science into religion. Extreme positions resemble each other. There is a line from Manuel González Prada (1979): "War against mean sentiments, divine cult to reason." The position of the provincial intellectuals who formed the initial nucleus of Shining Path falls within this register. They take on Marxism-Leninism in such a way as to convert it into a "divine cult of reason." Given the degree of passion that Shining Path develops

How Difficult It Is to Be God

and unleashes, it seems strange to define it as a hyperrationalist movement, but we should take Blaise Pascal's phrase "the heart has its reasons that reason does not know" and turn it on its head to say about Sendero's leadership that "reason has passions that the heart does not know." I cite just one phrase as an example: when Shining Path leader Laura Zambrano Padilla, comrade "Meche," was asked about love, she replied: "Love has a class character and it is at the service of the popular war" (1985, 9).

Significantly, the provincial elite that constituted the initial nucleus of Shining Path leadership was neither original nor unique; rather, they came from a long tradition of opposition by provincial elites confronting oligarchic centralism. In the first half of the century, such people tended to adopt *indigenist* positions. From the 1920s onward, but especially from the middle of the century, in many places these elites adopted Marxism — in the majority of cases combining it with a revalorization of Andean culture that linked them with the previous *indigenismo*. José Carlos Mariátegui is the precursor of this revalorization. This is not the case, though, with Sendero, whose official documents entirely omit the ethnic dimension or directly reject Andean cultural reevaluation as "folklore" or bourgeois manipulation.[7]

In the initial Shining Path nucleus we find, then, both continuities with this intellectual tradition and also ruptures. In this sense, the Senderista turns out to be the "coldest" of all the versions of Marxism that arose in Peru during the 1960s and 1970s. Nevertheless, a vision claiming to be absolutely scientific became tremendously effective and ended up offering its members an enormously strong, quasi-religious, and fundamentalist identity. I cite a critical phrase from one of the most important Shining Path documents, where communism is defined as:

> The society of "great harmony," the radical and definitive new society towards which 15 billion years of matter in motion, the part that we know of eternal matter, have necessarily and irrepressibly led. . . . The unique new society, for which there is no substitute, without exploited or exploiters, without oppressed or oppressors, without classes, without State, without parties, without democracy, without arms, without wars. (PCP-SL 1989c, 20)

A society without movement, one should add. It is not strange that people should long for this type of nirvana, the society of great harmony, since these are social strata that have been pulverized terribly by the course of history in Peru. The nirvana of Sendero, however, has the trappings of a great cosmic journey. To complete it, the Senderistas have to order it and plan it all in accordance with the Book of Marxism-Leninism-Maoism, as warrior-intellectuals in the service of that entirely exact science that regulates the universe like a boundless cosmic ballet, conquering or destroying whatever stands in the way of inescapable laws.[8]

Thus, after four hundred years, a new Sacred Book has invaded Peru at another critical moment in our history. And it turns out that according to the Book of Marxism-Leninism-Maoism, Peruvian society is "semifeudal." Perhaps this Shining Path thesis would not have generated as much violence in China in the 1930s, because there they would not have encountered, for example, engineers repairing electricity pylons, agronomists organizing rural extension programs, or anthropologists advising peasant federations. The possibility of assassinating them would not have arisen, as such tokens of modernity simply did not exist. I believe that the level of violence that Shining Path develops is so great—among other reasons—because Senderistas have to fit reality to the idea, and in order to do so, they must not only stop time but have to turn it backward. It is as if in Peru, with the development of what they define as bureaucratic capitalism, too many rotten stems have grown, or, to cite González Prada once more, too many "fruits with a noxious aroma." They have to prune them back. When they turn the pages and reach a blank sheet, they can write a pamphlet for "their" Indians on it.[9]

When I state that they want to adapt reality to their own idea, I don't wish to say that there is no point of contact between the two. If that were the case, Shining Path would not have found it possible to construct a social base. Seen from Ayacucho, or from the south-central sierra in general, Peru has much that is "semifeudal." While the land-owners have practically disappeared, there are still local bosses with their economic bases of support—pre-capitalist commercial capital that leaves its trail of coercion and abuses (Manrique 1989). The intellectual elite that gave rise to Shining Path emerges from that background of "semifeudal" decadence—mercantile weakness—yet at the same time, it displays an exaggerated hope in progress, which is channeled through the drive for education.

It is not surprising that this elite figured so prominently in the University of Huamanga, the most modernized house of learning of the provinces, tucked away in the poorest region of the Peruvian Andes, or that the most important social movement in that region between the 1950s and 1970 was not a movement for land, as was the case in the rest of the Andes, but a movement for free education in 1969 (Degregori 1990).

Emerging in a region with little tradition of independent democratic organization and where, as we have noted, ideas arrived first, Shining Path took up and magnified both registers. The eagerness for progress was taken to its limit through Marxism-Leninism-Maoism. But at the same time, the authoritarianism of the old provincial elite of the *mistis* was also taken to extremes, running against the broader current in Peru that aimed to break up the power of the *mistis* and an end to their "total domination."

In effect, from the perspective of the rural and urban popular sectors, possibly the most important development that had occurred in Peru since the uprising of Túpac Amaru II in 1780 was the broad and multistranded process of organization that, in spite of its limitations, had made Peru at the beginning of the 1980s a country with one of the most dense networks of independent popular organizations in Latin America. In this context, if "total domination" (Portocarrero 1984) or the "triangle without base" (Cotler 1968) are considered to define the traditional or semifeudal relation between *misti* and Indians, then Shining Path in its practice constitutes a new form of being *misti*. This is because a fundamental feature of its actions is the repudiation of popular organization, such as *campesino* communities, workers' unions, neighborhood associations, and so on, and their replacement with the so-called generated organizations, their "*own* movements as organizations generated on different fronts by the proletariat" (PCP-SL 1988a, vii). That is to say, generated by themselves, by the party that "decides all," just as in the past everything was decided by the *patrones* and local power holders, by the party that has replaced the proletariat and the people in general, depriving them of their very being and their capacity for decision-making.[10]

Thus, in referring to rural areas I speak of Shining Path and *their* Indians because of the vertical manner in which Shining Path relates to the Andean peasantry. As divine representatives of a religion that is belligerently monotheistic, Senderistas do not admit anyone else onto their Olympus; they must be the only ones who organize the rural world. But, in contemporary Peru, unlike China in the 1930s, and despite the growing weakness of the state and civil society by the 1980s, those spaces where they wanted to be the solitary creator-gods are relatively populated by *campesino* organizations, unions, the parties or the Left, the progressive church, NGOs, and so on. Shining Path violence therefore strikes not only against the state but also against these other actors, because Sendero has to be unique with regard to the masses in order, finally, to "educate them in the popular war" (PCP-SL 1988a, vi).

This is why Sendero's documents can express the relationship between the party and the masses in such terms as: "the popular war is a political fact that goes pounding ideas into the minds of men with forceful actions" (PCP-SL 1988a, iv). Let me cite Abimael Guzmán himself, known to his followers as President Gonzalo:

> The masses *must be taught with convincing facts*. You must *drive home ideas* into them. . . . The masses in Peru need the direction of a Communist Party, we hope that with more revolutionary theory and practice, with

more armed actions, with more popular war, with more power, we may arrive at the very heart of the class and of the people, and really win them over. What for? To serve them, that is what we want. (Guzmán 1988, 36, emphasis added)

The language is one of an astonishing violence against the masses, although in the same paragraph it claims to be of love and service. It is an ambiguous relationship and one that is thoroughly Peruvian. This is why Shining Path can be seen as the third Aragón de Peralta brother, the synthesis of modernizing Don Fermín and authoritarian Don Bruno: tortuous, violent love from the superior to his subordinate, from the teacher toward his favorite but somewhat slow pupil to whom he must teach that "literacy comes with blood."

When classic Marxism says that "practice is the criterion of truth," the phrase is assumed to refer fundamentally to the practice of the broad masses. But in the previous quotation it is basically the practice of the *vanguard* that determines the criterion for truth, which must be *pounded in* from the outside. For Shining Path, "except power, everything is illusion." If that is so, if power is the only reality, then the party, which is the central instrument in conquering power, is the only thing that is real. Except for the party, everything is illusion. Society, for example, only becomes real when the party collides with it.

I offer just one example: Sendero's attitude toward the national work stoppages. Between 1977 and 1988, nine nationwide stoppages took place in Peru. In the most impressive (June 1977 and May 1978), millions of people participated throughout the country, turning them into possibly the most important movements in the history of contemporary Peru. The position of Shining Path toward the first eight stoppages swung between absolute indifference and head-on opposition since, according to Sendero Luminoso, the stoppages were led by "revisionism" and served "the imperialism of the socialist bloc." Then, for the first time, in January 1988, they decided to back the ninth national stoppage, which turned out to be much less well supported.

Sendero's participation, in turn, was limited to small-scale, specific actions, the main one being the disruption of the meeting convened by the General Confederation of Peruvian Workers (Confederación General de Trabajadores del Perú, CGTP) in the center of Lima where they lit firecrackers.[11] Nevertheless, the following day the headline in *El Diario* (the unofficial voice of Shining Path) read: "A Historic Day for the Peruvian Proletariat" (*El Diario*, 28/29/30 January 1988). Evidently, it was not a historic day because of the level of struggle but because the party had decided to support it, producing a kind of proletarian Pentecost that marked a "new direction for the working class"

How Difficult It Is to Be God

(*El Diario*, 30 January 1988, 7), such that "for the first time it was nourished by a more elevated experience of struggle" (*El Diario*, 1 February 1988, 10).

For Shining Path, then, we are a kind of clay, a mud that has to be molded by the party and its all-powerful ideology, in its image and in its likeness.

Epilogue

Open Wounds and
Elusive Rights: Reflections
on the Truth and Reconciliation
Commission

Early in 2000, to predict that soon there would be a Truth and Reconciliation Commission (hereafter CVR, the acronym in Spanish for Comisión de la Verdad y Reconciliación) in Peru would have sounded eccentric. How is it, then, that a window of opportunity appeared for its creation only eighteen months later?[1] How did the commission's work impact the dispute over the hegemonic narrative about the internal armed conflict that the country endured during the 1980s and 1990s? How did the *Final Report* presented on 28 August 2003 affect the intellectual and political agenda? This epilogue reflects on some of these questions.

The Emergence of the CVR

In April 1992, in the context of a serious national crisis and after twelve years of the bloodiest internal armed conflict in the republic's history, majority public opinion supported the coup by then-president Alberto Fujimori, giving up liberties in exchange for order and security. Five months later, Abimael Guzmán was taken prisoner, and in subsequent months the majority of his national leadership was also arrested. At the same time, the principal leaders of MRTA (Túpac Amaru Revolutionary Movement), also an armed insurgent group, were captured.[2] The military and political capacity of the subversive organizations collapsed. Taking advantage of the favorable political context, in the following years the principal spokespeople for the regime insistently spread a message supported by important opinion leaders and amplified by most of the media, which became the received wisdom: human rights violations committed by state agents during the conflict had been the necessary cost that the country had to pay for ending the subversive violence unleashed by Shining Path in 1980 and by MRTA four years later. It was better to turn the page, look to the future, not open the wounds caused by the conflict. By mid-decade, forgetting appeared to have been imposed. The 1995 Amnesty Law seemed like its consecration.

But arguably, what had been imposed was a particular narrative of the years of political violence.[3] There was a "memory of salvation" (Stern 1998) in which the central protagonists of the pacifying gesture were Alberto Fujimori and Vladimiro Montesinos. The military and police appeared as supporting actors and civilian institutions and citizens occupied the footlights like mere passive spectators of this black-and-white drama in which the incarnation of evil was not only Sendero and MRTA but everyone who differed with the official version of what happened in those years.

Nevertheless, narratives that questioned the official story always existed. The most visible ones were those that emerged from human rights organizations or the opposition press. But there were also silenced memories held close within communities or families out of fear or lack of outlets for expression in the public sphere.

Exploring these questioning versions, these hidden memories, their evolution over the past decade, and their impact on public opinion and the social mobilizations at the end of Fujimori's regime leads to a sketching of a genealogy of the CVR. It is also a means for questioning generalizations about the supposed irredeemably authoritarian "Peruvian culture."

Thus, even during the debate on the 1993 Constitution, at the height of general acceptance that "mano dura" (iron fist) was the only response not only to violent terrorism but to almost any problem, between 30 and 40 percent of Peruvians were opposed to restoring the death penalty in the new constitution. About 85 percent opposed the amnesty law passed in June 1995, only a few weeks after Fujimori's overwhelming electoral victory that allowed him to be reelected for a second term. Shortly afterward, the National Coordinating Committee for Human Rights (CNDDHH) did a survey on citizen perceptions of human rights. The survey participants' greatest request was for the CNDDHH to focus on the "right to life, understood as the protection of all people against all forms of abuse and discriminatory treatment, particularly in access to justice" (IMASEN 1996). Equally revealing are the perceptions conveyed through focus groups asked about the massacre of students at the National University of Education "La Cantuta" in 1992 and the recent amnesty: "La Cantuta might be hazily remembered but it is synonymous with the assassination of students and it is condemned even if the disappeared had effectively been Senderistas. The amnesty is rejected, it violated human rights, especially the obligations to know the truth and receive justice. These are values that are appreciated."[4]

This sensibility in favor of truth and against impunity came to occupy an important place in the package of complaints about the government that crystallized in the second half of the decade. The rejection of authoritarianism was among the most pronounced demands; initially urged by middle-class urban sectors, it began to gain force with the 1996 "law of authentic interpretation" that opened the door to a second reelection for Fujimori. In the following years, as the regime concentrated on its own perpetuation and the economic crisis deepened, demands for employment and wages, and against centralization, grew. Finally, especially after the first *vladivideo* appeared in September 2000, rejection of the regime's corruption spread.[5]

In 2000, these concerns found common ground around the demand to respect representative democracy, specifically condemning electoral fraud and supporting respect for the vote of the citizenry. The centrality of this demand shows the degree to which the national and international scenario had changed since the earlier transition to democracy (1977–80), when the demands of social movements pushing for withdrawal of the military government (1968–80) were primarily economic and social.[6]

The objection to human rights violations was successfully incorporated into this package of anti-authoritarian demands when *fujimorismo* reached a crisis point. This happened because, in addition to the sensibility previously mentioned, beginning in the 1980s, "memory entrepreneurs" emerged in oppositional public narratives and the silenced memories of the victims; they were building bridges and creating organizations like the CNDDHH.[7] Even if they were not mass based, these organizations were coherent, and they had managed to establish beachheads in various regions and social sectors of the country. These "memory entrepreneurs" allied with groups close to them, from organizations of victims of the violence to youth collectives, who during Fujimori's second government expressed the democratic aspiration for the respect for human rights. At the same time, especially after the public exposure of crimes committed by the *Colina* death squad and its relationship with the strongman of the regime, Vladimiro Montesinos, the political opposition began to devote greater space on its agenda to the issue of respect for human rights (Rospigliosi 2000; CVR 2003, vols. 2 and 5).

Nevertheless, the inclusion of this demand is not sufficient to explain the creation of the CVR in Peru. This is especially the case given that the concerns were concentrated on the human rights violations during the regime of Alberto Fujimori. Those committed in the 1980s, which were equally serious and much more extensive, remained completely in the dark. Another factor that helps explain the existence of the CVR is the weakness of the political parties during the transition. In reality, political parties did not play a decisive role in either of the two most recent transitions in Peru. In the earlier case (1977–80), this role was played by "popular organizations." In this instance it was "civil society." Simplifying somewhat, both terms refer to popular and middle-class sectors that played important roles as activators of the transition in 2000.[8] After the fraudulent elections that year, their role became more manifest; for example the CNDDHH participated as one of the four representatives of civil society in an OAS-sponsored dialogue that to a great extent informed the transition.[9] If the traditional political parties had taken a central role in the transition, as in Chile for example, it would have been almost impossible to create a CVR that would investigate as far back as 1980, since the Popular Action (1980–85) and APRA (1985–90) governments would have come under scrutiny.

Changes at the international level also contributed to the creation of the CVR. The consolidation of representative democracy was a necessary credential to access globalization, but even more critically, other Latin American countries had formed truth commissions to deal with the military dictatorships in the Southern Cone and the armed conflicts in Central America. By 2000, truth commissions were part of a menu of options in countries that underwent democratic transitions following internal armed conflict.[10]

Thus, unlike in Argentina after the fall of the military dictatorship, in Peru at that time there was not a massive outcry for truth and justice, but there was a strong demand for transparency and an end to impunity in a favorable international context.[11]

Moreover, in Peru there was not a transition by pact, but a collapse of the authoritarian regime. Unlike in Chile or Guatemala, where the armed forces not only retained their prerogatives but actually monitored the transition, in Peru the guardians of forgetting beat a retreat, fled the country, or were imprisoned. Finally, transitions, or at least the early stages, are highly fluid moments in which the possibilities for agency or "political will" expand, the official histories begin to crack, and crevices open up, ceding space to other memories and other readings of the past.

Thus, the space for a truth commission opened up. The result could have been different.[12] Additionally, the CVR in Peru had a broad mandate. It was not limited to clarifying executions and disappearances, like in Chile; rather, it investigated: "(a) assassinations and kidnappings; (b) forced disappearances; (c) torture and other serious injuries; (d) violations of the collective rights of Andean and native communities; (e) other crimes and serious violations of rights against individuals."[13] Finally, this mandate was endorsed by the principal candidates for the presidency in the 2001 elections. Everyone agreed in writing to adopt as their own the recommendations of the CVR's *Final Report* in the event they were elected.

Speaking Out

Sixteen months after its formation, the full commission of the CVR stated in a meeting with regional headquarters and investigatory staff that the spaces that had opened for the CVR seemed to be fading. Economic difficulties monopolized the attention of the majority of poor people. The fragility of the regime sharpened the tension between democratic governability and truth and justice. Authoritarian enclaves strongly persisted in important sectors like the media. Skepticism detracted from the credibility of institutions. The spaces for retelling the past thinned and the temptation of forgetting returned. These tendencies were reinforced after the terrorist attacks on the United States on 11 September 2001, which dramatically changed the international scene. The principal risk that the CVR faced was that its *Final Report* would be received with total indifference.

Nevertheless, the political moment continued to be fluid, and the country was far from having regressed to the pre-2000 situation, which by then would have been impossible. The very existence of the CVR, inscribed within the process of the fight against forgetting and impunity previously described, was sustained by this very process while simultaneously facilitating its development and consolidation.[14]

Here I will mention just a few examples. To dare to speak about crimes and human rights violations in Peru's recent history in such a direct manner would have been unthinkable three years earlier. I am not only referring to the public hearings, which were the line of work in which the CVR had the greatest impact. There were several other arenas in which multiple actors rose to report, for example, the existence of burial sites or common graves. This was not because they were recently discovered, but because the disintegration of fear created the possibility of reporting their existence. Thus, when the CVR initiated its work, there were around 50 burial sites reported to the human rights defense organizations or the Ombudsman. When the CVR finished its work, the number of sites reported was greater than 4,000, of which the CVR's forensic team managed to do preliminary reviews of more than 2,000. Furthermore, given the experience of other commissions, the dimensions of the conflict in Peru, and our own capacity, the CVR planned to collect around 12,000 testimonies. But the demand grew steadily and the CVR ended up gathering more than 17,000.

Wounds, Rights

Did the CVR reopen wounds that were already healed, exacerbating unnecessary pain in the victims by encouraging them to speak? If anything became clear from the CVR's work, it was that the wounds were not healed, and were significantly more serious and painful than might have been imagined. The voices that expressed themselves had been silenced by distance or indifference, since in contrast with the Southern Cone countries, where the political violence took place in urban spaces and in a context of greater development of citizenship, in our country the group most heavily affected by the political violence was poor rural indigenous youth. And the women of this social segment overwhelmingly suffered the greatest effects.

It can be said that in Peru there coexist different experiences of time that are marked by differentiated access to power. What for the elites and the majority of the urban population is past, continues to be present for the *insignificantes*: this term was coined by Gustavo Gutiérrez.[15] They were insignificant economically, because the domestic armed conflict impacted mostly in zones of the country that mattered very little in macroeconomic terms, in that they contributed very little to GDP. They were insignificant politically, because elections are not decided in the countryside. And they were insignificant culturally, given the deep-rooted racism toward indigenous groups: 75 percent of the victims who died in the conflict had Quechua as their mother tongue.[16]

The CVR brought to the public sphere a reality that had been relegated to the past: the reality that thousands of relatives of the disappeared, for example, were trapped in a present of suffering, kept from having closure on their grief and moving on as long as they could not locate their loved ones. Once they were able to do so, an alteration in the balance of power could occur, even if only by making those who held it uncomfortable, which was noticeable in their reactions to the final report of the CVR.[17]

One of the dangers of public hearings was establishing an asymmetric, paternalistic relationship with people who could appear to be, or worse, could be constructed as *victims*, and only as such be able to access the public sphere and obtain recognition.[18] Nevertheless, the very fact of daring to speak confirmed the witnesses as agents. When they spoke in languages other than Spanish, the testimony constituted a double symbolic reparation, because their silence was broken and because their voice was heard in languages silenced from the public sphere.

However, rarely did the witnesses adhere to mere petition; overcoming the pain, the majority made demands. And the range of demands was not limited to economic restitution; they also prominently included requests for justice, education, and psychological support, just to name a few of the most frequent claims.[19] The prevailing tone in the hearings tracked the sensibility observed in the IMASEN survey (1996). Those who gave their testimony protested "against the abuses and discriminatory treatment, especially in access to justice," which worsened beyond any threshold of tolerance during the years of political violence.

These were, in other words, testimonies that included claims for equality before the law, made by those who to begin with *were* victims, understanding this word as a legal category that provides rights to demand criminal and civil restitution.[20] In the decades prior to the domestic armed conflict, important sectors of Peruvians entered the public space as unionists or through urban land or hacienda invasions as a basis for obtaining rights of citizenship. In the last two decades, other Peruvians entered the public scene, unfortunately as victims of political violence. It is possible that on that basis, they will be able to achieve citizenship rights. One positive indicator would be the formation— taking advantage of the window of opportunity provided by the CVR's work—of a federation of victims' organizations, which would partially rectify the weakness of these organizations compared to those in the Southern Cone.

This requires that those who are disposed to speak, and to make claims, find interlocutors in the state. In this respect, the CVR's work also represented a less dramatic but important change: victims of the political violence who expressed their desire to speak found an official space (public, or private in the case of collecting testimonials) for being heard. There were precedents within the state for this type of work, especially by the Ombudsman (Defensoría del Pueblo), that were able to create a list of detainees-disappeared. But the space for being heard was (and continues to be) tremendously insufficient, not only from the state but within society itself. Nevertheless, especially in this last aspect, the *temporalities of memory* must be considered. As Jelin (2002, 31–32) observes, "There are conjunctures of political transition—such as Chile at the end of the 1980s, or postwar France—in which the desire for reconstruction is experienced as contradictory to messages linked to the horrors of the past. . . . Finding others with the capacity to listen is central to the process of breaking silences."

In some cases, like the Holocaust,

> The outside world was not able to recognize it. . . . The available cultural interpretive frameworks lacked the symbolic resources needed to account for and make sense of the events. . . . Sufficient time had to elapse, and a new generation born after the end of the war had to come of age and begin questioning their elders, in order to recognize and attempt to give meaning to the historical void that had been created in the social ability to convey and listen to testimony, . . . since testimonial narratives could not be conveyed or interpreted at the time the events were taking place. Only with the passing of time was it possible to bear witness to testimony, which implies the social ability to listen and give meaning to the narrative of the survivors. Here we encounter one of the paradoxes of "historical trauma," which reveals the double void in the narrative: the inability or impossibility of constructing a narrative due to the dialogical void—there is no subject, and there is no audience and no listening. When dialogue becomes possible, he or she who speaks and he or she who listens begin the process of naming, of giving meaning and constructing memories. (Jelin 2002, 83–84)

The work of the CVR's *Final Report* has revealed the reticence to listening to "messages linked to the horrors of the past," as well as to creating spaces for dialogue that previously did not exist or were scarce.

Final Report, Will to "Forget," Spaces for Dialogue

As noticeable as the presentation of the *Final Report* was the demolition campaign taken up by sectors of the press and the media outlets of several political parties in the two months before its presentation, in effect, before seeing it. In their harshest edges, the attacks were reminiscent of the media campaigns launched against the opposition in the final years of Alberto Fujimori's regime (see Degregori 2000a, section 2).

The principal criticisms of the *Final Report* concerned the bias against the armed forces and in favor of the subversive groups. Nevertheless, in the context of a crisis of legitimacy of all institutions, the CVR maintained a high approval rating in public opinion polls.[21] Moreover, aside from the approval or lack thereof of the work of the commissioners, more than 80 percent of survey respondents supported the view that the *Final Report* should be delivered to the government and its content made public. This is an important point, since one of the proposals of the critics was that the delivery be delayed, or that it be conducted strictly in private to the president.

What these polls showed was the desire for the retraction of the aggressively militarized "memory of salvation" of the previous decade with its proposal of "forgetting." However, even if momentarily in retreat, this refusal to recognize what happened is inscribed in what could be called a long period of forgetting, or perhaps a habit of repressing subaltern memories. The reluctance to accept the figure of more than 60,000 dead and disappeared suggested in CVR's report, as opposed to the 25,000 deaths maintained until then as the official tally of the years of violence, prompted the following reflection from Mirko Lauer:

> In addition to constituting a horrific figure, the 35,000 "new victims" simultaneously reveal a new category that in reality is quite old: the twice dead and disappeared. They are people who suffered a tragedy, and the country—not just officialdom, but society as well—simply were unaware that they had died or disappeared. This is the same as more or less saying that those Peruvians did not exist for the country long before they stopped existing in reality. . . . The poverty into which they were born covered the hole without being perturbed. (Lauer 2003, 6)

Rather than the lack of culturally available symbolic resources within a national community victimized by traumatic events, Peru is facing old symbolic frameworks within a community that excludes or discriminates, especially toward the poor who are, in addition, culturally distinct—in this case Quechuas and Asháninkas.

At the same time, in contrast to the initial silence and the weak earlier response from the government, it was established that there were subjects available to listen. The public success of the CVR's photography exposition— *Yuyanapaq: Para recordar* (To remember)—as well as a proliferation of events, many of them organized and attended by youth, which perhaps indicate the arrival of a generation "disposed to question their elders," make it difficult at the time of this writing, November 2003, to evaluate whether the CVR's *Final Report* will be capable of recasting the intellectual and political agenda of the country. However, given the reluctance of the majority of the political parties, the attorney general, and the government itself, there is no guarantee that its recommendations will be taken up by the government and supported by important sectors of public opinion.

Other experiences of truth commissions established in periods of democratic transition lead to the conclusion that "skipping phases, finding shortcuts in the road to truth and justice with the argument of sustaining governability erodes the possibilities of strengthening the very democracy that one is attempting to defend" (Valdéz 2001, 128). But they also teach that the commissions are successful to the extent that important social and political actors agree to the recommendations and take ownership of the new reading of the past proposed by the commissions. Moving from a kind of passive sympathy to an active memory of the past that is not only in solidarity with the victims but also capable of creating new meanings of the past and political proposals for the future—that is the difficult challenge of the coming years.

Notes

Introduction. Beyond Orientalism in Twentieth-Century Peru

1. The essays in this book are drawn from those that appeared in Carlos Iván Degregori, *Qué difícil es ser Dios: El Partido Comunista del Perú–Sendero Luminoso y el conflicto armado interno en el Perú: 1980–1999* (Lima: IEP, 2010), and are adapted for the English-language edition with permission from Degregori before he passed away, and by the Instituto de Estudios Peruanos (IEP).

For narrative, analysis, and statistics of the war, the fundamental starting point is Comisión de la Verdad y Reconciliación (CVR), *Informe final*, 9 vols. (Lima: CVR, 2003), esp. vols. 1, 4, 9; also published online at www.cverdad.org.pe (accessed 11 July 2011), and ably summarized in one volume as *Hatun Willakuy: Versión abreviada del Informe Final de la Comisión de la Verdad y Reconciliación Perú* (Lima: Comisión de Entrega de la CVR, 2004). The CVR's careful revision of the estimated toll from perhaps 30,000 lives to 69,000 lives was a major shock. All volumes of CVR are available in both print and online editions.

For increasingly well-researched scholarship since the mid to late 1990s on grassroots experiences and consequences of the war, see Carlos Iván Degregori, Ponciano del Pino Huamán, Orin Starn, and José Coronel Aguirre, *Las rondas campesinas y la derrota de Sendero Luminoso*, 2nd ed. (Lima: IEP, 1996); Steve J. Stern, ed., *Shining and Other Paths: War and Society in Peru, 1980–1995* (Durham, NC: Duke University Press, 1998); Carlos Iván Degregori, ed., *Jamás tan cerca arremetió tan lejos: Memoria y violencia política en el Perú* (Lima: IEP, 2003); Kimberly Theidon, *Entre prójimos: El conflicto armado interno y la política de la reconciliación en el Perú* (Lima: IEP, 2004); Jo-Marie Burt, *Political Violence and the Authoritarian State in Peru: Silencing Civil Society* (New York: Palgrave Macmillan, 2007); Ponciano del Pino Huamán, "'Looking to the Government': Community, Politics and the Production of Memory and Silences in Twentieth-Century Peru, Ayacucho" (PhD diss., University of Wisconsin–Madison, 2008); Olga M. González, *Unveiling Secrets of War in the Peruvian Andes* (Chicago:

University of Chicago Press, 2011); and for historical backdrop, also Jaymie Heilman, *Before the Shining Path: Politics in Rural Ayacucho* (Palo Alto, CA: Stanford University Press, 2010). For pioneering work already by 1990–92, with special attention on origins and early war years, see Carlos Iván Degregori, *El surgimiento de Sendero Luminoso: Ayacucho 1969–1979: Del movimiento de la gratuidad de la enseñanza al inicio de la lucha armada* (Lima: IEP, 1990; 2nd ed., 2010); Gustavo Gorriti Ellenbogen, *Sendero: Historia de la guerra milenaria en el Perú* (Lima: Editorial Apoyo, 1990); David Scott Palmer, ed., *The Shining Path of Peru* (rev. ed., New York: St. Martin's Press, 1994).

2. For exoticist sensibilities, their historical and moral contexts, and the necessity to build historicized analysis of Shining Path, see Steve J. Stern, "Beyond Enigma: An Agenda for Interpreting Shining Path and Peru, 1980–1995," in Stern, *Shining and Other Paths*, 1–9.

3. For regional histories and expansion of the war, with detailed accounting of loss of life by major regions and subregions, see CVR, *Informe final*, vol. 4 (population of Ayacucho is taken from p. 30, and excludes the adjoining provinces of Acobamba and Angaraes in Department of Huancavelica and Andahuaylas/Chincheros in Department of Apurímac); and 1:69–70, for loss of life estimate for Ayacucho. If one includes the adjoining provinces, the weight of the greater Ayacucho region in the loss of life is that much greater—about half the national toll. See CVR, *Hatun Willakuy*, 77–78. The total deaths and disappearances reported directly to the CVR amounted to 23,969 of the 69,280 estimated dead and disappeared. For explanation of estimate methodology at a 95 percent confidence level, see CVR, *Informe final*, vol. 9, Anexo 2.

4. On expansion into Lima, see CVR, *Informe final*, 4:439–505; Burt, *Political Violence and the Authoritarian State*, cf. Jo-Marie Burt, "Shining Path and the 'Decisive Battle' in Lima's Barriadas: The Case of Villa El Salvador," in Stern, *Shining and Other Paths*, 267–307.

5. Nelson Manrique, "La caída de la cuarta espada y los senderos que se bifurcan," *Márgenes, encuento y debate* 13–14 (November 1995): 22; for astute analysis of Fujimori and manipulation of Guzmán's image, see Patricia Oliart, "Alberto Fujimori: 'The Man Peru Needed'?" in Stern, *Shining and Other Paths*, 411–24.

6. Edward W. Said, *Orientalism* (New York: Pantheon, 1978); for evolution and adaptation of thought to other imperial experiences, see Said, *Culture and Imperialism* (New York: Alfred A. Knopf, 1993); for foundational research on the national question in the making of republican Peru, see Nelson Manrique, *Las guerrillas indígenas en la guerra con Chile* (Lima: Centro de Investigación y Capacitación, 1981); Florencia E. Mallon, *The Defense of Community in Peru's Central Highlands: Peasant Struggle and Capitalist Transition, 1860–1940* (Princeton, NJ: Princeton University Press, 1983); Florencia E. Mallon, *Peasant and Nation: The Making of Postcolonial Mexico and Peru* (Berkeley: University of California Press, 1995); see also Mark Thurner, *From Two Republics to One Divided: Contradictions of Postcolonial Nationmaking in Andean Peru* (Durham, NC: Duke University Press, 1997); Cecilia Méndez, *The Plebeian Republic: The Huanta Rebellion and the Making of the Peruvian State, 1820–1850* (Durham, NC: Duke University Press, 2005); and for how such issues played out specifically in the

twentieth-century sociopolitical history of rural Ayacucho, see Heilman, *Before the Shining Path*. See also the sources in n. 10 below. The colonial foundations of the problem of the national Other, both within and beyond Peru, are evident from a literary perspective in the compelling and masterful study of Rolena Adorno, *The Polemics of Possession in Spanish American Narrative* (New Haven, CT: Yale University Press, 2007).

7. On conceptualizing Orientalism in relation to internal national dynamics, see Jane Schneider, ed., *Italy's "Southern Question": Orientalism in One Country* (New York: Berg, 1998); Barbara Weinstein, "Developing Inequality," *American Historical Review* 113.1 (February 2008): 1–18; and Barbara Weinstein, *Race, Region, Nation: São Paulo and the Formation of National Identities* (forthcoming; I am grateful to Weinstein for presenting a preview of the argument at the Merle Curti Lectures, University of Wisconsin–Madison, 18–20 October 2011); and for additional fascinating study of ethnographic mapping of peoples in a context of state building, see Francine Hirsch, *Empire of Nations: Ethnographical Knowledge and the Making of the Soviet Union* (Ithaca, NY: Cornell University Press, 2005). For photo-images in Peru, *indigenismo*, and de-Indianization, the best starting points are Deborah Poole, *Vision, Race, Modernity: A Visual Economy of the Andean Image World* (Princeton, NJ: Princeton University Press, 1997); Marisol de la Cadena, *Indigenous Mestizos: The Politics of Race and Culture in Cuzco, Peru, 1919–1991* (Durham, NC: Duke University Press, 2000); cf. José Luis Rénique, *Los sueños de la sierra: Cusco en el siglo XX* (Lima: CEPES, 1991); for education and intellectuals, see also the chapters by Degregori in this book; and Marisol de la Cadena, "From Race to Class: Insurgent Intellectuals *de provincia* in Peru, 1910–1970," in Stern, *Shining and Other Paths*, 22–59; and for a fine one-volume history that sets the centralization of power in Lima and the politico-cultural dynamics of the "Indian question" in long-term context, see Peter Flindell Klarén, *Peru: Society and Nationhood in the Andes* (New York: Oxford University Press, 2000).

8. Scholarly fascination with *lo andino* (or *andinismo*) was an international as well as Peruvian phenomenon, and vivid during my periods of field and archival work in Peru during the run-up to and start of the war, 1976–81. For an important critique amidst the war crisis, see Orin Starn, "Missing the Revolution: Anthropologists and the War in Peru," *Cultural Anthropology* 6, no. 1 (February 1991): 63–91; for illuminating debate, see the special issue of *Allpanchis* 23.39 (1992); cf., for insightful retrospective, Pablo F. Sendón, "Ecología, ritual y parentesco en los andes: Notas a un debate no permitido," *Debate agrario* 40–41 (2006): 273–97. A focal point was the well-regarded ethnographic study of Chuschi in the 1970s by anthropologist Billie Jean Isbell, *To Defend Ourselves: Ecology and Ritual in an Andean Village* (Austin: University of Texas Press, 1978), but the debate used Isbell's work (and Starn's critique) less as the main focus than as a point of entry for wide-ranging discussion of scholarship and assumptions about *lo andino*, within and beyond Peru. For a broader vision of anthropology in Peru and Latin America, engaged with essentialism but also competing currents, see Carlos Iván Degregori and Pablo Sandoval, eds., *Saberes periféricos: Ensayos sobre la antropología en América Latina* (Lima: IEP, 2007).

9. Juan Ansión, "¿Es luminoso el camino de Sendero?" *El Caballo Rojo*, no. 108 (1982): 4–5; Pablo Macera, *Las furias y las penas* (Lima: Mosca Azul, 1983), cf. Gonzalo Portocarrero, *Razones de sangre: Aproximaciones a la violencia política* (Lima: Pontificia Universidad Católica del Perú, 1998), 83–88; see also chapter 2 of the present volume. A foreign author produced the most sensationalist—intellectually crude and politically irresponsible—work: Simon Strong, *Shining Path: Terror and Revolution in Peru* (New York: Times Books, 1992).

10. Alberto Flores Galindo, *Buscando un Inca: Identidad y utopía en los andes* (1986; 3rd rev. ed., Lima: Horizonte, 1988); for distinct editions and impact, including debate and critique by Degregori, an excellent overview is given in Carlos Aguirre and Charles F. Walker, "Alberto Flores Galindo: Historian and Public Intellectual," in Alberto Flores Galindo, *In Search of an Inca: Identity and Utopia in the Andes*, ed. and trans. Carlos Aguirre, Charles F. Walker, and Willie Hiatt (New York: Cambridge University Press, 2010), xiii–xxix; see also Portocarrero, *Razones de sangre*, 114–19. For a distinct focus on Andean utopia by a colleague who worked closely with Flores Galindo, see Manuel Burga, *Nacimiento de una utopía: Muerte y resurrección de los Incas* (Lima: Instituto de Apoyo Agrario, 1988).

11. Mario Vargas Llosa et al., eds., *Informe de la Comisión Investigadora de los sucesos de Uchuraccay* (Lima: Editora Perú, 1983); for critical analysis and inside-story research in Uchuraccay, see, respectively, Enrique Mayer, "Peru in Deep Trouble: Mario Vargas Llosa's 'Inquest in the Andes' Reexamined," *Cultural Anthropology* 6.4 (1991): 466–504; and Ponciano del Pino Huamán, "Uchuraccay: Memoria y representación de la violencia política en los andes," in *Jamás tan cerca arremetió lo lejos: Memoria y violencia política en el Perú*, ed. Carlos Iván Degregori (Lima: IEP, 2003), 49–93.

12. The best journalistic account is the superb study by Gorriti Ellenbogen, *Sendero: Historia de la guerra milenaria*; for Sendero within a broader national context of competing political events and currents, an excellent account is Deborah Poole and Gerardo Rénique, *Peru: Time of Fear* (London: Latin American Bureau, 1992). For important early reflections on violence and race (some specifically on Sendero, some analyzing the problem in wider or long-term contexts), see Alberto Flores Galindo and Nelson Manrique, *Violencia y campesinado* (Lima: Instituto de Apoyo Agrario, 1985); Nelson Manrique, "La década de la violencia," *Márgenes, encuentro y debate* 5–6 (December 1989): 137–82 (cf. his *El tiempo del miedo: La violencia política del Perú, 1980–1996* [Lima: Fondo Editorial del Congreso del Perú, 2002]); Henrique Urbano, ed., *Poder y violencia en los andes* (Cusco: Centro de Estudios Regionales Andinos Bartolomé de Las Casas, 1991); Gonzalo Portocarrero, *Racismo y mestizaje* (Lima: Sur, 1993) (cf. his *Razones de sangre*, and later expanded essays, *Racismo y mestizaje y otros ensayos* [Lima: Fondo Editorial del Congreso del Perú, 2007]). The interest in violence as a long-standing phenomenon was also evident in the superb and much-commented study of late colonial Lima by Alberto Flores Galindo, *Aristocracia y plebe: Lima, 1760–1830* (Lima: Mosca Azul, 1984).

13. Degregori passed away on 18 May 2011. He had suffered from pancreatic cancer since 2008, but remained lucid and himself—analytical and engaged with society and

politics, soft-spoken and humorous, interested in others—until the end. The discussion of Degregori's life experiences, Ayacucho connection, and evolution that follows in this subsection is based on several sources: (a) personal knowledge, through a thirty-five-year relationship of intellectual exchange and collaboration, and friendship, that began in Ayacucho in the 1970s, included joint teaching and conference collaboration in Wisconsin, the reckonings with truth and memory of atrocity in Peru during the 2000s, and conversation during the late phase of his illness; (b) his updated 2011 CV, kindly provided by Degregori and the Instituto de Estudios Peruanos; (c) his written reflection, as presented in chapter 2; and (d) retrospective reflections and comments in Peruvian media and websites by those who knew him, esp. Carlos Tapia, "Carlos Iván Degregori," *La Primera*, 25 April 2011; Salomón Lerner Febres, "Degregori: La tradición de la palabra crítica," *La República*, 13 February 2011, www.larepublica.pe; Gustavo Gorriti, "El tiempo, la muerte, la lucidez," orig. *Caretas*, reposted 20 May 2011 at IDL-Reporteros, http://idl-reporteros.pe; Esteban Valle-Riestra, "Adiós al maestro Carlos Iván Degregori," *Redacción mulera*, 18 May 2011, http://redaccion .lamula.pe; Sinesio López Jiménez, "Carlos Iván Degregori," *La República*, 18 May 2011, reposted 20 May at "Sociología 7's Blog colaborativo de Sociología . . . ," http:// sociologia7.wordpress.com (all last accessed 18–20 May 2011). For additional insightful essays that appeared after this introduction was drafted, see also the special issue of the Instituto de Estudios Peruanos's online journal *Revista Argumentos* 5.3 (July 2011), http://www.revistargumentos.org.pe/.

14. For illuminating discussion of intellectual life and the imperative of social critique in a Latin American context, for the case of anthropology, see Carlos Iván Degregori and Pablo Sandoval, eds., *Saberes periféricos: Ensayos sobre la antropología en América Latina* (Lima: IEP, 2007).

15. For political parties, Shining Path as poor kin, and zones of political ambiguity in rural and urban places of strong Left influence, see Stern, "Introduction to Part I," Iván Hinojosa, "On Poor Relations and the Nouveau Riche: Shining Path and the Radical Peruvian Left," Florencia E. Mallon, "Chronicle of a Death Foretold? Velasco's Revolution, Vanguardia Revolucionaria, and 'Shining Omens' in the Indigenous Communities of Andahuaylas," Stern, "Introduction to Part III," Burt, "Shining Path and the 'Decisive Battle' in Lima's Barriadas," and José Luis Rénique, "Apogee and Crisis of a 'Third Path': Mariateguismo, 'People's War,' and Counterinsurgency in Puno, 1987–1994," all in Stern, *Shining and Other Paths*, 13–21, 60–117, 261–338; Burt, *Political Violence and the Authoritarian State*. The forthcoming PhD dissertation of Tamara Feinstein (University of Wisconsin–Madison) on the legal Left during the era of Sendero will add much to our understanding of this issue.

16. I collaborated with the SSRC project and therefore had opportunities to observe its impact on Degregori's intellectual evolution and mentoring experiences. The training program, directed by Jelin and Degregori, supported research by some 60 fellows from Argentina, Brazil, Chile, Paraguay, Peru, the United States, and Uruguay. Much of their research was published in a twelve-book series titled *Memorias de la represión* (Madrid and Buenos Aires: Siglo Veintiuno, 2002–6), and in Degregori, *Jamás tan cerca arremetió lo lejos*.

17. See note 1 for the nine-volume CVR report and one-volume summary.

18. Chapters 1, 2, 4, 5, and the epilogue are first-time publications in English. Chapters 3 and 7 are updated and newly translated.

19. The 54 percent of deaths and disappearances attributed to Sendero Luminoso refers to cases (n = 23,969) directly reported to the Commission. In its statistical methodology appendix that explains rigorously the process of database cross-comparison and estimated totals with 95 percent confidence levels, the statistical weighting effect reduces to 46 percent the share attributed to Sendero Luminoso. This is far more than the 30 percent weighted attribution to state agents, and the 24 percent to other circumstances (e.g., peasant civil patrols, non-Senderista guerrillas, para-military groups, unidentified perpetrators), and very far out of line with the share of state responsibility in Southern Cone dictatorships such as Chile, just south of Peru; or civil war experiences such as Guatemala, a country that also had a large indigenous population. In those two cases, the truth commissions attributed, respectively, over 95 percent and 90 percent responsibility to the state for deaths and disappearances. For Peru, see CVR, *Informe final*, 1:187; 9: Anexo Estadístico: Anexo 2: esp. 1, 17, 21: cf. Anexo 4: Cuadro 1. For Chile and Guatemala, see, respectively, Steve J. Stern, *Reckoning with Pinochet: The Memory Question in Democratic Chile, 1989–2006* (Durham, NC: Duke University Press, 2010), 84–89 (cf. 290–97 on state torture); Elizabeth Oglesby, "Educating Citizens in Postwar Guatemala: Historical Memory, Genocide, and the Culture of Peace," *Radical History Review* 97 (Winter 2007): 77–98.

Shining Path's unique scale of responsibility complicated enormously the work of human rights defenders, whose classic doctrine had focused on the state as perpetrator. For insightful accounts, see Carlos Basombrío Iglesias, "Sendero Luminoso and Human Rights: A Perverse Logic that Captured the Country," Hortensia Muñoz, "Human Rights and Social Referents: The Construction of New Sensibilities," both in Stern, *Shining and Other Paths*, 425–69; Coletta Youngers, *Violencia política y sociedad civil en el Perú: Historia de la Coordinadora Nacional de Derechos Humanos* (Lima: IEP, 2003).

20. Degregori's positive and negative objectives, while clear in the essays that appear in this edition, are presented more explicitly (albeit not at the outset) in the full Spanish edition: *Qué difícil es ser Dios*, 72–73, 109–14. They emerged over time, by engaging a series of related topics, rather than as a full-blown research agenda set early in the war. From a more urban perspective, focused on the social profile of the imprisoned, see the work of another early pioneer of de-Indianization of Sendero, Dennis Chávez de Paz, *Juventud y terrorismo: Características sociales de los condenados por terrorismo y otros delitos* (Lima: IEP, 1989). For additional insight based on the culture of political imprisonment, see José Luis Rénique, *La voluntad encarcelada: Las "luminosas trincheras de combate" de Sendero Luminoso del Perú* (Lima: IEP, 2003).

21. Two essays in *Qué difícil es ser Dios*, 109–58, do not appear in this English-language edition. They were early works in progress—thoughtful essays to build key ideas and analysis, and to spark responses. "Sendero Luminoso: Los hondos y mortales desencuentros" is a two-part essay, originally published in 1985. The key ideas of "Los hondos" were refined and incorporated in the other essays that appear in this book. The other essay, "Los Robin Hood ya pasaron a la historia: Abimael Gúzman y la

izquierda latinoamericana," originally published in 1992, sketched some basic differences between Shining Path and the rest of the Left. Degregori was not able fully to develop and refine that essay, whose topic is complementary rather than central to the purpose of this book.

22. The concept of "resistant adaptation" refers to the ways that real and apparent accommodations to authorities (in this case insurgent authorities) incorporate a sense of "right"—of resistant assertion and self-protection—that render such accommodations partial and contingent. "Resistant adaptation" by peasants or comuneros implies that they retain a set of political values and engage in ongoing political evaluations that provide a basis for defiance or rebellion, if the sense of "right" incorporated into an adaptive accommodation is violated. For fuller discussion, in dialogue with trends in Andean history and anthropology, see Steve J. Stern, "New Approaches to the Study of Peasant Rebellion and Consciousness," in Stern, ed., *Resistance, Rebellion, and Consciousness in the Andean Peasant World, 18th to 20th Centuries* (Madison: University of Wisconsin Press, 1987), 3–25, esp. 10.

23. See, e.g., Carlos Iván Degregori, Cecilia Blondet, and Nicolás Lynch, *Conquistadores de un nuevo mundo: De invasores a ciudadanos en San Martín de Porres* (Lima: IEP, 1986); Carlos Iván Degregori, *La década de la antipolítica: Auge y huida de Alberto Fujimori y Vladimiro Montesinos* (Lima: IEP, 2000).

24. Portocarrero, *Razones de sangre*, 107–14 (quote on 109); and for rejoinder, see Degregori, *Qué difícil es ser Dios*, 78–79, 83.

25. Manrique, "La década de la violencia," 137–82, esp. 196; cf. Degregori, *Qué difícil es ser Dios*, 83–84.

26. My comments on Degregori's open and collaborative intellect and capacity for self-critique draw on personal knowledge, but see also the commentaries cited in n. 13, and his self-critiques in chapter 2, and in the Spanish edition, *Qué difícil es ser Dios*, 15–16, 57, 67–68, 70–71, 80–81.

27. Quoted in Ponciano del Pino Huamán, "Family, Culture, and 'Revolution': Everyday Life with Sendero Luminoso," in Stern, *Shining and Other Paths*, 163. Chuto is an insult applied to indigenous peoples of the high punas (in contrast to people of mountain valleys of somewhat lower altitude), and signifies both brutishness and ignorance. The implication is that such people are savages—monolingual Quechua speakers who are uneducated and rather isolated from cities or markets, compared to indigenous and mestizo peoples who live in the valleys.

28. For statistics, see CVR, *Informe final*, 1:169 (Gráfico 13, national and regional); 9: Anexo Estadístico: Anexo 3: 85 (Cuadro 3, national), 216 (Cuadro 3, regional); cf. 8:149–54. The comparative counts are based on the population five years of age or older in the 1993 census.

Chapter 1. The Years We Lived in Danger

1. Juan Velasco Alvarado was president of Peru from 1968 to 1975.

2. This desire corresponds with the Leninist definition of a "party of cadres," although we cannot know to what extent Guzmán felt obliged to make a virtue out of

necessity. In any case, in 1988, in the only interview given before his capture, he asked: "How many Bolsheviks were there when the Russian revolution triumphed? Seventy thousand in a country of more than a million people!" (Guzmán 1988).

3. The Huallaga Valley was (and is) the major producer of coca leaf in the country. The numbers do not include members of the Popular Guerrilla Army (EGP), which reached a membership of five thousand, many of whom were not fully integrated into Sendero.

4. On the first years of war, see Degregori (1985a, 1985b); Gorriti Ellenbogen (1990). See also CVR (2003, vol. 2, chap. 1).

5. The justification was offered by Guzmán in what was referred to as the "Interview of the Century," given in 1988 to *El Diario*, his official newspaper, and later confirmed in conversations with members of the Truth and Reconciliation Commission (CVR 2003, vol. 2, chap. 1). In both cases, he said it was a decision of the Central Directorate of the Shining Path. On the Lucanamarca massacre, see an extensive report in CVR (2003, vol. 5, chap. 2.2).

6. The term Guzmán used was *mesnadas*, an archaic term referring to troops recruited by feudal lords.

7. One of the most revealing aspects of this declaration is that when Guzmán refers to "them," the ones they had to "restrain" and attack, he is not referring to the peasants of Lucanamarca, or not entirely, but to the armed forces. Both sides fought during these years through *interposita persona*. Twenty years later the CVR found no signs of remorse among the top Shining Path leaders. To them, "these are things we say are errors, excesses committed. But they are not a party line problem."

8. See Guzmán (1988). From 1986 to 1988, *El Diario* was published legally as Sendero's official organ. Shortly after this interview, it was declared illegal but continued to be published clandestinely, in an increasingly irregular manner, until 1993. Its director during the legal years, Luis Arce Borja, exiled in Brussels, also published *El Diario Internacional* until 1994. In mid-1996, a new clandestine version of *El Diario* went into circulation but never with any regularity.

9. Despite the obvious asymmetry between the CAD and the armed forces, and the degree of coercion often exercised by the military and the "*ronderos*" to force the peasants to organize into a CAD, there is a significant difference between them and the Patrullas de Autodefensa Civil (Civil Self-Defense Patrols, PAC) of Guatemala.

10. There were some at the Huallaga military base, as part of their "war against drugs," but the logic of that mandate was different. According to Carlos Tapia (1997), Guzmán was conscious of his strategic weakness. His escalation in Lima was calculated to provoke bloody repression by the State and American intervention—which was completely improbable in the international scenario at the time—as the only way out of his trap.

11. Assuming that the two previous instances were conducted by Hitler and Pol Pot.

12. During the critical Plenary of its Central Committee that took place during its escalation in Lima in July 1992, Shining Path decided to profoundly modify certain

aspects of its strategy. For example, it started abiding by the Geneva Conventions in acts of war, sparing the civilian population as much as possible. Perhaps the repudiation provoked by bloody terrorist attacks, such as in Tarata and Villa El Salvador (Lima), among many others, influenced this decision. But it appeared there were more pragmatic motives as a part of major changes of direction, including the preparation for a purported American intervention that would change the character of the war, which would become a "war of national liberation." Sendero called for the construction of a National Liberation Front (FLN) and decided to change the name of its so-called Popular Guerrilla Army (EGP), which became the National Liberation Army (ELN).

13. On the state's anti-subversive strategy, see CVR (2003, vol. 2, chaps. 3 and 4). See also Degregori and Rivera (1993); Obando (1991); Mauceri (1989); Tapia (1997).

14. The two members who fell were both women: Laura Zambrano (Meche) and Elena Iparraguirre (Miriam). The latter was Guzmán's romantic partner and, in the tradition of Qian Qing, second in the Shining Path line of command. The third member of the bureau, Alberto Ramírez Durand (Feliciano), who was responsible for the party's military work, was not captured because he was in a remote rural location.

15. The antiterrorist legislation of 1992 granted broad powers to the military tribunals, which operated through faceless judges without minimum due process. The legislation was challenged by the Inter-American Court of Human Rights in Costa Rica, after which the government effected a "partial withdrawal" from the American Convention on Human Rights, in order to evade the court's decisions. After the fall of the Fujimori government and the restoration of the Constitutional Tribunal, the antiterrorist legislation was modified, and beginning in 2004, hundreds of convictions were retried and sentenced, among them the principal leaders of Shining Path and MRTA (Túpac Amaru Revolutionary Movement).

16. Since the mid-1980s, Shining Path formed part of the Internationalist Revolutionary Movement (MRI). This movement was made up of a little over a dozen microparties nostalgic for Maoism, among them the Revolutionary Communist Party of the USA, and groups in Iran, Italy, New Zealand, India, Bangladesh, Colombia, Sri Lanka, Nepal, Turkey, Great Britain, Haiti, and the Dominican Republic. The MRI found almost the only reason for its existence—the other one was the Kurdish Communist Party (before Occalam's capture) and currently the Nepalese party—in its support of Shining Path, which treated them with an undisguised and sometimes offensive attitude of superiority. See the MRI magazine, *A World to Win*.

17. See *El Diario Internacional* (1993).

18. Guzmán adopted this title in keeping with the Maoist model and as part of his personality cult, but he was also president of the Organizing Committee for the "Republic of New Democracy," which Shining Path intended to build in what it considered "liberated zones." Conceiving itself from early on as a counterstate or "new state" was one of the strong points in Sendero's strategy, allowing it to exploit, from a perspective I would call Hobbesian, the population's need for order, for example in the drug-trafficking zones of Amazonia.

19. With his popularity at a peak for having tamed the hyperinflation inherited from the previous government, and only two months after Guzmán's capture, Fujimori had achieved a comfortable majority in the elections for a Constitutional Congress in November 1992. The new Parliament dedicated itself to drafting a new constitution to fit the authoritarianism and neoliberal reforms of the regime. All this correspondence took place a few weeks before a referendum scheduled for 31 October, in which the population would decide on the new Magna Carta.

20. *Gonzalo, the Myth* was the title of a book written by an admirer. See Roldán (1990).

21. On Guzmán in the 1970s, see Degregori (1990, chap. 15). On Guzmán's transformation from bureaucrat to prophet toward the end of that decade, see chapter 3 of this volume.

22. See chapters 3, 4, and 7 of this volume; cf. Degregori (2010, 132–44).

23. In fact, jails became a sort of prefiguration of the future Shining Path society. During the 1980s, Sendero was able to create a Foucauldian reality, a "panopticon" situation. The state was left only with the power to lock up (and not for very long, since corruption and fear among judges and jailers had turned jails into veritable sieves), while the party was in charge of "watching and punishing" its militants, of organizing and regimenting their lives twenty-four hours a day, indoctrinating them, "pounding and riveting" ideas through lectures, study groups, talks, hymns, plays, and all types of nonstop activity.

24. The interview was conducted in 1986 by Rita Márquez, who generously provided it to me.

25. Only with this self-deception is it possible for the decapitated to continue fighting and, moreover, to attempt to recruit new followers. In reality, both factions would have great difficulty in recruiting; few would join Sendero to develop a "political war," and fewer to fight in a cornered army abandoned by its field marshal.

26. The phrase "hammer their hard heads . . ." is from a speech by Guzmán (1990b). Similar images show up repeatedly in his writings, referring to the need to "educate the masses" or the party militants on the "correct line." See, for example, chapter 7 of this volume.

Chapter 2. How Social Sciences Failed?

1. For information on the United Left and its behavior during the internal armed conflict, see CVR (2003, vol. 3, chapter 2.4, 118–43).

2. All the statistics provided for the 1960s are from the chronology of Guzmán and Vargas (1981). In these years, the most important land takeovers occurred in Cerro de Pasco, the central Andes, and during movements in La Convención, Cusco. During the first of these, between December 1959 and July 1962, twenty-five peasants lost their lives. In La Convención, during the high point of the mobilization, between 20 October 1962 and 2 January 1963, fifteen people died: seven peasants, five people listed as guerrillas, and three policemen. On peasant movements in this period, see Blanco

(1964); Neyra (1968); Quijano (1965). For an important literary quintet inspired by the Cerro de Pasco movements, see Churampi (2004).

3. An analysis of these movements, which lasted less than a year and which have also received little attention, is beyond the scope of this book. For information on the 1965 guerrillas, see Béjar (1973); Mercado (1982).

4. The numbers were almost absurdly low. Two peasants died during the movement in Andahuaylas—the most important in that decade (García Sayán 1982, 83; Quintanilla 1981, 88–89; Sánchez 1981, 197, 207). Four more died in Huacataz, Cajamarca, in 1977 (García Sayán 1982, 61); a cooperative member was accidentally killed in Lucrepata, Cusco in 1978 (ibid., 154); and another peasant died in Piura in February 1979 (ibid., 48).

5. The largest massacre took place in 1971 during a miners' strike at the Cobriza mine in Huancavelica that belonged to the U.S. company Cerro Corporation, which was nationalized in 1974.

6. One source on the democratic transition (1977–80) is Lynch (1992a, 1992b).

7. The candidate was the respected leader of the Peruvian Teachers' Union SUTEP, Horacio Zevallos. He was running as the candidate of the UNIR (Union of the Revolutionary Left), whose strongest member was the Patria Roja (Communist Party of Peru–Red Fatherland), a Maoist-inspired group. Patria Roja was the last Leftist political party to enter into legal political activity during the transition and it did so with the most reservations. It refused to participate in the elections for the Constituent Assembly in 1978, and it participated in the 1980 presidential elections on the basis of strictly Leninist conceptions: as a way of raising the consciousness of the "masses" and unmasking the bourgeois state.

8. Although these mobilizations reached their apogee between 1976 and 1978, they continued until 1980. In February of that year, the worker takeover of a textile factory in Lima, Cromotex, ended with the death of five workers, a bloody epilogue that was a harbinger of the future.

9. Sendero was especially referring to PCP-UNIDAD (Peruvian Communist Party–Unity), an influential member of the General Confederation of Peruvian Workers (CGTP), which convened the strikes. The PCP-UNIDAD was aligned—though ever less so—with the Soviet Union, which the Shining Path considered "socio-imperialist."

10. On the military regime (1968–80), see, for example Kruijt (1991a, 1991b); Lowenthal (1975); McClintock and Lowenthal (1989); Pease (1979).

11. Later, the idea that the state and society are constructed reciprocally was expanded upon. For Latin American history, see texts compiled by Joseph and Nugent (1994), and for historical anthropology, see works by Muratorio (1994) and Mallon (1995).

12. And later, emphasis was found in an abundant literature on the "new" social movements inspired in a long theoretical genealogy that had its most suggestive reflections in the volumes by Álvarez et al. (1988) and Escobar and Álvarez (1992). For Peru, see Blondet (1991); Degregori et al. (1986); Golte and Adams (1985); Huber (1995); Starn (1991b, 1999).

13. Gramsci became known in Latin America primarily through the works of José Aricó (1978, 1988) together with those of Juan Carlos Portantiero (1977). In Peru, the works of Sinesio López (1977, 1987) stand out, as does a publication for university students by Francis Guibal (1981).

14. For more on the "Copernican revolution," see Ames (1985). In addition, see a set of articles that appeared between 1985 and 1987 in the journal I edited, *El Zorro de Abajo*.

15. At the beginning of the 1980s, many social scientists, both in Lima and in other cities, sympathized with or were members of the United Left Party. Many worked with its Platform Commission (Comisión de Plan de Gobierno).

16. After the armed forces took charge of countersubversive activities, the number of victims grew exponentially. The years 1983 and 1984 were the bloodiest of the conflict—approximately one-third of the total number of victims died during these two years. See CVR (2003, vol. 1, chap. 3, 133).

17. Anthropology was a discipline that from the beginning was influenced by U.S., French, and Mexican anthropologies both theoretically and through physical presence. Peruvians went for graduate studies first to France and Mexico and, in recent decades, to the United States. Since 1959, there has been a School of Anthropology at the University in Ayacucho from which several of the principal Sendero leaders graduated.

18. A quite exhaustive guide to the development of anthropology in Peru can be found in an anthology edited by Degregori (2000b).

19. For *indigenismo* as an urban vision of the Andes, see Kristal (1991). For *indigenismo* as a ventriloquistic representation, see Guerrero (1993).

20. The most important effort was Rodolfo Stavenhagen (1976).

21. *Campesinista* comes from *campesino*, which means peasant.

22. See especially Ortiz Rescanieri (1972); Ossio (1973, 1992); Zuidema (1989). For a critical review of this type of approach, see Roel (2000).

23. The best known was the anthropologist Osmán Morote, a member of the National Directorate of Shining Path. While in other universities, monographs about indigenous communities or studies of "Andean verticality" or rural development predominated, the School of Anthropology of the Universidad Nacional de San Cristóbal de Huamanga (UNSCH), as well as the diploma on the Agrarian Reform offered by the same university, systematically produced studies about large estates (*latifundios*) and their contradictions during the 1960s.

24. All the statistics provided in this and the following two paragraphs are from CVR (2003, vol. 1, chap. 3, 120–23).

25. If we add the victims from the departments of Junín, Huánuco, Huancavelica, Apurímac, and San Martín (see map 1), the number goes up to 85 percent of the total victims. It should be noted that only 9 percent of all Peruvian household income is produced in these six departments. In addition, Huancavelica, Ayacucho, Apurímac, and Huánuco are the four poorest departments in Peru.

26. This projection had a 95 percent confidence interval so that the real number could vary between 61,000 and 77,000 victims.

27. According to the 1940 national census, 65 percent of the population lived in rural areas and 35 percent in urban areas. By 1981, the numbers had been inverted—only 35 percent of Peruvians lived in rural areas while the urban population had reached 65 percent (INEI 1998). Many of those who continued to work on rural areas concentrated on "Andean rationality" (Golte 1980; Golte and de la Cadena 1986), Andean thought throughout the centuries, or the advance of the mercantile economy and production on small plots in rural areas (Montoya 1980, 1989).

28. Until 1990, these zones covered 32 percent of Peruvian territory and included 49 percent of its population (Senado de la República del Perú 1992). The statistic for the percentage of population is technically exaggerated because while Lima was under a state of emergency, it was not under the control of a political military command, which involved more radical limitations on democracy. Lima was a kind of "gray area" where popular sector neighborhoods and, more important for my argument, some national universities found themselves in conditions similar to those in the regions most affected by the violence (i.e., under military rule).

29. For information on developments in anthropology at national universities, see Degregori and Sandoval (2009).

30. The gap and tensions between intellectuals from Lima and those from the provinces always existed but the processes of urbanization, violence, and later neoliberal reforms have increased the distance between the two groups to the point where they are insurmountable without a joint and sustained effort to rebuild bridges. See Degregori and Sandoval (2009).

31. A third such work was *Historia del Tawantinsuyu* by María Rostworowski (1988).

32. One of the most influential books of the decade belongs to this approach: *Buscando un Inca* (*In Search of an Inca*) by Alberto Flores Galindo (1988). This book develops the concept of an "Andean utopia" and views Sendero as a "nightmarish" vision of this utopia. Portocarrero (1991), more influenced by psychoanalysis, stresses the importance of "colonial ghosts" in contemporary Peru. In addition, a book by psychoanalyst César Rodríguez Rabanal (1991) is titled, precisely, *Cicatrices de la pobreza* (Scars of Poverty).

33. Although in 1940, Lima was home to less than 20 percent of the total population of the country, by 1981, the number had grown to more than 30 percent. At the same time, 80 percent of the industrial and manufacturing production and the best national and private universities were also in Lima.

34. Or who were children of people from the provinces who were born in Lima.

35. Sendero believed that it possessed the *science* of Marxism-Leninism, "which is all-powerful because it is accurate."

36. *Cholificación* comes from "cholo." Although originally a derogatory colonial reference to people of indigenous origin, it has increasingly been embraced as a positive descriptor of the mixed heritage of all Peruvians.

37. CVR (2003, vol. 1, chap. 2, 81). The text continues: "The gaps between the modernity and progress expressed in political discourse and in expectations, but only

initiated in a fragmentary manner [on the one hand], and backwardness and poverty [on the other], undermined the understandings that had made these conditions bearable and habitual for a very long time."

38. One of the few exceptions was an article by Bonilla (1989) that was specifically about communities in Ayacucho.

39. The *Final Report* of the CVR clearly establishes that the Peruvian conflict was not an ethnic one. Nevertheless, ethnic and racial discrimination was evident in a variety of strategies, actions, and discourses.

40. The concept "racial formation" is from Omi and Winant, cited in de la Cadena (2004, 12).

41. MRTA tried to be a "media" guerrilla group, holding press conferences and inviting journalists to witness some their most dramatic actions.

42. In addition, the task of denouncing human rights crimes and violations committed by state agents and Shining Path fell to human rights groups that quite early in the conflict were able to form the National Coordinating Committee for Human Rights (Coordinadora Nacional de Derechos Humanos, CNDDHH), which gave more national, and especially international, credibility to their denunciations. In contrast to other countries in the region, the CNDDHH early on condemned Sendero's crimes as well as human rights violations by state agents and set itself apart from the Shining Path's legal support group, the Democratic Lawyers (Abogados Democráticos). See CVR (2003); Youngers (2003).

43. See CVR (2003, vol. 1, chap. 3).

44. The principal limitation of DESCO's database became evident during the CVR's work. DESCO created its database primarily from information published in newspapers and magazines or announced on radio or television. Events that did not make the news were not included. Nevertheless, there was a substantial difference between the 25,000 victims who it was thought had perished in the conflict on the basis of DESCO's information and the 69,000 victims projected by the CVR. Still, in those years and with the resources DESCO had available, it was not possible to do more. The database served as an excellent starting point to prepare a chronology and plan other CVR tasks.

45. We never came close to the number of researchers or the quantity of publications produced by the Colombian "violentólogos," for example.

46. Comments on texts published before 1990 are based extensively on Degregori (1992).

47. The principal criticism was directed against Billie Jean Isbell's *To Defend Ourselves* (1978), a classic of Andean anthropology based on extensive fieldwork carried out in the 1970s in the community of Chuschi in Ayacucho, the exact place where the Shining Path initiated its armed actions in 1980.

48. In several cases, early publication was not synonymous with an accurate interpretation or analysis. One critique of the work of North American "senderologists" can be found in Poole and Rénique (1991).

49. See the articles by Raúl Gonzáles in *Quehacer* (1982, 1983, 1984a, 1984b) or those by Gorriti Ellenbogen in *Caretas* (1981, 1983a, 1983b); these are only a few of the articles by these authors who continued to work on the issue in later years as well.

50. This section is based extensively on the *Final Report* of the CVR (2003, vol. 5, chap. 4) and the excellent work of Ponciano del Pino Huamán (2003).

51. None of the commissioners spoke Quechua and they only made one visit to Uchuraccay, on 11 February 1983, obtaining testimonies of community members in an assembly in which only males spoke. The transcription of this assembly was never published.

52. For an explanation of the causes of the community silence, see CVR (2003, vol. 5, chap. 4).

53. In May 1983, when a search patrol was sent out by order of a judge, a suitcase was found hidden in a small cave that contained rolls of film and personal documents of three of the assassinated journalists. A camera belonging to journalist Willy Retto was also found that contained a roll of film with nine photos that captured the moments just before the killings (Notice of Seizure, folio 1544 of the Uchuraccay case file).

54. The Sinchis were special counterinsurgency units of the Civil Guard (Guardía Civil, GC), now called the National Police of Peru.

55. The name "Iquichano" and the town of Iquicha were created in the third decade of the nineteenth century, according to recent historical studies (Méndez 2002).

56. *Varayoc* is a Quechua word for a type of traditional indigenous community leader.

57. An excellent and balanced critique of the IVL can be found in Mayer (1991).

58. For a description of the trial see CVR (2003, vol. 5, chap. 4).

59. See the opinions of anthropologists Juan Ossio and Rodrigo Montoya, who analyzed the magical-religious elements of the massacres to support contrasting interpretations of the event: "Uchuraccay: ¿crimen sin castigo?" *La República* (Lima), 19 March 1983.

60. This does not mean that peasants did not frequently consider Senderistas or the military to be demons or *pishtacos*. See the articles compiled in Ansión (1989b).

61. In February 1982, after a successful Shining Path attack on the jail in Ayacucho that freed dozens of its members, the police assassinated three wounded Shining Path members in the hospital in Ayacucho. Indignation against state agents was generalized. A few months later, the funeral of a young Shining Path member, Edith Lagos, was attended by tens of thousands of people from Ayacucho who marched through the streets of the city. See CVR (2003, vol. 1, chap. 1); Uceda (2004, 39).

62. See many of the works collected in Cristóbal (2003) and Montoya (2004).

63. The CVR used del Pino Huamán (2003) as a starting point. This article was the product of a decade of work with Uchuraccay. The CVR carried out open interviews and, in addition, collected twenty-two testimonies and sponsored two assemblies during which *comuneros* reconstructed the history of those years and prepared a "list of people from Uchuraccay who were assassinated" that included 135 names.

64. Between 1983 and 1984, 135 members of the Uchuraccay community were assassinated, some by armed forces patrols or *rondas* (peasant patrols) from neighboring communities but the majority at the hands of Shining Path. At the end of 1984, the few survivors fled from the village, which remained abandoned until 1993. In that year, those who had left decided to return (CVR 2003; del Pino Huamán 2003).

65. Flores Galindo (1988, 81) defines the Andean utopia as "the millenarian or messianic dream of a cataclysmic inversion of the actual social order in order to inaugurate a new age, a new idyllic world that in the Andes was identified with the return of the Inca, the restoration of Tawantinsuyu or, in more recent times, with a world in which the *mistis* disappear."

66. Chuschi is the place where Shining Path started its armed actions on 17 May 1980.

67. "Wamanis" are supernatural beings.

68. I use the adjective "agonizing" in the same sense as Flores Galindo (1980) applies it to the trajectory of José Carlos Mariátegui. For works that continue to use the millenarian approach, see, for example, Ossio (1990, 15–64). An extreme and dishonest case can be found in Strong (1992).

69. On displaced persons, who came to number more than half a million, see CVR (2003, vol. 8, part 3, chap. 2).

70. *Misti* is a Quechua term that refers to mestizos, especially those linked to traditional local powers.

71. The Granados article was a summary of a pioneering thesis, which he defended at the university in Ayacucho in 1981: "La conducta política: Un caso particular" (Political behavior: A particular case). The title itself is totally hermetic and, by not mentioning the specific issue studied (Sendero's ideology), illustrated how difficult it was to speak about this subject in Ayacucho, even before the armed forces appeared on the scene and the Political Military Command was established in the region.

72. During the *yarqa aspiy* (cleaning irrigation ditches) festival, a dance revives the history of a priest and a captain who, in a drunken state, fired against a multitude during a fair. Both were tied up and forced to walk 120 kilometers to the capital of the department where they were handed over to the prefect.

73. This line of analysis is continued in the piece "Youths, Peasants, and Violence: Ayacucho, 1980–1983." See chapter 5 in this book.

74. For information about the SAIS, see Montoya et al. (1974).

75. Two of the authors had studied communications; one was a sociologist and the other was a journalist.

76. For information on the PAC in Guatemala, see Carmack (1988), Kruijt (1999), Remijnse (2002), Stoll (1993), as well as the Comisión para el Esclarecimiento Histórico (1999). For the Colombian self-defense groups, see Romero (2004).

77. Especially through the work of Elizabeth Jelin (2002 and 2003). Later, the issue of memory and violence was featured in a collection of articles edited by Belay et al. (2004).

78. Sandoval (2002) wrote on the same topic in his honor's degree thesis in anthropology at San Marcos University.

79. Once again, the exception in the 1980s were the investigative articles of Raúl González (1987, 1988b, 1991, and others) and one by José Gonzáles (1989, 207–22). In the 1990s, most of the research was on the economic and legal aspects of the issues, as well as U.S. policy in its "war on drugs."

80. Except for articles such as Burt (1999) and Smith (1992).

81. Some exceptions are worth mentioning, such as the article by Portocarrero (1998, 105–46) on some of the academic discourses about Shining Path and the Andean world or the book by Peralta (2000), which was among the few dealing with the press during the years of violence.

82. The CVR worked from July 2001 to August 2003. During this period, it collected nearly 17,000 testimonies throughout the country; it carried out about 2,000 open-ended interviews, hundreds of these in jails; it held more than a dozen public hearings and was the first truth commission in Latin America to hold these types of events; it interviewed the principal political and military leaders of the era as well as the main Sendero and MRTA leaders who were imprisoned; it found more than 2,000 secret burial sites and was able to exhume three of them. For the purpose of this book and future research, it is important to point out that the CVR also prepared six Regional Histories (CVR 2003, vol. 4); twenty-three brief ethnographies, which it called "representative histories of the violence" (CVR 2003, vol. 5); and seventy-three judicial cases (CVR 2003, vol. 6). The results of the CVR's work were presented to the President of Peru on 28 August 2003 in a *Final Report*, which included nine volumes in addition to appendixes. In addition to the printed version, the *Final Report* is available on the Internet: www.cverdad.org.pe. In February 2004, a compendium titled *Hatun Willakuy* was widely disseminated.

83. The ethical position of the CVR was very clear from the first sentence of the speech the CVR's president delivered before the President of Peru when he presented the *Final Report*: "The history of Peru has included more than one period that was difficult, painful, and of authentic national prostration but certainly none of these so emphatically deserves the stamp of shame and dishonor as the fragment of history that we are obliged to recount in these pages. The two final decades of the twentieth century are—it must plainly be said—a mark of horror and dishonor for the Peruvian state and society" (CVR 2003, vol. 1, chap. 31, preface).

84. Only one of the studies mentioned was written by a Peruvian: Hinojosa (1992).

85. The United Front of Students (El Frente Único de Estudiantes, FUE), the SUTE teachers' union (Sindicato Único de Trabajadores de la Educación) of the UNSCH (SUTEUNSCH), the Federation of Peasants of the Apurímac River Valley (Federación de Campesinos del Valle del Río Apurímac, FECVRA), the Departmental Federation of Workers of Ayacucho (Federación Departamental de Trabajadores de Ayacucho, FEDETA).

86. On rereading these texts, I discovered that they contained many of the principal ideas that I later developed in more detail in my academic publications between 1985 and 1990.

Chapter 3. The Maturation of a Cosmocrat and the Construction of a Community of Discourse

1. Guzmán cites Lenin, who promoted a boycott of the Duma, keeping in mind "the rise of the popular struggle that led to insurrection." He states, "In our country the path is not insurrection in the city but rather armed struggle, surrounding the cities by the countryside through a prolonged popular war. For us uprising is, in essence, the uprising of the peasant movement and this is what will become armed struggle, the history of the country, and the decade of the 1960s proves this beyond a doubt" (Arce Borja 1989, 110).

This interpretation is particularly interesting because it is made at a moment when the urban popular movement was overwhelmingly more significant. Guzmán, nonetheless, prefers to look back to the decade of the 1960s, the height of the peasant movements, so that reality might "coincide" with his project and diverge from positions of other parties of the Left, which began to assign more importance to the cities and to an eventual urban insurrection.

2. See for example "Contra las ilusiones constitucionales y por el Estado de Nueva Democracia" (PCP-SL 1989b [1978]), peppered with charts on the distribution of land and the evolution of the GDP; and "Desarrollemos la creciente protesta popular" (PCP-SL 1989d [1979]), in which he attempts to explain the weakness of the Peruvian state based on citations from Mao and the existence of a revolutionary situation recurring to Mao and Lenin. These reflections are mediocre in their statistical interpretation, confused in their political analysis.

3. For a detailed description of the inner struggles during which these texts/speeches were produced, see Gorriti Ellenbogen (1990, chap. 3).

4. The text was delivered as a speech on 7 June 1979, during the Ninth Expanded Session of the PCP Central Committee, on the occasion of the pledge of allegiance to the party's flag. The flag, of course, is red; the day coincided with the Peruvian armed forces' annual pledge of fidelity to the Peruvian flag (Guzmán 1989b, 141–45).

5. Regarding this acceptance of destiny, according to Gorriti Ellenbogen (1990, chap. 3), in a meeting held a few months later, Guzmán gave one of those present a copy of one of his favorite books, *The Life of Mohammed*, by Washington Irving. If we keep in mind that from the 1980s onward, Senderista militants had to sign a "letter of submission" to President Gonzalo, we might imagine that Guzmán embodied not only matter but also destiny or divine will.

6. If something stands out in Senderista discourse it is the echoes of the god of wrath, the god of vengeance, the inquisitor god, the god of fear, very similar to the God brandished by the crusades of Francisco Franco in Spain and preached by many La Salle brothers when young Abimael sat in their classrooms, before the profound

changes that swept that Order subsequently, thanks to the influence of theologians of the stature of Noé Cevallos.

7. The speech was given in the National Expanded Conference of the PCP, on the occasion of the decision to "build through action" the First Company of the First Division of the People's Army (Arce Borja 1989, 145–50).

8. Speech delivered on 28 March 1980, during the Second Plenary Session of the PCP Central Committee, according to Arce Borja (1989–90).

9. According to Sendero's interpretation, one consequence of this "strategic offensive of the world revolution" is that the next 50 to 100 years are destined to be an age marked by violence "indicating a world war" (PCP-SL 1989a, 2–3).

10. Recall that the cult of Lenin's personality takes off after his death. In the cases of Stalin, Mao, or Kim Il Sung the cult is launched upon the seizure of power.

11. This personalization is evident in the very title of some of the chapters. Thus, one is titled "President Gonzalo and the Democratic Revolution" and begins with these words: "Brandishing, defending and applying Marxism-Leninism-Maoism, principally Maoism, President Gonzalo establishes that the Peruvian revolution in its historic course is destined to be the first democratic revolution" (PCP-SL 1988b). Another chapter, "Military Line: Sendero and the Popular Guerrilla Army," begins as follows: "Brandishing, defending and applying Marxism-Leninism-Maoism, President Gonzalo has established the military line of the Party" (PCP-SL 1988c).

12. In this process "Gonzalo Thought" begins to resemble a "Tibetan" version of Marxism, in which the revolutionary "idea" is incarnated in given individuals or "swords"—Marx, Lenin, Mao, Gonzalo—much the way the spirit of Buddha is reincarnated in each new Dalai Lama. Recall that the idea of Peru as the center of world revolution, and later that of Gonzalo as the "Fourth Sword," begins to germinate shortly after Mao's death and that, if one takes Sendero's viewpoint, there has never been more than one living sword: Stalin assumed the role after Lenin's death and in a struggle against his rivals; Mao does so after Stalin's death.

13. This epilogue was written in 2000. The ideas are further developed in Degregori (2000b).

Chapter 4. Revolution by Handbook

1. This chapter presents results of the first part of a research project on "Radicalism and political violence: A study of the relationship between social sciences, state and society in contemporary Peru," sponsored by FOMCIENCIAS. We developed our study in the universities of San Marco, San Antonio Abad de Cuzco, San Cristóbal de Huamanga, and Nacional de Trujillo, where we carried out interviews and reviewed theses and archives. We also surveyed participants in the Séptimo Congreso del Hombre y la Cultura Andina (Seventh Congress on Man and Andean Culture), held in Trujillo. In this chapter, we present the core ideas that shape the case studies. I wish to convey my thanks to Iván Rivas Plata and Pedro Roel of the Universidad Nacional Mayor de San Marcos, who participated as research assistants.

2. Among the best known are the texts on historical materialism by F. V. Konstantinov or Victor Afanasiev; the *Handbook on Political Economy* by E. V. Spiridonova; and the *Philosophical Dictionary* of M. Rosenthal and P. Yudin. Additional works included texts by the French author Georges Politzer and a more recent and somewhat more sophisticated manual by the Chilean Martha Harnecker.

3. I have addressed several of these themes elsewhere. See Degregori (1985b, 1989b, 1990).

4. The decline is noteworthy in the context of the entire educational sector, which only falls from 25 percent of the budget during the previous decade to 20 percent in the first phase of the military government. This is explained because the regime, embarked on a long-term education reform, placed emphasis on other levels of education, such as primary or vocational education, reducing its investment in a university system that it aimed to resize.

5. Public sector demand for social science professionals began to increase already at the end of the 1940s with the creation of agencies such as the Instituto Indigenista Peruano (Peruvian Indigenist Institute), and it gained significant momentum during the 1960s, when under the military junta of 1962 the National Planning Institute (INP) and Casa de Cultura (Culture House) were created, as well as the first agrarian reform agencies. During the first government of Belaúnde (1963–68), the number of civil servants dedicated to agrarian reform is increased and Cooperación Popular (Community Development) is created, among other organizations.

The military government made use of social scientists, among other reasons, because it had a negative view of political parties and politics in general. To connect directly with the "bases" without intermediaries, the regime sought social engineers: scientific, objective, integrating, and mobilizing. It was thought that social scientists fulfilled those requirements.

6. It is important to recall that at the beginning of the decade, Abimael Guzmán was university director of personnel at the Universidad de Huamanga. Antonio Díaz Martínez, killed in 1986 in the massacre of Lurigancho, was director of student welfare, and Sendero at the time advocated the tactic of "defense of the university."

7. Guillermo Bonfil, lecture delivered at the Instituto de Estudios Peruanos, 28 August 1987, titled "Antropología y Estado" (Anthropology and State).

8. A summary of the many versions of the myth of Inkarrí: the Inca King (Inkarrí) was conquered by the king of Spain; he was decapitated and his head was buried. But the body is reconstructing itself from the head. When this reconstruction is complete, Inkarrí will reemerge to the earth's surface and with him the idealized times of the Incan Empire will return.

9. I cite a lecture delivered by Webb at the Instituto de Estudios Peruanos in April 1987.

10. Of the 103,500 students in non-university higher education, 68,900 (66.6 percent of the total) studied in public institutions and 34,600 (33.4 percent) in private ones. But moreover there existed countless "higher technological institutes," "centers of education and professional training" (CENACAPES), and other similar institutions—the enormous majority private and some of them even informal—that offered career

training in fields ranging from accounting to computer science, even encompassing secretarial training, "etiquette," or tailoring. This is without even going into the many pre-university academies.

11. Economics is included in the social sciences because, in most universities, training in the field was overwhelmingly slanted toward political economy.

12. This thesis was defended in 1970. At the request of its author, we withhold mention of the title and author.

13. An interesting phenomenon is to see how the expansion of "Marxism by handbook" adapted itself regionally. The final product was not the same in the Universidad de San Marcos, which reflected in some ways the profound transformations of the capital, than in Cuzco, with its rich *indigenista* tradition among the middle classes, or in Trujillo, where there was a powerful political and cultural presence of APRA. Not to mention in Ayacucho, where the power vacuum created by the decay or migration of regional elites was notorious.

Chapter 5. Youth, Peasants, and Political Violence

1. I refer to the title of Hernando de Soto's book about the paths he calls informal: *El otro sendero* (*The Other Path*, 1985).

2. The exact opposite occurred: massive migration to the cities in those zones where the violence was being unleashed and the dirty war was beginning.

3. Andean, but not necessarily indigenous. It must be noted that Andean tradition is lengthy and heterogeneous. It includes pre-Hispanic elements, both statist and imperial, as well as those of ethnicity and kinship groups (*ayllus*). It also includes colonial elements, *señoriales*, *mistis*, and landholders, along with peasants, serfs, and community members (*comuneros*). Finally, this tradition includes contemporary elements.

4. *Mita* was a form of mandatory public service, a form of forced or corveé labor.

5. I think here of the Revolutionary Guards, Iranians dying as martyrs on the border with Iraq.

6. The Guardía Civil is a component of the police force.

Chapter 6. Harvesting Storms

This chapter focuses on the northern provinces of the department of Ayacucho. It includes a reworking of materials from Degregori 1991a, which includes testimonies collected in the communities of Cangallo, Huanta, La Mar, Sucre, and Huancasancos, and, in particular, an interview with "Nicario," a youth from "Rumi" (a pseudonym for a community in Cangallo), who was a senderista *miliciano* between 1980 and 1983. In the testimonies real names do not appear, only pseudonyms. I do not mention the specific places where the testimonies were recorded, only the provinces.

1. This weakness was, in part, the consequence of a trajectory that Shining Path developed over the course of the 1970s. The resulting project was fundamentalist in ideology, a social antimovement (Wieviorka 1988) in its political stance, and, in its

practical organization, a "war machine" that did not prioritize political work in social organizations, communities, or federations, except in the party's own "generated organizations." These party organizations were to form the "transmission belt" between the party and the "masses." On the composition of Shining Path up to 1980 and the evolution of the Shining Path project, see Degregori (1996).

2. This occurred in the *punas* of Huanta, as José Coronel explains in his essay in Degregori (1996).

3. The state as a route to mobility was not an alien notion for them, if we take into consideration that the bureaucracy of the small towns traditionally formed part of the old *misti* power structure.

4. Nicario's younger brother, for example, joined the guerrilla column and lived as a "night walker" (*tuta pureq*) between 1983 and 1986 until, ill, he responded to the call of his family and went down to Lima. But even some time afterward, when he no longer had an organizational connection to Shining Path, he did not want to say anything to me about his experience beyond reciting the official party line.

5. For the peasantry, attending school and receiving an education—understood as literacy in Spanish—signified passing from blindness to vision, or from night to day. See Montoya (1980); Degregori (1989b).

6. The complete opposite occurred: massive migration to the cities from those rural zones where violence had been unleashed and a "dirty war" had begun. Regarding the utopian ideals of Shining Path youth, see the complete testimonial of Nicario in Degregori (1991c).

7. Nicario participated in the first party-organized planting in Chuschi (Cangallo Province), a community where Shining Path initiated its armed struggle on 17 May 1980. His account is reminiscent of sowing crops, in early times, in the land designated for the Sun, the Inca, or the landowner. In the eight hectares of communal land were congregated sixty teams of oxen of Chuschi and of neighboring communities; in the four corners of the plot they planted a red flag. "At the beginning, twelve sticks of dynamite were blown up; then at midnight, six sticks of dynamite; then in the afternoon twelve. The work was successful, . . . but the party wasn't able to harvest the crops because the army came in" (Nicario). In Chaca (Huanta province), according to a personal communication from José Coronel, the party did carry out the harvest in 1983, which resulted in the first rupture with peasants.

8. Lima is an extreme case, but not even the medium-sized cities of the sierra depended principally on their immediate rural hinterlands. See Gonzáles de Olarte (1992).

9. In other cases, cadres from outside received negative evaluations, and the local *milicianos* appeared to be more understanding. Alejandro, a young university student, the son of peasants, expressed his opinion about one of these cases, in which the irresponsible manner in which the cadres faced military confrontation was evident. "It appears that they were not good cadres those who led the group in Allpachaka; they argued that we were going to win the war, that we were going to take their helicopters, that not to worry because there would be arms for everyone." And he adds, "I think

that it depends on the zone, in others there were good elements." This comment is important because it illustrates the wide variety of situations that emerged.

10. Regarding those Senderistas who had opposed the position of initiating armed struggle, Guzmán (1990b) stated: "We will uproot the poison herbs, this is pure poison, cancer of the bones will take us over; we cannot permit it, it is putrefaction and sinister pus, we cannot permit it . . . we will burn, and uproot this pus, this poison, to burn it is urgent." Regarding Shining Path discourse and purifying violence in the context prior to the beginning of the armed struggle, see Degregori (1996). On the necessity of intensifying the violence for the advance of the revolution around 1982, see Gorriti Ellenbogen (1990, chap. 5).

11. "They talked to us about how there was so much bureaucracy in Peru and many delinquents, many thieves, rapists—and that the objective of Sendero was to make all of that disappear" (Nicario).

12. PCP-SL, December 1982, quoted in Gorriti Ellenbogen (1990, 283).

13. A sharp contrast is provided by the example of the Guards of the Iranian Revolution, who died as martyrs on the frontier with Iraq. In an interesting work on the Iranian Revolution of 1979, Khosrokhavar (1993) presented a profile of the revolutionaries that showed similarities with the Peruvian case: middle-range provincial intellectuals (in the Iranian case, ayatollahs) and radicalized educated youth who were marginalized by and disillusioned with the Shah's modernization process. But the dynamics and results, as is well known, were very different.

14. A discussion of political violence versus structural violence is beyond the scope of this chapter. It is sufficient to note that the latter type of violence substantiated Mao's famous phrase, which Shining Path adopted: "rebellion is justified." The question is: what type of rebellion?

15. Many times the conflicts were resolved in competitions or even ritualized battles, for example, in carnivals. Underlying this vocation for restitution of unity after the conflict is the concept of *tinkuy*. See Ansión (1985).

16. An analysis of the violence of the state and the armed forces in Ayacucho also exceeds the limits of this chapter. A testimonial regarding the raving, racist violence exercised by members of the armed forces in these same years can be found in Degregori and López Ricci (1990).

17. Nicario, for example, was torn between his younger brother, who pressured him to join the guerrilla column, and his other brothers, who called from "the other path" (the informal economic sector) in Lima. In 1983, he opted for this second option and began a minibusiness. Over the following years there were other, isolated cases of deserters (*arrepentidos*), which became a significant flow with the expansion of the *rondas*.

18. Shining Path promised to do so: "Don't worry, we will protect you," said the youth to the women of Rumi who wept as they saw the army trucks descending the highway toward the community. But in the majority of cases, the Senderistas were not in any condition to fulfill their promise and the population became a "terrain of dispute" between the two competing armies.

19. "Cabitos" was the name used for soldiers in the region. It referred to the Los Cabitos military garrison located in the outskirts of the departmental capital.

20. For a sharp contrast with Shining Path, consider the Zapatista Army of National Liberation (Ejército Zapatista de Liberación Nacional, EZLN) in Mexico: see Collier and Lowery (1994).

21. On this dynamic in the 1970s, see Degregori (1985b, 1990).

22. It is beyond the scope of this chapter to discuss the extreme voluntarism that led Guzmán to believe that Shining Path could achieve strategic equilibrium at that time. Tapia (1997) analyzes in detail the differences between Mao's equilibrium in China and the situation that Peru experienced leading up to 1990. See also Manrique (1995).

23. In Junín and other departments of the central sierra with a greater mercantile development, events progressed at a quicker pace. Until 1987–88, the peasantry in the high zones had witnessed with astonishment, not without sympathy, Shining Path's destruction of the great SAIS (Sociedades Agrícolas de Interés Social, large agrarian units created by the agrarian reform program of the Velasco regime). But soon the majority of the population passed into opposition, especially in the valley of the Mantaro, Cunas, and Tullumayo, the breadbaskets of Lima, when Shining Path sought to cut off commerce, directly or indirectly, by blowing up bridges and destroying roads. See Manrique (1989).

24. The distributions began in 1990, as Alan García's administration breathed its last gasps. The situation was legalized in 1992 by Legislative Decree 747, which recognized the Self-Defense Committees and permitted "the possession and use of arms and munitions for civil use."

25. Military repression continued to produce victims, however. During these same years, Peru also became the world's leading country in persons "disappeared" by the state (see *Ideele*, 1992; cf. IDL 1992).

26. If one believes erroneously that these personages, a mixture of Andean humanoid monsters (*pishtacos*) and the Rambos of video-movie culture, are exclusively the product of the hallucinatory imagination of our informant, consider the ferocious testimony of "Pancho," who served in the marine infantry in Ayacucho (Degregori and López Ricci 1990).

27. In Purus, in October 1994, recalling the ways in which Sendero killed, a former leader insisted that the Senderistas were not human but rather devils. On the identification of Shining Path with the anti-Christ, see del Pino Huamán (1996). On the identification of Shining Path with the *ñakaq* of the Andean tradition, who assassinates his victims in order to rob their body grease, see Isbell (1992).

28. Ponciano del Pino Huamán, in a personal communication, called my attention to this episode. TV Cultura filmed a video of a convoy of vehicles that were attacked—some were burned—in 1991, on the Libertadores highway that runs between Ayacucho and Pisco.

29. It is evident that at least this part of this document is a transcription of an oral intervention by Guzmán. The decree is analyzed article by article, with numerous

notations such as "are [the directives] for the emergency zones or not? This is the problem, the previous article does not say anything" (PCP-SL 1991, 53).

30. For a more specific analysis of Senderista strategy, which lies beyond the scope of this chapter, see Manrique (1995); Tapia (1997).

31. We do not overestimate the changes in the armed forces, nor do we forget the high degree of demoralization that the military suffered by the end of the 1980s. Nor can we say that would have come to pass had Guzmán not been captured. Toward the end of the decade of the 1980s, the counterinsurgency actions seemed to verge toward a "Guatemalan solution." Fortunately, history took a different path, and the armed forces developed a strategy that can be described as "nongenocidal authoritarianism" (Degregori and Rivera 1993).

32. The utilization of Quechua language, Ayacuchan music, and "chicha" music by the Senderistas remains to be studied. The use of Quechua by Senderistas seems instrumentalist. The *huayno*, music of the sierra, with a simple change of lyrics, becomes "art of a new type." But we still do not know, nor in what measure, if behind the political instrumentalism of the new art is hidden a secret enjoyment of the music—desiring without wanting to desire. In any case, the Montoya brothers (Montoya et al. 1987, 40) have noted perceptively that "strange and terrible is our country; the dominant class that disdains and abuses the Indians also uses their language to express its deepest emotions."

Chapter 7. How Difficult It Is to Be God

1. I have limited myself to only a few of the characteristics of education in the Andes. I do not elaborate, for example, on the clear aspects of ethnocide, or the use of education as an instrument of domination by the new bourgeois classes. With respect to this, see Montoya (1980, 310 ff.)

2. It was Rodrigo Montoya (1980, 309 ff.) who first drew attention to the significance of education for Andean *campesinos*: it enabled them to pass from night to day, and from blindness to light. Those same associations appear in these testimonies and others as well: education vs. absence of education aligned with progress vs. backwardness, freedom vs. slavery, truth vs. deception, well-being vs. poverty, equality vs. exploitation, a guide vs. absence of a guide, virtue vs. vice (coca, alcohol, etc.). But there is a difference in our positions. For Montoya, education has a liberating role only in opposition to domination by feudal ideology, but it is at the same time a means of implanting a much greater domination by capitalist ideology. In other articles I have questioned this generalization (Degregori 1986b, 1989a). The testimonies cited here suggest that education is not necessarily an "ideological state apparatus." The expansion of Marxism in the universities, for example, spreads anticapitalist ideological elements among youth. In the schools, too, what Portocarrero and Oliart (1989) have called the "critical idea of Peru" is spreading. Even so, it is important to note that Marxism shares the same faith in progress as capitalism and, at least in the hard-line Marxist-Leninist versions taught in our universities, a similar authoritarianism, as well

as an objective of liquidating Andean culture comparable to that which Montoya detects in schools.

3. In the 1970s, Marxist manuals by Georges Politzer, Martha Harnecker, and especially from the USSR's Academy of Sciences were widely disseminated in the national universities and later among secondary schools and the *insititutos superiores*, resulting in the creation of a certain "common sense" favoring the subsequent expansion of a project like that of Shining Path among some sectors of university youth. On this issue, see chapter 4 of this volume.

4. We need not discuss the concept of modernity here. It is sufficient to note that for the inhabitants of Papua, modernity appeared in the form of manufactured goods separated from their broader context and without any indication of how and where they were produced. In the case of Andean populations linked to the European economy for four centuries, the situation is different. After the defeat of Túpac Amaru II and throughout the existence of the Republic of Peru, the category of "Indian" was fused with that of "poor *campesino*," and the *mistis* took on the role of intermediaries who controlled and often blocked communication between the world of the Indians and that of modernity. In recent decades, the expansion of the market and the state into rural areas—through market fairs, roads, bureaucracy, and so on—has opened the way to modifying the traditional relationship between *misti* and Indian. Through new organizations and their struggles for basic rights such as land, work, and education, the Indians have obtained direct access to the urban world that brings not only manufactured goods but also ideas.

5. Jürgen Golte and Billie Jean Isbell, among others, have shown me that this comparison is not accurate. Pidgin is something different. I accept the correction, but wish to reiterate the importance of the anxiety that results from the fragmentary and incoherent way in which modernity reaches us. I will develop this idea more satisfactorily in the future.

6. The novel *Todas las sangres* (1964) is by the great Peruvian writer Jose María Arguedas, whose books portray the richness of Andean cultures and the complexities of Indian relations with the *mistis*, and vice versa.

7. This rejection included even José María Arguedas, whom an editorial in *El Diario* described as "a fervent disciple and cheerleader for North American anthropology in Peru," who at the height of World War II "prided himself on his little Hitler mustache" (*El Diario*, 9 June 1988, 12).

8. In these pages we have been referring mainly to the contingent of intellectuals and young people educated in the 1960s and 1970s with whom Shining Path initiated their armed actions in the early 1980s. Subsequently, as Sendero incorporated new cadres and supporters, especially when it expanded into the coca-growing zone of Alto Huallaga and into Lima, the situation became more complicated. With respect to its ideology, we might depict the relationship between the established top-level cadres, the new middle-level cadres, and the militants and sympathizers at the base who are active in the "generated organizations" and/or the "popular guerrilla army" as that which exists between theologians, village priests, and simple parishioners. The further

we go from the leadership, the more the motivations and modes of action vary. I believe, nevertheless, that in a vertically structured and hyper-ideologized party that is defined as a "war machine"—which emphasizes constantly that ideological unity is fundamental—that those to whom we refer as "theologians" continued to exert a decisive influence.

9. Sendero's violence is exacerbated by the belief that practically everything that is not "generated" by the party is contaminated and is part of or serves the interests of some system, particularly the old bureaucratic, landowning state, bureaucratic capitalism, imperialism, or the imperialism of the socialist bloc. This wholesale condemnation covers *campesino* communities, village mayors elected by popular vote, nongovernmental development organizations, and trade union and popular organizations, especially those influenced by other parties of the Left.

10. The most notorious examples are the so-called armed stoppages that have occurred since 1987 in different cities, convened not by trade unions or regional bodies but by the party (Shining Path) or its generated organizations.

11. The truth is that, for Shining Path, the struggle was against the government and *also* against the organizers of the stoppage, that is the CGTP (see "Todos contra el APRA y el oportunismo," *El Diario*, 28 January 1988, 1).

Epilogue. Open Wounds and Elusive Rights

1. In July 2001, President Valentín Paniagua's government created a Truth Commission made up of seven members charged with "clarifying the process, facts and responsibilities for the terrorist violence and human rights violations that occurred from May 1980 through November 2000, attributable to the terrorist organizations as well as the State, as well as proposing initiatives to promote peace and harmony among Peruvians" (PCM 2001, art. 1). In August of that year, a few days after his inauguration, President Alejandro Toledo ratified the commission's existence; he changed the name to the Commission for Truth and Reconciliation and included five new members, but kept its mandate, which ended on 13 July 2003.

2. An extended discussion of the causes of the defeat of Sendero and MRTA is beyond the scope of this work. See the *Final Report* of the CVR (2003), especially volume 2.

3. On memory, forgetting, and politics, see, among others, Jelin (2002).

4. The survey was carried out by IMASEN in Lima, Iquitos, and Huancayo. Additionally, a qualitative study was done with popular sectors (poor and lower classes) in metropolitan Lima. On the events in 1992 at La Cantuta, see Sandoval (2002, 2003).

5. The *vladivideo* is the famous video in which the head of the National Intelligence Service (SIN) and the strongman of the regime, Vladimiro Montesinos, hands over piles of cash to an elected representative so that he would renounce his political affiliation and join the governing bloc. On his role as advisor during the governments of Alberto Fujimori, see Rospigliosi (2000); Bowen (2000); Bowen and Holligan (2003).

6. The purpose of this discussion is not to address the "paradigm of democratic transitions," which is widely debated today. The term is used in the sense of a change from an authoritarian government that resulted from a rupture with the rule of law, to another that is elected by universal suffrage in elections that comply with minimal international standards.

7. The term "memory entrepreneurs" is from Jelin (2003, 48).

8. Thus, just as in the late 1970s, forms of protest originally connected to labor unions—strikes, marches, soup kitchens—spread to middle-class sectors who were becoming impoverished. This time the flag-washings and other performative strategies, initially planned by groups of middle-class intellectuals and artists, were replicated in various cities by diverse regional and popular social actors.

9. The other three members were the General Confederation of Peruvian Workers (CGTP), the Peruvian Chamber of Commerce (CONFIEP), and the Peruvian Episcopal Conference (CEP).

10. The first in the region was the National Commission on the Disappeared in Argentina in 1983. Subsequently, state commissions were created in Chile, El Salvador, and Guatemala. In recent years a specialized literature on truth commissions has developed. See, among others, Hayner (2001); IIDH (2001).

11. This demand emerged even before *fujimorismo* was in crisis, at which time it became more publically visible. In the study by IMASEN, for example, it was notable: "From a clear consciousness of equality there were objections to the lack of equal procedural justice, institutionalized corruption and the multiple manifestations of abuse and mistreatment that they could be or had been subjected to" (IMASEN 1996, 57).

12. In Uruguay, for example, after a timid investigatory commission appointed by Congress with limited mandate, the government sponsored a referendum on a "Law of expiration on the punitive efforts by the state," which was approved.

13. PCM (2001, art. 3). Truth Commissions are not generally binding. On the variability of their mandates, see Hayner (2001).

14. Unlike countries such as Guatemala, the Peruvian CVR did not have to initiate its investigations from practically zero. In the Peruvian case, it was able to take advantage of investigations done by human rights defense organizations and the Ombudsman, as well as by independent journalists and social science researchers.

15. Literally, the term has a dual sense: "the insignificant ones" or those who "have no signifier." From the international seminar "From Denial to Recognition: Post-CVR Scenarios," Lima, June 1993.

16. Whereas in the national census of 1993, the percentage of Quechua speakers did not reach 20 percent.

17. On the impossibility of working out grief in traumatic situations, see Ernst van Alphen (1999); Kaufman (1998).

18. The asymmetry was accentuated by the composition of the CVR itself, which did not fail to reflect the gaps in the country that were partly underlying the political violence. For example, ten of the commissioners were men and only two were women,

all from the urban middle class. All lived in Lima. Only one spoke or understood Quechua, and another partially understood the maternal language of 75 percent of the victims.

19. The objections that politicians and businesspeople have made to the possibility of individual restitution to the victims of violence are a good reflection of the hegemonic ideology in which everything is measured in economic terms and in which macroeconomic measures are more important than the pockets or the dignity of citizens. At times in a derogatory manner, some politicians have stated that those who gave their testimony did so in order to "earn a little something for themselves" (Víctor Andrés García Belaúnde). Almost always on the defensive, many have made reference to the economic difficulties of the state: "I would like it if all the poor people could receive a million dollars, but it isn't possible" (Rafael Rey).

20. The *Final Report* of the CVR avoids presenting them as victims in the sense of passive individuals, trapped between two fires, and needing only protection. Emphasizing the responsibility of the state to protect the life of its citizens, the report recovers the agency of the social sectors damaged by the violence; it is full of episodes of resistance and heroism but also, in cases like the Comités de Autodefensa (Self-Defense Committees, CAD), for example, they are implicated in the abuses and human rights violations.

21. The CVR had more than 60 percent before the demolition campaign and reached the end of its work with an approval rating of 48 percent. The president, Congress, and the judiciary did not receive 20 percent approval at that time.

References

Adorno, Rolena. 2007. *The Polemics of Possession in Spanish American Narrative*. New Haven, CT: Yale University Press.

Aguirre, Carlos, and Charles F. Walker. "Alberto Flores Galindo: Historian and Public Intellectual." In *In Search of an Inca: Identity and Utopia in the Andes*, by Alberto Flores Galindo, ed. and trans. Carlos Aguirre, Charles F. Walker, and Willie Hiatt, xiii–xxix. New York: Cambridge University Press, 2010.

Alarcón Tipe, Rafael. 1976. "El movimiento de Ayacucho y Huanta, 1969." Research seminar, Historic and Social Sciences Department, UNSCH, Ayacucho.

Alfaro, Glicerio. 1985. "Cuadro histórico del Colegio González Vigil." In *Libro Jubilar 1933–1983*, 30–43. Huanta: González Vigil, UNSCH.

Allpanchikrayku. 1969. "Ayacucho: Un año de gran actividad popular." *Allpanchikrayku* 1, no. 2 (20 December): 19–21.

Álvarez, Sonia E., Evelina Dagnino, and Arturo Escobar. 1998. *Cultures of Politics/Politics of Cultures: Re-Visioning Latin American Social Movements*. Boulder, CO: Westview Press.

Americas Watch. 1986. *Civil Patrols in Guatemala*. New York: Americas Watch Committee.

Ames, Rolando. 1985. "Movimiento popular y política nacional: Nuevos horizontes." *Tarea Revista de Cultura*, no. 12: 3–7.

Anderson, James. 1983. *Peru's Maoist Guerrillas*. London: Control Risks.

Ansión, Juan. 1982. "¿Es luminoso el camino de Sendero?" *El Caballo Rojo*, no. 108: 4–5.

———. 1985. "Violencia y Cultura en el Perú." In *Siete ensayos sobre la violencia en el Perú*, edited by Felipe Mac Gregor, José Luis Rouillón, and Marcial Rubio, 59–78. Lima: Fundación Friedrich Ebert, Asociación Peruana de Estudios e Investigaciones para la Paz.

———. 1989a. *La escuela en la comunidad campesina*. Lima: Proyecto Escuela, Ecología y Comunidad Campesina.

———. 1989b. *Pishtacos: De verdugos a sacaojos*. Lima: Tarea.

——. 1994. "Transformaciones culturales en la sociedad rural: El paradigma indigenista en cuestión." In *Perú: El problema agrario en debate*, SEPIA V, edited by Óscar Dancourt, Enrique Mayer, and Carlos Monge, 69–101. Lima: SEPIA.

Apter, David. 1993. *Democracy, Violence and Emancipatory Movements: Notes for a Theory of Inversionary Discourse*. Geneva: UNRISD.

——. 1997. "Political Violence in Analytical Perspective." In *The Legitimization of Violence*, edited by David Apter, 1–32. London: UNRISD, Palgrave Macmillan.

Arce Borja, Luis, ed. 1989. *Guerra popular en el Perú: El pensamiento Gonzalo*. Brussels: L. A. Borja.

Arguedas, José María. 1941. *Yawar Fiesta*. Lima: Populibros Peruanos.

——. 1958. "Notas elementales sobre el arte popular religioso y la cultura mestiza en Huamanga." *Revista del Museo Nacional*, no. 27: 140–94.

——. (1964) 1980. *Todas las sangres*. Lima: Milla Batres.

——. 1968. Prologue to *Poesía y prosa quechua, selección de francisco carillo*. Lima: Biblioteca Universitaria.

Aricó, José, ed. 1978. *Mariátegui y los orígenes del marxismo latinoamericano*. Mexico City: Ediciones Pasado y Presente.

——. 1988. *La cola del diablo: Itinerario de Gramsci en América Latina*. Buenos Aires: Puntosur.

Bandera Roja (Red Flag). 1969. "¡Abajo la represión! ¡Viva la revolución!" *Bandera Roja* 7, no. 42: 9–10.

Barbero, Jesús Martín. 1997. "Nosotros habíamos hecho estudios culturales mucho antes que esa etiqueta apareciera." Interview by Jesús Martín-Barbero. *Dissens*, no. 3: 47–53.

Basombrío, Carlos. 1994. "Para la historia de una guerra con nombre: ¡Ayacucho!" *Ideele* 62 (April): 27–33.

Béjar, Héctor. 1973. *Las guerrillas de 1965: Balance y perspectivas*. Lima: Ediciones Peisa.

Belay, Raynald, Jorge Bracamonte, Carlos Iván Degregori, and Joinville Jean Vacher, eds. 2004. *Memorias en conflicto: Aspectos de la violencia política contemporánea*. Lima: IEP, IFEA, RED, and Embassy of France.

Benavides, Gustavo. 1988. "Poder político y religión en el Perú." *Márgenes, encuentro y debate* 4 (December): 21–54.

Benavides, Margarita. 1990. "Levantamiento de los asháninkas del río Pichis." *Página Libre*.

——. 1992. "Autodefensa asháninka, organizaciones nativas y autonomía indígena." In *Perú: el problema agrario en debate*, SEPIA IV, edited by Carlos Iván Degregori, Javier Escobal, and Benjamín Marticorena, 539–59. Lima: Seminario Permanente de Investigación Agraria, Universidad Nacional de la Amazonía Peruana.

Berg, Ronald. 1986. "Sendero Luminoso and the Peasantry of Andahuaylas." *Journal of Interamerican Studies and World Affairs* 4, no. 28 (Winter): 165–96.

——. 1988. "Explaining Sendero Luminoso." Program in Latin American Studies Occasional Papers Series no. 22, University of Massachusetts at Amherst.

——. 1992. "Peasant Responses to Shining Path in Andahuaylas." In *Shining Path of Peru*, edited by David Palmer, 83–104. New York: St. Martin's Press.

Bernales, Enrique. 1981. *El desarrollo de las ciencias sociales en el Perú*. Lima: Universidad del Pacífico.

Biondi, Juan, and Eduardo Zapata. 1989. *El discurso de Sendero Luminoso: Contratextos educativos*. Lima: CONCYTEC.

Blanco, Hugo. 1964. "Los sindicatos campesinos: Desarrollo del poder dual." In *El camino de nuestra revolución*. Lima: Ediciones Revolución Peruana.

Blondet, Cecilia. 1991. *Las mujeres y el poder: Una historia de Villa el Salvador*. Lima: IEP.

Bobbio, Norberto. 1986. *El futuro de la democracia*. Mexico City: Fondo de Cultura Ecónomica.

Bonilla, Heraclio. 1989. *La defensa del espacio comunal como fuente de conflicto: San Juan de Ocros vs. Pampas, Ayacucho, 1940–1970*. Lima: IEP.

——, ed. 1994. *Perú en el fin del milenio*. Mexico City: Consejo Nacional para la Cultura y las Artes.

Bourdieu, Pierre. 1997. *Razones prácticas: Sobre la teoría de la acción*. Barcelona: Anagrama.

——. 1999. "La causa de la ciencia: Cómo la historia social de las ciencias sociales puede servir al progreso de estas ciencias." In *Intelectuales, política y poder*, 111–27. Buenos Aires: Editorial Universitaria de Buenos Aires.

Bowen, Sally. 2000. *El expediente Fujimori: El Perú y su presidente 1990–2000*. Lima: Consultoría Editorial Richard Bauer.

Bowen, Sally, and Jane Holligan. 2003. *El espía imperfecto: La telaraña siniestra de Vladimiro Montesinos*. Lima: PEISA.

Burga, Manuel. 1988. *Nacimiento de una utopía: Muerte y resurrección de los Incas*. Lima: Instituto de Apoyo Agrario.

Burt, Jo-Marie. 1999. "Sendero Luminoso y la 'batalla decisiva' en las barriadas de Lima: El caso de Villa El Salvador." In *Los senderos insólitos del Perú: Guerra y sociedad, 1980–1995*, edited by Steve Stern, 263–300. Lima: IEP, UNSCH.

——. 2007. *Political Violence and the Authoritarian State in Peru: Silencing Civil Society*. New York: Palgrave Macmillan.

Camborda, Juan. 1981. "Evolución de la hacienda en Huamanga: 1900–1970." Final Investigation Seminar Report, Historical-Social Science Department, UNSCH, Ayacucho.

Cameron, Maxwell, and Philip Mauceri. 1997. *The Peruvian Labyrinth: Polity, Society, Economy*. University Park: Pennsylvania State University Press.

Carmack, Robert. 1988. *Harvest of Violence: Guatemala's Indians in the Counterinsurgency War*. Norman: University of Oklahoma Press.

Castañeda, Jorge. 1993. *La utopía desarmada: Intrigas y dilemas de la izquierda en América Latina*. Mexico City: Joaquín Mortiz.

Castillo, Aracelio. 1972. "El movimiento popular de junio de 1969 (Huanta y Huamanga, Ayacucho)." PhD diss., Universidad Nacional Mayor de San Marcos, Lima.

Centro de Investigación y Promoción del Campesinado. 1988. *Bibliografía seleccionada sobre rondas campesinas*. Piura: Centro de Investigación y Promoción del Campesinado, Centro de Documentación.

Centro de Trabajo Intelectual "Mariátegui." 1973. *Esquemas de estudio*. Lima: Editorial Pedagógica Asencios.

Centro Universitario Huamanga. 1969a. *Informa*, Ayacucho, 1 August. Photocopy in author's possession.

———. 1969b. "Protesta del pueblo de Ayacucho hecho carne en la juventud del Centro Universitario Huamanga." *Boletín* 1, Ayacucho, 25 June, 5. Photocopy in author's possession.

Chávez de Paz, Denis. 1989. *Juventud y terrorismo: Características sociales de los condenados por terrorismo y otros delitos*. Lima: IEP.

Churampi, Adriana I. 2004. *Heraldos del Pachakuti: La pentalogía de Manuel Scorza*. Netherlands: Proefschrift, Leiden University.

Collier, George, and Elizabeth Lowery. 1994. *¡Basta! Land and the Zapatista Rebellion in Chiapas*. Oakland, CA: Food First Books.

Comisión de la Verdad y Reconciliación (CVR). 2003. *Informe final*. 9 vols. Lima: CVR.

———. 2004. *Hatun Willakuy: Versión abreviada del Informe Final de la Comisión de la Verdad y Reconciliación, Perú*. Lima: CVR.

Comisión Económica para América Latina y el Caribe (CEPAL). 1985. *Anuario estadístico de América Latina/Statistical Yearbook for Latin America and the Caribbean, 1984*. New York: United Nations, Economic Commission for Latin America and the Caribbean.

Comisión para el Esclarecimiento Histórico (CEH). 1999. *Guatemala: Memoria del Silencio*. 12 vols. Guatemala: CEH.

Comité de Defensa de Ayacucho. 1969. "A la opinión pública." Flier, Lima, July. Photocopy in author's possession.

CONAI (Consejo Nacional Universitario). 1986. *Boletín del Consejo Nacional Universitario*. Lima: CONAI.

Contreras, Carlos. 1981. *La ciudad del mercurio: Huancavelica 1570–1700*. Lima: IEP.

Coral, Isabel. 1994. *Desplazamiento por violencia política en el Perú*. Lima: IEP, Centro de Promoción y Desarrollo Poblacional.

———. 1997. "Women in War: Impact and Responses." In *Shining and Other Paths: War and Society in Peru, 1980–1995*, edited by Steve J. Stern, 345–74. Durham, NC: Duke University Press.

Coronel, José. 1983. "Pugnas por el poder local: Don Manuel J. Urbina y la creación del colegio 'González Vigil.'" In *Libro Jubilar 1933–1983*, 217–40. Huanta: González Vigil, UNSCH.

———. 1984. "Mistis e indios en Huanta: 1870–1915." PhD diss., Universidad Nacional de San Cristóbal de Huamanga, Ayacucho.

———. 1996. "Violencia política y respuestas campesinas en Huanta." In *Las rondas campesinas y la derrota de Sendero Luminoso*, edited by Carlos Iván Degregori, 29–116. Lima: IEP.

Cotler, Julio. 1968. "La mecánica de la dominación interna y del cambio social en la sociedad rural." *Perú Problema*, no. 1: 153–97.

———. 1982. "Respuesta a 'Una encuesta sobre Sendero.'" *Quehacer* 20 (November–December): 58–69.

Cotler, Julio, and Romeo Grompone. 2000. *El fujimorismo: Ascenso y caída de un régimen autoritario.* Lima: IEP.

Cotler, Julio, Romeo Grompone, and Fernando Rospigliosi. 1988. *El desarrollo institucional de las ciencias sociales en el Perú.* Lima: IEP.

Crabtree, Jim, and John Thomas, eds. 2000. *El Perú de Fujimori, 1990–1998.* Lima: Universidad del Pacífico, Centro de Investigación.

Cristóbal, Juan. 2003. *Uchuraccay o el rostro de la barbarie.* Lima: Editorial San Marcos.

Deas, Malcolm. 1997. "Violent Exchanges: Reflections on Political Violence in Colombia." In *The Legitimization of Violence*, edited by David E. Apter, 358–404. London: UNRISD, Palgrave Macmillan.

Debray, Regis. 1967. *¿Revolución en la revolución?* Lima: Ediciones de Cultura General.

———. 1975. *La crítica de las armas.* Mexico City: Siglo XXI Editores.

Degregori, Carlos Iván. 1983a. "En la selva de Ayacucho: No una sino muchas muertes." *El Diario de Marka*, Lima (22 January): 8–10.

———. 1983b. "Realidad socioeconómica de Ayacucho a través de los censos nacionales y otras fuentes estadísticas: 1961–1981." Thesis, Universidad Nacional de San Cristóbal de Huamanga, Ayacucho.

———. 1983c. "Reflexiones sobre ocho muerte peruanas." *El Diario de Marka*, Lima (14 February): 11.

———. 1985a. "Entre dos fuegos." *Quehacer* 37 (October–November): 53–54.

———. 1985b. *Sendero Luminoso.* Part 1, *Los hondos y mortales desencuentros*; Part 2, *Lucha armada y utopía autoritaria.* Lima: IEP.

———. 1986a. *Ayacucho, raíces de una crisis.* Ayacucho: Instituto de Estudios Regionales "José María Arguedas."

———. 1986b. "Del mito de Inkarrí al 'mito' del progreso: Poblaciones andinas, cultura e identidad nacional." *Socialismo y Participación*, no. 36 (December): 49–56.

———. 1989a. Prologue to *La escuela en la comunidad campesina*, edited by Juan Ansión, 13–20. Lima: Proyecto Escuela, Ecología y Comunidad Campesina.

———. 1989b. *Qué difícil es ser Dios: Ideología y violencia política en Sendero Luminoso.* Lima: El Zorro de Abajo Ediciones.

———. 1990. *El surgimiento de Sendero Luminoso: Ayacucho 1969–1979: Del movimiento por la gratuidad de la enseñanza al inicio de la lucha armada.* Lima: IEP.

———. 1991a. "Ayacucho 1980–1983: Jóvenes y campesinos ante la violencia política." In *Poder y violencia en los andes*, edited by Henrique Urbano, 395–417. Cusco: Centro de Estudios Regionales Andinos Bartolomé de Las Casas.

———. 1991b. "El aprendiz de brujo y el curandero chino: Etnicidad, modernidad y ciudadanía." In *Elecciones 1990: Demonios y redentores en el nuevo Perú: Una tragedia en dos vueltas*, edited by Carlos Iván Degregori and Romeo Grompone, 71–136. Lima: IEP.

———. 1991c. "Los hijos de la Guerra: Jóvenes andinos y criollos frente a la violencia política." In *Poder y violencia en los Andes*, edited by Henrique Urbano, 395–417. Cusco: Centro de Estudios Regionales Andinos Bartolomé de Las Casas.

———. 1992. "Campesinado andino y violencia: Balance de una década de estudios." In *Perú: El problema agrario en debate*, SEPIA IV, edited by Carlos Iván Degregori, Javier Escobal, and Benjamín Marticorena, 413–39. Lima: SEPIA, Universidad Nacional de la Amazonía Peruana.

———. 1996. "Cosechando tempestades: Las rondas campesinas y la derrota de Sendero Luminoso en Ayacucho." In *Las rondas campesinas y la derrota de Sendero Luminoso*, edited by Carlos Iván Degregori, José Coronel, Ponciano del Pino Huamán, and Orin Starn, 189–225. Lima: IEP.

———. 2000a. *La década de la antipolítica: Auge y caída de Alberto Fujimori y Vladimiro Montesinos*. Lima: IEP.

———, ed. 2000b. *No hay país más diverso: Compendio de antropología peruana*. Lima: Red para el Desarrollo de las Ciencias Sociales en el Perú.

———. 2000c. "Panorama de la antropología en el Perú: Del estudio del otro a la construcción de un nosotros diverso." In *No hay país más diverso: Compendio de antropología peruana*, edited by Carlos Iván Degregori, 20–73. Lima: Red para el Desarrollo de las Ciencias Sociales en el Perú.

———, ed. 2003. *Jamás tan cerca arremetió lo lejos: Memoria y violencia política en el Perú*. Lima: IEP.

———. 2004. *Ilave: Desafíos de la gobernabilidad, la democracia participativa y la descentralización*. Cuadernos Descentralistas 13. Lima: Grupo Propuesta Ciudadana.

———. 2010. *Qué difícil es ser Dios: El Partido Comunista del Perú–Sendero Luminoso y el conflicto armado interno en el Perú: 1980–1999*. Lima: IEP.

Degregori, Carlos Iván, Cecilia Blondet, and Nicolás Lynch. 1986. *Conquistadores del nuevo mundo: De invasores a ciudadanos en San Martín de Porres*. Lima: IEP.

Degregori, Carlos Iván, Ponciano del Pino Huamán, Orin Starn, and José Coronel Aguirre. 1996. *Las rondas campesinas y la derrota de Sendero Luminoso*. 2nd ed. Lima: IEP.

Degregori, Carlos Iván, Jürgen Golte, Walter Pariona, and Hugo Reynoso. 1973. "Cambios económicos y cambios ideológicos en Ayacucho." *Ideología*, no. 3: 14–41.

Degregori, Carlos Iván, and José López Ricci. 1990. "Los hijos de la guerra: Jóvenes andinos y criollos frente a la violencia política." In *Tiempos de ira y amor: Nuevos actores para viejos problemas*, edited by Carlos Iván Degregori, Marfil Francke, Nelson Manrique, Gonzalo Portocarrero, Patricia Ruiz Bravo, and Antonio Zapata, 183–219. Lima: DESCO.

Degregori, Carlos Iván, and Carlos Rivera. 1993. *Perú 1980–1990: Fuerzas armadas, subversión y democracia; Redefinición del papel militar en un contexto de violencia subversiva y colapso de régimen democrático*. Lima: IEP.

Degregori, Carlos Iván, and Pablo Sandoval. 2007. *Saberes periféricos: Ensayos sobre la antropología en América Latina*. Lima: IEP.

———. 2009. *Antropología y antropólogos en el Perú: La comunidad académica de ciencias sociales bajo la modernización neoliberal.* Lima: IEP.

Degregori, Carlos Iván, and Jaime Urrutia. 1983. "Reflexiones sobre ocho muertes peruanas." *El Diario de Marka,* 14 February, 11.

Degregori, Carlos Iván, Jaime Urrutia, and Edwige Balutansky. 1979. "Apuntes sobre el desarrollo del capitalismo y la destrucción del área cultural Pokra-Chanka." *Investigaciones, Ciencias Histórico Sociales* 2, no. 2, part 2: 243–52.

de la Cadena, Marisol. 2003. "Escribir otra historia del Perú." *Cuestión de Estado,* no. 32 (November): 12–13.

———. 2004. *Indígenas mestizos: Raza y cultura en el Cusco.* Translated by Montserrat Cañedo y Eloy Neyra. Lima: IEP. Originally published as *Indigenous Mestizos: The Politics of Race and Culture in Cuzco, Peru, 1919–1991* (Durham, NC: Duke University Press, 2000).

del Pino Huamán, Ponciano. 1992. "Los campesinos en la guerra o de cómo la gente comienza a ponerse macho." In *Perú: El problema agrario en debate,* SEPIA IV, edited by Carlos Iván Degregori, Javier Escobal D'Angelo, and Benjamín Marticorena, 487–508. Lima: SEPIA, Universidad Nacional de la Amazonía Peruana.

———. 1996. "Tiempos de guerra y de dioses: Ronderos, evangélicos y senderistas en el valle del río Apurímac." In *Las rondas campesinas y la derrota de Sendero Luminoso,* edited by Carlos Iván Degregori, 117–88. Lima: IEP.

———. 2003. "Uchuraccay: Memoria y representación de la violencia política en los Andes." In *Jamás tan cerca arremetió lo lejos: Memoria y violencia política en el Perú,* edited by Carlos Iván Degregori, 49–93. Lima: IEP.

———. 2008. "'Looking to the Government': Community, Politics and the Production of Memory and Silences in Twentieth-Century Peru, Ayacucho." PhD diss., University of Wisconsin–Madison.

DESCO (Centro de Estudios y Promoción del Desarrollo). 1989. *Violencia política en el Perú, 1980–1988.* Vol.1, *Estadísticas de la violencia.* Lima: DESCO.

de Soto, Hernando. 1986. *El otro sendero: La revolución informal.* Lima: Instituto Libertad y Democracia. Translated by June Abbott as *The Other Path: The Invisible Revolution in the Third World* (New York: Harper & Row, 1989).

de Trazegnies, Fernando. 1983. "Informe." In *Informe de la Comisión Investigadora de los sucesos de Uchuraccay,* edited by Mario Vargas Llosa et al., 127–52. Lima: Editora Perú.

Díaz Martínez, Antonio. 1969. *Ayacucho, hambre y esperanza.* Ayacucho: Ediciones Waman Puma.

Dirección Nacional de Estadística y Censos. 1965. *VI Censo Nacional de Población.* Lima: República del Perú, Dirección Nacional de Estádistica y Censos.

Earls, John, and Irene Silverblatt. 1979. "Ayllus y etnías en la región Pampas-Qaracha: El impacto del imperio incaico." In *Investigaciones UNSCH,* vol. 2. Ayacucho: Universidad Nacional de San Cristóbal de Huamanga.

Eco, Umberto. 1986. "La nueva edad media." Supplement, *La República,* 19 November, 7–8.

Eguren, Fernando. 1988. "Democracia y sociedad rural." In *Democracia, sociedad y gobierno en el Perú*, edited by Luis Pásara and Jorge Parodi, 125–49. Lima: Centro de Estudios de Democracia y Sociedad.

Eguren, Fernando, Raúl Hopkins, Bruno Kervyn, and Rodrigo Montoya, eds. 1988. *Perú: El problema agrario en debate*, SEPIA II. Lima: Universidad Nacional de San Cristóbal de Huamanga, Seminario Permanente de Investigaciones Agrarias.

El Diario. 1989. "El 'contraelviento' de Yuyachkani." *El Diario*, 24 May, 16.

———. 1991a. "Inició la Década del Triunfo." *El Diario*, 2–4 December.

———. 1991b. "Mejores condiciones para Gran Salto en Equilibrio Estratégico." *El Diario*, 2–4 December.

El Diario Internacional. 1993. "Presidente Gonzalo responde." *El Diario Internacional*, no. 21 (September–October).

Escobar, Arturo, and Sonia E. Álvarez. 1992. *The Making of Social Movements in Latin America: Identity, Strategy, and Democracy*. Boulder, CO: Westview Press.

Espinosa, Óscar. 1994. *La repetición de la violencia: Informe sobre la situación de los Asháninka del río Ene y Tambo*. Lima: Centro Amazónico de Antropología y Aplicación Práctica.

Favre, Henri. 1984. "Perú: Sendero Luminoso y horizontes oscuros." *Quehacer* 31 (September–October): 25–36.

———. 1989. "Violencia y descomposición social." *Debate* 11, no. 57 (September–October): 31–33.

Flores Galindo, Alberto. 1980. *La agonía de Mariátegui: La polémica con la Komintern*. Lima: Centro de Estudios y Promoción del Desarrollo.

———. 1984. *Aristocracia y plebe, Lima 1760–1830*. Lima: Mosca Azul.

———. 1988. *Buscando un Inca: Identidad y utopía en los Andes*. 3rd rev. ed. Lima: Horizonte. Translated by Carlos Aguirre, Charles F. Walker, and Willie Hiatt as *In Search of an Inca: Identity and Utopia in the Andes* (New York: Cambridge University Press, 2010).

Flores Galindo, Alberto, and Nelson Manrique. 1985. *Violencia y campesinado*. Lima: Instituto de Apoyo Agrario.

Fonseca Martel, César, and Enrique Mayer. 1988. *Comunidad y producción en la agricultura andina*. Lima: FOMCIENCIAS.

Franco, Carlos. 1991. *Imágenes de la sociedad peruana: La otra modernidad*. Lima: Centro de Estudios para el Desarrollo y la Participación.

Fuenzalida, Fernando, J. L. Villarán, Jürgen Golte, and Teresa Valiente. 1967. *Estructuras tradicionales y economía de mercado, la comunidad de indígenas de Huayopampa*. Lima: IEP.

Fumerton, Mario. 2002. *From Victims to Heroes: Peasant Counter-Rebellion and Civil War in Ayacucho, Peru, 1980–2000*. Amsterdam: Rozenberg.

Fumerton, Mario, and Simone Remijnse. 2004. "Civil Defence Forces: Peru's Comités de Autodefensa Civil and Guatemala's Patrullas de Autodefensa Civil in Comparative Perspective." In *Armed Actors: Organised Violence and State Failure in Latin America*, edited by Kees Koonings and Dirk Kruijt, 52–72. London: Zed Books.

Gall, Norman. 1976. *La reforma educativa peruana*. Lima: Mosca Azul.

Gálvez, Modesto. 1977. "El enfoque regional en las investigaciones sociales." *Ideología*, no. 5: 53–58.

———. 1987. "El derecho en el campesinado andino del Perú." In *Derechos humanos y servicios legales en el campo*, edited by Diego García Sayán, 233–49. Lima: Comisión Andina de Juristas, Comisión Internacional de Juristas.

Gálvez, Modesto, and Lucía Cano. 1974. "El sistema latifundista en Huamanga, Ayacucho." Thesis, Universidad Nacional Mayor de San Marcos, Lima.

García Canclini, Néstor. 1990. *Culturas híbridas: Estrategias para entrar y salir de la modernidad*. Mexico City: Grijalbo.

García Sayán, Diego. 1982. *Tomas de tierras en el Perú*. Lima: Centro de Estudios y Promoción del Desarrollo.

Gitlitz, John, and Telmo Rojas. 1985. "Las rondas campesinas en Cajamarca-Perú." *Apuntes*, no. 16: 115–41.

Golte, Jürgen. 1980. *La racionalidad de la organización andina*. Lima: IEP.

Golte, Jürgen, and Norma Adams. 1985. *Los caballos de troya de los invasores: Estrategias campesinas en la conquista de la gran Lima*. Lima: IEP.

Golte, Jürgen, and Marisol de la Cadena. 1986. *La codeterminación de la organización social andina*. Lima: IEP.

Gonzáles, José. 1989. "Perú: Sendero Luminoso en el valle de la coca." In *Coca, cocaína y narcotráfico: Laberinto en los Andes*, edited by Diego García Sayán, 210–17. Lima: Comisión Andina de Juristas.

Gonzáles de Olarte, Efraín. 1982. *Economías regionales del Perú*. Lima: IEP.

———. 1992. *La economía regional de Lima*. Lima: Consorcio de Investigación Económica, IEP.

González, Olga M. 2011. *Unveiling Secrets of War in the Peruvian Andes*. Chicago: University of Chicago Press.

González, Osmar. 1996. *Sanchos fracasados: Los arielistas y el pensamiento político peruano*. Lima: Editorial PREAL.

———. 1999. *Señales sin respuesta: Los zorros y el pensamiento socialista en el Perú, 1968–1989*. Lima: Editorial PREAL.

González, Raúl. 1982. "Por los caminos de Sendero: Crónica desde Ayacucho; Entrevistas con el Prefecto y el Rector de la UNSCH: Estrategia militar." *Quehacer* 19 (September–October): 37–77.

———. 1983. "Las batallas de Ayacucho." *Quehacer* 21 (January–February): 14–27.

———. 1984a. "Ayacucho en el año de Noel." *Quehacer* 27 (January–February): 16–37.

———. 1984b. "Especial sobre Sendero Luminoso?" *Quehacer* 30 (July–August): 6–36.

———. 1987. "Coca y subversión en el Huallaga." *Quehacer* 48 (September–October): 59–73.

———. 1988a. "El retorno de lo reprimido: El Huallaga un año después." *Quehacer* 54 (August–September): 40–48.

———. 1988b. "MRTA: La historia desconocida." *Quehacer* 51 (March–April): 32–23.

———. 1988c. "Sendero: Los problemas del campo, la ciudad y además el MRTA." *Quehacer* 50 (January–February): 47–59.

———. 1991. "El Huallaga: Todos los conflictos." *Quehacer* 71 (May–June): 46–53.

González Galindo, Marcial. 1982. "De cofradía a empresa comunal de Huancasancos, 1953–1981." Research seminar final report. Universidad Nacional de San Cristóbal de Huamanga, Ayacucho.

González Prada, Manuel. 1979. *Páginas libres; Horas de lucha.* Caracas: Biblioteca Ayacucho.

Gorriti Ellenbogen, Gustavo. 1981. "La búsqueda de Sendero." *Caretas* 670 (26 October): 22–25.

———. 1983a. "¿Cómo se encendió la mecha? Entrevista a Efraín Morote Best." *Caretas* 733 (31 January): 26–31.

———. 1983b. "El ataque de Sendero al pueblo de Lucanamarca." *Caretas* 743 (11 April): 10–17.

———. 1990. *Sendero: Historia de la guerra milenaria en el Perú.* Lima: Editorial Apoyo.

Granados, Manuel. 1981. "La conducta política: Un caso particular." Thesis, Historical-Social Sciences Department, Universidad Nacional de San Cristóbal de Huamanga, Ayacucho.

———. 1987. "El PCP Sendero Luminoso: Aproximaciones a su ideología." *Socialismo y Participación* 37 (March): 15–36.

Guerrero, Andrés. 1993. "De sujetos indios a ciudadanos-étnicos: De la manifestación de 1961 al levantamiento indígena de 1990." In *Democracia, etnicidad y violencia política en los países andinos,* 83–101. Lima: Instituto Francés de Estudios Andinos, IEP.

Guerrero, Juan Carlos. 2002. "Las guerras del Tulumayo y las transformaciones del poder local en el marco de la guerra contrasubversiva en Concepción, Junín." In *Perú: El problema agrario,* SEPIA IX, edited by Pulgar Vidal, M. Zegarra, Eduardo Urrutia, and Jaime Urrutia, 514–89. Lima: SEPIA, Consorcio de Investigación Económica y Social, CARE Perú, and Oxfam.

Guibal, Francis. 1981. *Gramsci: Filosofía, política, cultura.* Lima: Tarea, Centro de Publicaciones Educativas.

Gutiérrez, Gustavo. 2003. "Propuestas para la reconciliación." Paper presented at the international seminar "Procesos Post Comisiones de la Verdad: De la negación al reconocimiento," Lima, Peru, 4–6 June.

Gutiérrez, Miguel. 1988. *La generación del 50: Un mundo dividido.* Lima: Editorial Labrusa.

Guzmán, Abimael. 1988. "Presidente Gonzalo rompe el silencio: Entrevista en la clandestinidad." *El Diario,* 24 July.

———. 1989a. "Forjar en los hechos." Orig. 1979. In *Guerra popular en el Perú: El pensamiento Gonzalo,* edited by Luis Arce Borja, 145–50. Brussels: L. A. Borja.

———. 1989b. "Por la Nueva Bandera." In *Guerra popular en el Perú: El pensamiento Gonzalo,* edited by Luis Arce Borja, 139–59. Brussels: L. A. Borja.

———. 1990a. "Comenzamos a derribar los muros y a desplegar la aurora." Orig. 1980. In *Guerra popular en el Perú: El pensamiento Gonzalo*, edited by Luis Arce Borja, 150–59. Brussels: L. A. Borja.

———. 1990b. "Somos los iniciadores." Orig. 1980. In *Guerra popular en el Perú: El pensamiento Gonzalo*, edited by Luis Arce Borja, 161–78. Brussels: L. A. Borja.

———. 1991a. "Construir la conquista del poder en medio de la guerra popular!" II Pleno del Comité Central. Sesión preparatoria, 1991. Accessed 16 August 2010. http://www.pagina-libre.org/MPP-A/Textos/PCP1991/Construir_2.html

———. 1991b. "Sobre campaña de rectificación con 'Elecciones no! Guerra Popular, sí!'" Intervención del Presidente Gonzalo en una Reunión de Campaña de Rectificación, 1991. Accessed 16 August 2010. http://www.pagina-libre.org/MPP-A/Textos/PCP1991/Rectificacion.html.

———. 1991c. "Sobre las dos Colinas: Documento de estudio para el balance de la II Campaña, 1991." Accessed 16 August 2010. http://www.pagina-libre.org/MPP-A/Textos/PCP1991/Colinas.html.

———. 1992. "Comentarios acerca del golpe de Estado." II Pleno del Comité Central, April.

———. 1993. "Yo admiraba a Stalin." Excerpts of interview of Guzmán by the National Counter-Terrorist Directorate (DINCOTE) in September 1992. *Semanario Sí* 310 (8 February).

———. 1994a. "Asumir la nueva decisión y la nueva definición y combatir por ellas." Special supplement, *La República*, 25 January.

———. 1994b. "Asumir y combatir por la nueva gran decisión y definición." Movimiento Popular Perú, Francia. Accessed 16 August 2010. http://www.pagina-libre.org/MPP-A/Textos/PCP1993/Asumir_Resumen.html.

Guzmán, Virginia, and Virginia Vargas. 1981. *El campesinado en la historia: Cronología de los movimientos campesinos, 1956–1964*. Lima: Ideas.

Hayner, Priscilla. 2001. *Unspeakeable Truths: Confronting State Terror and Atrocities*. New York: Routledge.

Heilman, Jaymie. 2010. *Before the Shining Path: Politics in Rural Ayacucho*. Palo Alto, CA: Stanford University Press.

Hinojosa, Iván. 1992. "Entre el poder y la ilusión: Pol Pot, Sendero y las utopías campesinas." *Debate agrario* 15 (October–December): 69–93.

Hirsch, Francine. 2005. *Empire of Nations: Ethnographical Knowledge and the Making of the Soviet Union*. Ithaca, NY: Cornell University Press.

Huber, Ludwig. 1995. *Las rondas campesinas en Piura: "Después de Dios y la Virgen está la ronda."* Lima: IEP, Instituto Francés de Estudios Andinos.

Huber, Ludwig, and Karin Apel. 1990. "Comunidades campesinas en Piura." *Boletín del Instituto Francés de Estudios Andinos* 19, no. 1: 165–82.

Huertas, Lorenzo. 1981. "Poblaciones indígenas en Huamanga colonial." In *Etnohistoria y antropología andina*, edited by Amalia Castelli, Marcia Koth de Paredes, Mariana Mould de Pease, 131–44. Lima: Centro de Proyección Cristiana.

Husson, Patrick. 1983. "Guerre indienne et revolte du sel dans la provience de Huanta

(Department de Ayacucho, Perú) au XIX siècle." Thesis, Universidad de París IV, Paris.

———. 1986. "¿Los campesinos contra el cambio social? El caso de los sublevaciones en la provincia de Huanta (Perú) en el siglo XIX." In *Estados y naciones en los Andes: Hacia una historia comparativa: Bolivia, Colombia, Ecuador, Perú*, vol. 1, edited by Jean Paul Deler and Y. Saint-Geours, 153–68. Lima: IEP, Instituto Francés de Estudios Andinos.

IMASEN. 1996. *A la intemperie: Percepciones sobre derechos humanos*. Lima: Coordinadora Nacional de Derechos Humanos.

Instituto de Defensa Legal (IDL). 1990. *Perú 1989: En la espiral de la violencia*. Lima: Instituto de Defensa Legal.

———. 1991. *Perú 1990: La oportunidad perdida*. Lima: Instituto de Defensa Legal.

———. 1992. *Perú hoy: En el oscuro Sendero de la guerra*. Lima: Instituto de Defensa Legal.

———. 1994. "Sendero en cifras: Terror y figura . . . hasta la sepultura." *Ideele* 71–72 (December): 32–37.

Instituto Interamericano de Derechos Humanos (IIDH). 2001. *Verdad y justicia: Homenaje a Emilio F. Mignone*. San José: IIDH.

Instituto Nacional de Estadística e Informática (INEI). 1983a. *Censos Nacionales de Población: VIII de Población y III de Vivienda, 12 de julio de 1981; Nivel Nacional: Resultados de Prioridad*. 2 vols. Lima: INEI.

———. 1983b. *Censos Nacionales de Población: VIII de Población y III de Vivienda, 12 de julio de 1981; Departamento de Ayacucho, Resultados Definitivos*. 3 vols. Lima: INEI.

———. 1983c. *Producto Bruto Interno por Departamentos: 1971–1981*. Lima: Dirección General de Cuentas Nacionales.

———. 1986. *Informe estadístico: Cuarto semestre 1986*. Lima: Dirección General de Indicadores Económicos y Sociales—Dirección de Coyuntura.

———. 1987. *Las migraciones internas en el Perú por departamento y provincias, período: 1976–1981*. Boletín de Análisis Demográfico 30.

———. 1989. *Perú: Compendio estadístico 1989–1990*. Lima: INEI.

———. 1994. *Censos nacionales 1993, IX de Población, IV de Vivienda, Departamento de Ayacucho*. Vols. 1–4. Lima: INEI.

Instituto de Pedagogía Popular. 1987. *Mapa de la pobreza educativa en el Perú*. Lima: Instituto de Pedagogía Popular.

Isbell, Billie Jean. 1978. *To Defend Ourselves: Ecology and Ritual in an Andean Village*. Long Grove, IL: Waveland Press.

———. 1988. *The Emerging Patterns of Peasant's Responses to Sendero Luminoso*. Latin American, Caribbean and Iberian Occasional Papers no. 7. New York: Consortium of Columbia University Institute of Latin American and Iberian Studies and New York University Center for Latin America and Caribbean Studies.

———. 1992. "Shining Path and Peasant Responses in Rural Ayacucho." In *Shining Path of Peru*, edited by David S. Palmer, 59–81. New York: St. Martin's Press.

J. C. F. 1988. "Pensamiento Gonzalo: Marxismo del nuevo siglo (VIII)." *El Diario*, 9 June, 12.

Jelin, Elizabeth. 2002. *Los trabajos de la memoria*. Mexico City: Siglo XXI Editores.

———. 2003. "Memorias y luchas políticas." In *Jamás tan cerca arremetió lo lejos: Memoria y violencia política en el Perú*, 29–48. Lima: IEP.

Joseph, Gil, and David Nugent, eds. 1994. *Popular Culture and State Formation in Revolutionary Mexico: Revolution and the Negotiation of Rule in Modern Mexico*. Durham, NC: Duke University Press.

Jurado, Joel. 1983. "Política económica y condiciones de vida en la región central." Servicios Populares (SERPO), Lima. Photocopy in author's possession.

Kapsoli, Wilfredo. 1981. *Ayllus del sol: Anarquismo y utopía andina*. Lima: Tarea Educativa.

Kaufman, Susana. 1998. "Sobre violencia social, trauma y memoria." Paper presented at Social Science Research Council seminar on "Memoria colectiva y represión: Perspectivas comparativas sobre el proceso de democratización en el Cono Sur de América Latina." Montevideo, Uruguay, 6–17 November.

Khosrokhavar, Farhad. 1993. *L'Utopie Sacrifiée de la révolution iranienne*. Paris: Presses de la Fondation Nationale des Sciences Politiques.

Kiernan, Ben. 1985. *How Pol Pot Came to Power: A History of Communism in Kampuchea, 1930–1975*. London: Verso.

Kirk, Robin. 1991. *La década de chaqwa: Los desplazados internos del Perú*. Lima: Coordinadora Nacional de Derechos Humanos.

———. 1993. *Grabado en piedra: Las mujeres de Sendero Luminoso*. Lima: IEP.

Klarén, Peter Flindell. 2000. *Peru: Society and Nationhood in the Andes*. New York: Oxford University Press.

Koonings, Kees, and Dirk Kruijt, eds. 2003. *Ejércitos políticos: Las Fuerzas Armadas y la construcción de la nación en la era de la democracia*. Lima: IEP.

Kristal, Efraín. 1991. *Una visión urbana de los Andes: Génesis y desarrollo del indigenismo en el Perú: 1848–1930*. Lima: Instituto de Apoyo Agrario.

Kruijt, Dirk. 1991a. *La revolución por decreto: Perú durante el gobierno militar*. 2nd ed. San José: Mosca Azul.

———. 1991b. *Perú: Entre Sendero y los militares, seguridad y relaciones cívico-militares, 1950–1990*. Barcelona: Ed. Robles.

———. 1999. "Exercises in State Terrorism: The Counter-Insurgency Campaigns in Guatemala and Peru." In *Societies of Fear: The Legacy of Civil War, Violence and Terror in Latin America*, edited by K. Koonings and D. Kruijt, 33–62. London: Zed Books.

Kruijt, Dirk, and María del Pilar Tello. 2003. "De los reformistas militares a la dictadura civil: La política militar peruana desde los años sesenta hasta el presente." In *Ejércitos políticos: Las Fuerzas Armadas y la construcción de la nación en la era de la democracia*, edited by Kees Koonings and Dirk Kruijt, 70–103. Lima: IEP.

Kurtz, Paul. 1989. "El manantial de los adeptos." *El País*, 20 July, 3–5.

Lauer, Mirko. 2003. "La desaparición de la desaparición." *La República*, 19 June, 6.

Lenin, Vladimir Illich. 1970a. "Las enseñanzas de la insurrección de Moscú." Orig. 1906. In *Obras escogidas en tres tomos*, vol. 1, 594–600. Moscow: Editorial Progreso.

———. 1970b. "¿Qué hacer? Problemas candentes de nuestro movimiento." Orig. 1902. In *Obras escogidas en tres tomos*, vol. 1, 117–278. Moscow: Editorial Progreso.

———. 1973. "Una gran iniciativa." In *Marx, Engels, Marxismo*, 479–82. Moscow: Editorial Progreso.

———. 1975. *La enfermedad infantil del "izquierdismo" en el comunismo*. Orig. 1920. 4th ed. Beijing: Ediciones en Lenguas Extranjeras.

León, Rafael. 1991. "Lecturas peligrosas." Interview in *El Suplemento de Expreso*, 26 May.

Linz, Juan J., and Alfred Stepan. 1996. *Problems of Democratic Transition and Consolidation: Southern Europe, South America, and Post-Communist Europe*. Baltimore: Johns Hopkins University Press.

Lomnitz, Claudio. 1996. "Insoportable levedad." *Fractal* 2 (July–September): 51–76.

López, Sinesio. 1979. "De imperio a nacionalidades oprimidas." In *Nueva historia general del Perú*, 231–63. Lima: Mosca Azul.

———. 1987. "Política, violencia y revolución." *El Zorro de Abajo*, no. 7.

———. 1991. *El Dios mortal: Estado, sociedad y política en el Perú del siglo XX*. Lima: Instituto Democracia y Socialismo.

Lowenthal, Abraham. 1975. *The Peruvian Experiment: Continuity and Change under Military Rule*. Princeton, NJ: Princeton University Press.

Lumbreras, Luis Guillermo. 1974. *Las fundaciones de Huamanga*. Lima: Ediciones Club Departamental de Huamanga.

———. 1985. "De señores, indios y subversivos." Interview in *El Zorro de Abajo*, no. 3 (November–December): 56–57.

———. 1986. "De cómo Lumbreras entiende el Perú de Sendero." Interview by Raúl González, in *Quehacer* 42 (August–September): 34–43.

Lynch, Nicolás. 1984. "El sentido común del izquierdismo en San Marcos." Unpublished manuscript based on *Boletín Eclesiástico* 9 (August 1984).

1990. *Los jóvenes rojos de San Marcos: Radicalismo universitario de los años 70*. Lima: El Zorro de Abajo Ediciones.

———. 1992a. *La transición conservadora: Movimiento social y democracia en el Perú, 1975–1978*. Lima: El Zorro de Abajo Ediciones.

———. 1992b. "Transiciones, democracia y movimientos sociales en el Perú." *Revista de Sociología* 6, no. 8.

Macera, Pablo. 1977. *Reflexiones a propósito de la polémica de indigenismo*. Lima: Centro de Investigación de la Universidad del Pacífico.

———. 1983. *Las furias y las penas*. Lima: Mosca Azul.

———. 1986. "Sendero y Mama Huaco." Portion of speech delivered at the Symposium on Andean Mythology presented at the Universidad Católica in 1984. *Cambio* 20 (28 August): 9.

Maletta, Héctor, and Alejandro Bardales. 1984. *Perú: Las provincias en cifras, 1876–1981*.

Vol. 1, *Población y migraciones*. Lima: Ediciones AMIDEP and Universidad del Pacífico.

Mallon, Florencia E. 1983. *The Defense of Community in Peru's Central Highlands: Peasant Struggle and Capitalist Transition, 1860–1940*. Princeton, NJ: Princeton University Press.

———. 1995. *Peasant and Nation: The Making of Postcolonial Mexico and Peru*. Berkeley: University of California Press.

———. 2001. "Bearing Witness in Hard Times: Ethnography and Testimonio in a Postrevolucionary Age." In *Reclaiming the Political in Latin America History: Essays from the North*, edited by Gilbert Joseph, 311–54. Durham, NC: Duke University Press.

Manrique, Nelson. 1981. *Las guerrillas indígenas en la guerra con Chile*. Lima: Centro de Investigación y Capacitación.

———. 1989. "La década de la violencia." *Márgenes, encuentro y debate* 5–6 (December): 137–82.

———. 1995. "La caída de la cuarta espada y los senderos que se bifurcan." *Márgenes, encuentro y debate* 13–14 (November): 11–42.

———. 2002. *El tiempo del miedo: La violencia política del Perú, 1980–1996*. Lima: Fondo Editorial del Congreso del Perú.

Mao Zedong. 1971a. "Informe sobre una investigación del Movimiento Campesino de Junan." In *Obras escogidas*, vol. 1. Beijing: Ediciones en Lenguas Extranjeras.

———. 1971b. "La revolución china y el Partido Comunista de China." In *Obras escogidas*, vol. 2. Beijing: Ediciones en Lenguas Extranjeras.

———. 1971c. "Sobre la Guerra Prolongada." In *Obras escogidas*, vol. 2. Beijing: Ediciones en Lenguas Extranjeras.

Marcus-Delgado, Jane, and Martín Tanaka. 2001. *Lecciones del final del fujimorismo: La legitimidad presidencial y la acción política*. Lima: IEP.

Márquez, Gabriel. 1989. "¿Cuál arte alienante?" *El Diario*, 24 May, 16.

Marzal, Manuel. 1979. "Funciones religiosas del mito en el mundo andino cuzqueño." *Debates en Antropología*, no. 4: 11–22.

Mato, Daniel. 2003. "Estudios y otras prácticas latinoamericanas en cultura y poder: Crítica de la idea de 'estudios culturales latinoamericanos' y propuestas para la visibilización de un campo más amplio, transdisciplinario, crítico y contextualmente referido." In *Estudios culturales latinoamericanos: Retos desde y sobre la región andina*, edited by Catherine Walsh, 1–37. Quito: Universidad Andina Simón Bolivar, Ediciones Abya-Yala.

Matos Mar, José. 1984. *Desborde popular y crisis del estado: El nuevo rostro del Perú en la década de 1980*. Lima: IEP.

Mauceri, Philip. 1989. *Militares: Insurgencia y democratización en el Perú: 1980–1988*. Lima: IEP.

Mayer, Enrique. 1970. "Mestizo e indio: El contexto social de las relaciones interétnicas." In *El indio y el poder en el Perú*, edited by Fernando Fuenzalida, 87–152. Lima: IEP.

———. 1991. "Peru in Deep Trouble: Mario Vargas Llosa's Inquest in the Andes Re-examined." *Cultural Anthropology* 6.4: 466–504.

McClintock, Cynthia. 1983. *Democracies and Guerrillas: The Peruvian Experience.* International Policy Report 22. Washington, DC: Center for International Politics.

———. 1984. "Why Peasants Rebel: The Case of Peru's Sendero Luminoso." *World Politics* 37, no. 1 (October): 48–84.

———. 1998. *Revolutionary Movements in Latin America: El Salvador's FMLN and Peru's Shining Path.* Washington, DC: United States Institute of Peace Press.

McClintock, Cynthia, and Abraham Lowenthal, eds. 1989. *El gobierno militar: Una experiencia peruana 1968–1980.* Lima: IEP.

McCormick, Gordon. 1992. *From the Sierra to the Cities: The Urban Campaign of the Shining Path.* Santa Monica, CA: Rand Corporation.

Méndez, Cecilia. 2002. *El poder del nombre, o la construcción de identidades étnicas y nacionales en el Perú: Mito e historia de los iquichanos.* Lima: IEP.

———. 2005. *The Plebeian Republic: The Huanta Rebellion and the Making of the Peruvian State, 1820–1850.* Durham, NC: Duke University Press.

Mercado, Róger. 1982. *Las guerrillas del MIR, 1965.* Lima: Editorial de Cultura Popular.

Millones, Luis. 1983. "La tragedia de Uchuraccay: Informe sobre Sendero." In *Informe de la Comisión Investigadora de los sucesos de Uchuraccay*, edited by Mario Vargas Llosa et al., 85–102. Lima: Editora Perú.

Millones, Luis, and Mary Pratt. *Amor brujo: Imagen y cultura del amor en los Andes.* Lima: IEP.

Miró Quesada, Aurelio. 1947. "Ayacucho." In *Costa, sierra y montaña.* Lima: Editorial Cultura Antártica.

Montoya, Rodrigo. 1980. *Capitalismo y no capitalismo en el Perú: Un estudio histórico de su articulación en un eje regional.* Lima: Mosca Azul.

———. 1984. "Otra pista para entender lo que pasó en Uchuraccay." *La República*, 21 January, 8–16.

———. 1989. *Lucha por la tierra, reformas agrarias y capitalismo en el Perú del siglo XX.* Lima: Mosca Azul.

———. 2004. "Informe de la Comisión de la Verdad y Reconciliación: Un doloroso espejo del Perú." Presentation at a conference at the Institute des Hautes Etudes sur l'Amérique Latin (IHEAL) at the Université de Paris III, Sorbonne Nouvelle, January.

Montoya, Rodrigo, Luis Montoya, and Edwin Montoya. 1987. *La sangre de los cerros: Antología de la poesía quechua que se canta en el Perú.* Lima: Centro Peruano de Estudios Sociales.

Montoya, Rodrigo, and Universidad Nacional Mayor de San Marcos. 1974. *La SAIS Cahuide y sus contradicciones.* Lima: Universidad Nacional Mayor de San Marcos.

Mora, Daniel, Fernando Rospigliosi, Samuel Abad Yupanqui, and Carlos Basombrio Iglesias. 2001. *Las fuerzas armadas en la transición democrática en el Perú.* Lima: IEP.

Morote Best, Efraín, comp. 1974. *Huamanga, una larga historia.* Lima: Consejo Nacional de la Universidad Peruana.

———. 1977. Introduction to the first recording of the Tuna Universitaria de Huamanga. In *Universidad Nacional de San Cristóbal de Huamanga, 1677–1977, Libro jubilar en homenaje al tricentenario de su fundación*. Ayacucho: Universidad Nacional de San Cristóbal de Huamanga.

Morote, Osmán. 1971. "El latifundio en Chaca." Thesis, Universidad Nacional de San Cristóbal de Huamanga, Ayacucho.

Morse, Richard. 1982. *El espejo de Próspero: Un estudio de la dialéctica del Nuevo Mundo*. México City: Siglo XXI Editores.

Movimiento Popular Perú. 1994. "Proletarios del mundo unios!" Undated flier in author's possession.

Muratorio, Blanca, ed. 1994. *Imágenes e Imagineros: Representaciones de los indígenas ecuatorianos, siglos XIX y XX*. Quito: FLACSO.

Murra, John. 1975. *Formaciones económicas y políticas del mundo andino*. Lima: IEP.

Neyra, Hugo. 1968. *Los Andes: Tierra o muerte*. Madrid: Editorial ZYX.

Noel, Roberto Clemente. 1989. *Ayacucho: Testimonio de un soldado*. Lima: Publinor.

Nugent, Guillermo. 1992. *El laberinto de la choledad*. Lima: Fundación Friedrich Ebert.

Nun, José. 1989. *La rebelión del coro: Estudios sobre la racionalidad política y el sentido común*. Buenos Aires: Ediciones Nueva Visión.

Obando, Enrique. 1991. "Diez años de guerra antisubversiva: Una pequeña historia." *Quehacer* 72 (July–August): 46–51.

———. 1993. "Subversion and anti-subversion in Peru, 1980–1992: A View from Lima." *Low Intensity Conflict and Law Enforcement* 2, no. 2: 318–30.

O'Donnell, Guillermo, Philippe Schmitter, and Laurence Whitehead, eds. 1986. *Transitions from Authoritarian Rule: Comparative Perspectives*. Baltimore: Johns Hopkins University Press.

Oglesby, Elizabeth. 2007. "Educating Citizens in Postwar Guatemala: Historical Memory, Genocide, and the Culture of Peace." *Radical History Review* 97 (Winter): 77–98.

Ortíz, Dionisio. 1968. "Pomacocha: Del latifundio a la comunidad." Thesis, Universidad Nacional de San Cristóbal de Huamanga, Ayacucho.

Ortíz, Renato. 2001. "Estudios culturales, fronteras y traspasos: Una perspectiva desde Brasil." *Punto de Vista* 71 (December): 36–40.

Ortíz Rescanieri, Alejandro. 1972. *De Adaneva a Inkarrí: Una visión indígena del Perú*. Lima: Retablo de Papel Editores.

Ossio, Juan M. 1973. *Ideología mesiánica del mundo andino*. Lima: Ediciones de Ignacio Prado Pastor.

———. 1992. *Parentesco, reciprocidad y jerarquía en los Andes: Una aproximación a la organización social de la comunidad de Andamarca*. Lima: Fondo Editorial de la Pontificia Universidad Católica del Perú.

Ossio, Juan M., and Fernando Fuenzalida. 1983. "Informe antropológico: La comunidad de Uchuraccay y la región iquichana." In *Informe de la Comisión Investigadora de los sucesos de Uchuraccay*, edited by Mario Vargas Llosa et al., 43–81. Lima: Editora Perú.

Ossio, Juan, and Rodrigo Montoya. 1983. "Uchuraccay: ¿crimen sin castigo?" *La República*, 19 March, 14–15.

Palmer, David Scott. 1986. "Rebellion in Rural Peru: The Origins and Evolution of Sendero Luminoso." *Comparative Politics* 18 (January): 127–46.

———, ed. 1994. *Shining Path of Peru*. Rev. ed. New York: St. Martin's Press.

Parodi, Carlos. 2004. "Readings of the Final Report of Peru's Truth and Reconciliation Commission." Paper presented to meeting of the Latin American Studies Association, Las Vegas, Nevada, 7–9 October.

Partido Comunista del Perú (fracción "Feliciano"). 1994. "Segunda campaña de 'Construir la conquista del poder.'" Manuscript in author's possession.

Partido Comunista del Perú–Sendero Luminoso (PCP-SL). 1988a. "Bases de discusión: El PCP llama a las masas a luchar por el poder: El pensamiento Gonzalo y los trabajadores." Special supplement, *El Diario*, 8 January.

———. 1988b. "Bases de discusión del PCP: El presidente Gonzalo y la revolución democrática: La guerra popular y el nuevo poder." Special supplement, *El Diario*, 4 January.

———. 1988c. "Bases de discusión del PCP: Línea militar; Sendero y el Ejército Guerrillero Popular: Estrategia y táctica para la toma del poder." Special supplement, *El Diario*, 6 January.

———. 1988d. "Bases de discusión del PCP: Sendero se prepara para la toma del poder; La guerra popular y los instrumentos de la revolución: El Partido, el Ejército y el Frente Único." Special supplement, *El Diario*, 7 January.

———. 1988e. "Documentos Fundamentales del Primer Congreso del Partido Comunista del Perú. (Congreso marxista-leninista-maoísta, pensamiento Gonzalo)." *El Diario*, 7 January.

———. 1989a. "Bases de discusión: Línea militar." Orig. 1978. In *Guerra popular en el Perú: El pensamiento Gonzalo*, edited by Luis Arce Borja, 341–65. Brussels: L. A. Borja.

———. 1989b. "Contra las ilusiones constitucionales y por el Estado de Nueva Democracia." Orig. 1978. In *Guerra popular en el Perú: El pensamiento Gonzalo*, edited by Luis Arce Borja, 93–111. Brussels: L. A. Borja.

———. 1989c. "Desarrollar la Guerra Popular sirviendo a la Revolución Mundial." Orig. 1986. In *Guerra popular en el Perú: El pensamiento Gonzalo*, edited by Luis Arce Borja, 219–304. Brussels: L. A. Borja.

———. 1989d. "Desarrollemos la creciente protesta popular." Orig. 1979. In *Guerra popular en el Perú: El pensamiento Gonzalo*, edited by Luis Arce Borja, 115–37. Brussels: L. A. Borja.

———. 1991. "¡Que el Equilibrio Estratégico remezca más el país!" Lima, November. Photocopy in author's possession.

———. 1992a. "Sobre las dos colinas: La guerra contrasubversiva y sus aliados." Photocopy in author's possession.

———. 1992b. "III Pleno del Comité Central del PCP." Photocopy in author's possession.

———. 1993. "Declaración." 7 October. Flier in author's possession.

Pease, Henry. 1979. *El ocaso del poder oligárquico: Lucha política en la escena oficial 1968–1975.* 2nd ed. Lima: Centro de Estudios y Promoción del Desarrollo.

Peralta, Víctor. 2000. *Sendero Luminoso y la prensa, 1980–1994: La violencia peruana y su representación en los medios.* Cuzco and Lima: Centro de Estudios Regionales Andinos Bartolomé de las Casas, Casa de Estudios del Socialismo.

Pizarro, Eduardo, ed. 1996. *Insurgencia sin revolución: La guerrilla en Colombia en una perspectiva comparada.* Bogotá: IEPRI, T/M Editores.

Poole, Deborah. 1997. *Vision, Race, Modernity: A Visual Economy of the Andean Image World.* Princeton, NJ: Princeton University Press.

Poole, Deborah, and Gerardo Rénique. 1991. "The New Chroniclers of Peru: U.S. Scholars End Their 'Shining Path' of Peasant Rebellion." *Bulletin of Latin American Research* 10, no. 1: 133–91.

———. 1992. *Peru: Time of Fear.* London: Latin American Bureau.

Portantiero, Juan Carlos. 1977. *Los usos de Gramsci.* Cuadernos de Pasado y Presente 54. Mexico City: Ediciones Pasado y Presente.

Portocarrero, Gonzalo. 1984. "La dominación total." Pontificia Universidad Católica del Perú, Lima. Mimeo in author's possession.

———. 1991. *Sacaojos: Crisis social y fantasmas coloniales.* Lima: Tarea.

———. 1993. *Racismo y mestizaje.* Lima: Sur, 1993.

———. 1998. *Razones de sangre: Aproximaciones a la violencia política.* Lima: Pontificia Universidad Católica del Perú.

———. 2007. *Racismo y mestizaje y otros ensayos.* Lima: Fondo Editorial del Congreso del Perú.

Portocarrero, Gonzalo, and Patricia Oliart. 1989. *El Perú desde la escuela.* Lima: Instituto de Apoyo Agrario.

Presidencia del Consejo de Ministros (PCM). 2001. Decreto Supremo 065-2001, 2 June. http://www.pcm.gob.pe/transparencia/Resol_ministeriales/2011/DS-065-2011-PCM.pdf.

Quijano, Aníbal. 1965. "El movimiento campesino en el Perú y sus líderes." *América Latina*, no. 4: 43–64.

———. 1971. *Nacionalismo, neoimperialismo y militarismo en el Perú.* Buenos Aires: Ediciones Periferia Colección Estados Unidos y América Latina.

Quintanilla, Lino. 1981. *Andahuaylas, la lucha por la tierra: Testimonio de un militante.* Lima: Mosca Azul.

Quispe Calderón, Edwin. 1983. "Historia colonial y republicana en Huanta." In *Libro Jubilar 1933–1983*, 95–123. Huanta: González Vigil, UNSCH.

Raimondi, Antonio. 1945. "Ayacucho: Año 1862; Libreta N. 28." In *Notas de viaje para su obra "El Perú,"* vol. 3, 306–19. Lima: Edit. Imprenta Torres Aguirre.

Rama, Ángel. 1984. *La ciudad letrada.* Hanover, NH: Ediciones del Norte.

Ramos, Factor, and Jorge Loli. 1979. "Historia del movimiento popular en Huamanga." Thesis, Universidad Nacional de San Cristóbal de Huamanga, Ayacucho.

Reátegui, Félix. 2004. "Comisiones de la verdad en América Latina: Lecciones para la protección de los derechos humanos en sociedades de posguerra." Paper presented at Human Rights, Political Violence and the Global South conference, University of Michigan, Ann Arbor, Institute for the Humanities, 4 November.

Remijnse, Simone. 2002. *Memories of Violence: Civil Patrols and the Legacy on Conflict in Joyabaj, Guatemala.* Amsterdam: Rozenberg.

Rénique, José Luis. 1987. "Estado, partidos políticos y lucha por la tierra en Puno." *Debate agrario* 1 (October–December): 55–76.

———. 1991a. "La batalla por Puno: Violencia y democracia en la sierra sur." *Debate agrario* 10 (January–March): 83–108.

———. 1991b. *Los sueños de la sierra: Cusco en el siglo XX.* Lima: Centro Peruano de Estudios Sociales.

———. 2003. *La voluntad encarcelada: Las "luminosas trincheras de combate" de Sendero Luminoso del Perú.* Lima: IEP.

Restrepo, Eduardo, and Arturo Escobar. 2005. "Other Anthropologies and Anthropology Otherwise: Steps to a World Anthropologies Framework." *Critique of Anthropology* 25, no. 2: 99–129.

Rivera Palomino, Jaime. 1971. *Geografía general del Ayacucho.* Ayacucho: Universidad Nacional de San Cristóbal de Huamanga.

———. 1974. *Geografía de la población de Ayacucho.* Ayacucho: Universidad Nacional de San Cristóbal de Huamanga.

Rodriguez Rabanal, César. 1991. *Cicatrices de la pobreza: Un estudio psicoanalítico.* 2nd ed. Caracas: Editorial Nueva Sociedad.

Roel, Pedro. 2000. "De Folklore a culturas híbridas: Rescatando raíces, redefiniendo fronteras entre nos/otros." In *No hay país más diverso: Compendio de antropología peruana*, edited by Carlos Iván Degregori, 74–122. Lima: Red para el Desarrollo de las Ciencias Sociales en el Perú.

Rojas, Álvaro. 1988. *Partidos políticos en el Perú.* 7th ed. Lima: Álvaro Rojas.

Rojas, Telmo. 1989. "Rondas, poder campesino y el terror." Thesis, Universidad Nacional de Cajamarca, Cajamarca.

Roldán, Julio. 1990. *Gonzalo, el mito.* Lima: Julio Roldán.

Romero, Mauricio. 2004. *Paramilitares y autodefensa, 1982–2003.* Bogotá: Instituto de Estudios Políticos y Relaciones Internacionales, Universidad Nacional de Colombia.

Roncalla, Fredy. 1972. "Chuschi, las canciones y la vida." *Runa* 1 (March): 8–9.

Rospigliosi, Fernando. 2000. *Montesinos y las fuerzas armadas: Cómo controló durante una década las instituciones militares.* Lima: IEP.

Rostworowski, María. 1988. *Historia del Tahuantinsuyo.* Lima: IEP.

Ruíz, Gamaniel. 1983. "Oswaldo N. Regal." In *Libro Jubilar 1933–1983*, 55–58. Huanta: González Vigil, UNSCH.

Said, Edward. 1978. *Orientalism.* New York: Vintage Books.

———. 1993. *Culture and Imperialism.* New York: Alfred A. Knopf.

Sánchez, Rodrigo. 1981. *Tomas de tierras y conciencia política campesina, las lecciones de Andahuaylas.* Lima: IEP.

Sandoval, Pablo. 2002. "El olvido está lleno de memoria: Juventud universitaria y violencia política en el Perú; La matanza de estudiantes de La Cantuta." Thesis, Universidad Nacional Mayor de San Marcos, Lima.

———. 2003. "El olvido está lleno de memoria: La matanza de estudiantes de La Cantuta." In *Jamás tan cerca arremetió lo lejos: Memoria y violencia política en el Perú*, edited by Carlos Iván Degregori, 175–222. Lima: IEP.

Schneider, Jane, ed. 1998. *Italy's "Southern Question": Orientalism in One Country*. New York: Berg.

Scott, James. 1976. *The Moral Economy of the Peasant: Rebellion and Subsistence in Southeast Asia*. New Haven, CT: Yale University Press.

———. 1985. *Weapons of the Weak: Everyday Forms of Peasant Resistance*. New Haven, CT: Yale University Press.

Senado de la República del Perú. 1988. *Informe al Congreso sobre los sucesos de los penales*. Commision presided over by Senator Rolando Ames. Lima: La Comisión.

———. 1990. *Comisión investigadora de grupos paramilitares: Una lucha cívica contra la impunidad*. Commission presided over by Senador Manuel Piqueras. Lima: n.p.

———. 1992. *Violencia y pacificación en 1991*. Comisión especial de investigación y estudio sobre la violencia y alternativas de pacificación. Commission presided over by Senator Enrique Bernales Ballesteros. Lima: Centro de Investigación Legislativa del Senado.

Sendón, Pablo F. 2006. "Ecología, ritual y parentesco en los andes: Notas a un debate no permitido." *Debate agrario* 40–41:273–97.

Smith, Carol. 1990. *Guatemala Indians and the State: 1540 to 1988*. Austin: University of Texas Press.

Smith, Michael. 1992. *Entre dos fuegos: ONG, desarrollo rural y violencia política*. Lima: IEP.

Starn, Orin. 1991a. "Missing the Revolution: Anthropologists and the War in Peru." *Cultural Anthropology* 6, no. 1 (February): 63–91.

———. 1991b. *Reflexiones sobre rondas campesinas y nuevos movimientos sociales: Con los llanques todo barro*. Lima: IEP.

———. 1991c. "Sendero, soldados y ronderos en el Mantaro." *Quehacer* 74 (November–December): 60–69.

———. 1999. *Nightwatch: The Politics of Protest in the Andes*. Durham, NC: Duke University Press.

Starn, Orin, Carlos Iván Degregori, and Robin Kirk, eds. 1995. *The Peru Reader: History, Culture, Politics*. Durham, NC: Duke University Press.

Stavenhagen, Rodolfo. 1976. *Las clases sociales en las sociedades agrarias*. Mexico City: Siglo XXI Editores.

Steinhauf, Andreas. 1991. "Diferenciación étnica y redes de larga distancia entre migrantes andinos: El caso de Sanka y Colcha." *Boletín del Instituto Francés de Estudios Andinos* 20, no. 2: 93–114.

Stern, Steve J. 1987. *Resistance, Rebellion, and Consciousness in the Andean Peasant World, 18th to 20th Centuries*. Madison: University of Wisconsin Press.

———. 1990. "Nuevas aproximaciones al estudio de la conciencia y las rebeliones campesinas: Las implicancias de la experiencia andina." Introduction to *Resistencia, rebelión y conciencia campesina en los Andes: Siglos XVIII al XX*, compiled by Steve J. Stern, 25–41. Lima: IEP.

———. 1998a. "De la memoria suelta a la memoria emblemática: Hacia el recordar y el olvidar como proceso histórico; Chile 1973–1998." Paper presented to seminar on Collective Memory and Repression, Social Science Research Council, Montevideo, Uruguay. Accessed 24 August 2010. http://www.cholonautas.edu.pe/memoria/stern.pdf.

———. 1998b. *Shining and Other Paths: War and Society in Peru, 1980–1995*. Durham, NC: Duke University Press.

———. 1999. *Los senderos insólitos del Perú, 1980–1995*. Lima: IEP, UNSCH.

———. 2010. *Reckoning with Pinochet: The Memory Question in Democratic Chile, 1989–2006*. Durham, NC: Duke University Press.

Stoll, David. 1993. *Between Two Armies in the Ixil Towns of Guatemala*. New York: Columbia University Press.

Strong, Simon. 1992. *Sendero Luminoso: El movimiento subversivo más letal del mundo*. Translated by Jessica McLauchlan and Mirko Lauer. Lima: The Peru Report. Originally published as *Shining Path: Terror and Revolution in Peru* (New York: Times Books, 1992).

Tapia, Carlos. 1968. "El latifundio en Socos Vinchos." Thesis, Universidad Nacional de San Cristóbal de Huamanga, Ayacucho.

———. 1995. *Autodefensa armada del campesinado*. Lima: Centro de Estudios para el Desarrollo y la Participación.

———. 1997. *Las fuerzas armadas y Sendero Luminoso: Dos estrategias y un final*. Lima: IEP.

Taylor, Lewis. 1983. *Maoism in the Andes: Sendero Luminoso and the Contemporary Guerrilla Movement in Peru*. Working Paper 2, Center for Latin American Studies, University of Liverpool, England.

Teivainen, Teivo. 2004. "Omisión de la verdad sobre actores transnacionales." *La República*, 12 March.

Theidon, Kimberly. 2004. *Entre prójimos: El conflicto armado interno y la política de la reconciliación en el Perú*. Lima: IEP.

Thompson, E. P. 1972. "Eighteenth-Century English Society: Class Struggle without Class?" *Social History* 3.2 (May): 133–65.

Thurner, Mark. 1997. *From Two Republics to One Divided: Contradictions of Postcolonial Nationmaking in Andean Peru*. Durham, NC: Duke University Press.

Touraine, Alain. 1978. *La voix et le regard*. Paris: Editions du Seuil.

———. 1984. *Le retour de l'acteur: Essai de sociologie*. Paris: Fayard.

Tuesta, Fernando. 1987. *Perú político en cifras: Élite política y elecciones*. Lima: Fundación Ebert.

TV Cultura. 2002. *Tarea pendiente*. Video. Ayacucho, Lima.

Uceda, Ricardo. 2004. *Muerte en el Pentagonito: Los cementerios secretos del ejército peruano*. Bogotá: Planeta.

Universidad Nacional de San Cristóbal de Huamanga. 1977. *Universidad de San Cristóbal de Huamanga, 1677–1977: Libro jubilar en homenaje al tricentenario de su fundación.* Ayacucho: UNSCH.

Urbano, Henrique, ed. 1991. *Poder y violencia en los Andes.* Cusco: Centro de Estudios Regionales Andinos Bartolomé de Las Casas.

Urrutia, Jaime. 1981. "Evolución de las comunidades en la región de Huamanga." *Ideología,* no. 7: 49–58.

———. 1982. "Comerciantes, arrieros y viajeros huamanguinos: 1770–1870." Thesis, Universidad Nacional de San Cristóbal de Huamanga, Ayacucho.

———. 1985a. "Ayacucho: Los frutos de la guerra." *El Zorro de Abajo,* no. 3 (November–December): 51–53.

———. 1985b. *Huamanga: Región e historia, 1536–1770.* Ayacucho: Universidad Nacional de San Cristóbal de Huamanga.

Urrutia, Jaime, Antonio Araujo, and Haydeé Joyo. 1983. *El empleo en el Perú: Un nuevo enfoque.* Lima: IEP.

———. 1988. "Las comunidades en la región de Huamanga: 1824–1968." In *Perú, el problema agrario en debate,* SEPIA II, edited by Fernando Eguren López, María Isabel Remy, and Patricia Oliart, 429–67. Lima: Universidad Nacional de San Cristóbal de Huamanga, Seminario Permanente de Investigación Agraria.

Valderrama, Ricardo, and Carmen Escalante. 1990. "Nuestras vidas (abigeos de Cotabambas)." In *Bandoleros, abigeos y montoneros: Criminalidad y violencia en el Perú, siglos XVIII–XX,* edited by Carlos Aguirre and Charles Walker, 309–32. Lima: Instituto de Apoyo Agrario.

Valdéz, Patricia. 2001. "Las comisiones de la verdad." In *Verdad y justicia: Homenaje a Emilio F. Mignone,* edited by Juan Méndez, Martín Abregú, and Javier Mariezcurrena, 123–28. San José: Instituto Interamericano de Derechos Humanos.

Van Alphen, Ernst. 1999. "Symptoms of Discursivity: Experience, Memory, and Trauma." In *Acts of Memory: Cultural Recall in the Present,* edited by Mieke Bal, Jonathan Crece, and Leo Spitzer, 24–38. Hanover, NH: University of New England Press.

Vargas Llosa, Mario. 1983. "Después del informe: Conversación sobre Uchuraccay." Interview of Mario Vargas Llosa by Alberto Bonilla. *Caretas* 738 (7 March).

Vargas Llosa, Mario, et al., eds. 1983. *Informe de la Comisión Investigadora de los sucesos de Uchuraccay.* Vargas Llosa Report (IVL). Lima: Editora Perú.

Vergara, Abilio. 1983. "Subregión de Huanta: Apuntes para su comprensión." In *Libro Jubilar 1933–1983,* 125–77. Huanta: González Vigil, UNSCH.

Vergara, Abilio, et al. 1985. "Culluchaca: Algunos elementos sobre la ideología comunal." In *Comunidades campesinas de Ayacucho: Economía, ideología y organización social.* Ayacucho: Instituto de Estudios Regionales "José María Arguedas," Comisión de Coordinación de Tecnología Andina.

Vich, Víctor. 2002. *El caníbal es el otro: Violencia y cultura en el Perú contemporáneo.* Lima: IEP.

Vidal, Ana María. 1993. *Los decretos de la guerra: Dos años de políticas antisubversivas y una propuesta de paz.* Lima: Instituto de Democracia y Socialismo.

Villapolo Herrera, Leslie. 2003. "Senderos del desengaño: Construcción de memorias, identidades colectivas y proyectos de futuro en una comunidad Asháninka." In *Jamás tan cerca arremetió lo lejos: Memoria y violencia política en el Perú*, edited by Carlos Iván Degregori, 135–73. Lima: IEP.

Webb, Richard. 1987. Lecture, Institute de Estudios Peruanos, April.

Weber, Eugene. 1976. *Peasants into Frenchmen: The Modernization of Rural France, 1870–1914*. Palo Alto, CA: Stanford University Press.

Weinstein, Barbara. 2008. "Developing Inequality." *American Historical Review* 113.1 (February): 1–18.

———. Forthcoming. *Race, Region, Nation: São Paulo and the Formation of Brazilian National Identities*.

Werlich, David. 1984. "Peru: The Shadow of Shining Path." *Current History* 83 (February): 78–90.

Wieviorka, Michel. 1988. *Sociétés et terrorisme*. Paris: Fayard.

———. 1997. *Un nouveau paradigma de la violence?* Paris: L'Harmattan.

Wolf, Eric. 1979. *Las luchas campesinas del siglo XX*. Mexico City: Siglo XXI Editores.

Youngers, Coletta. 2003. *Violencia política y sociedad civil en el Perú: Historia de la Coordinadora Nacional de Derechos Humanos*. Lima: IEP.

Zambrano Padilla, Laura. 1985. "Nuestra vida cotidiana es la guerra." Interview. *El Diario*, 14 March, 7–10.

Zuidema, Tom. 1989. *Reyes y guerreros: Ensayos de cultura andina*. Lima: FOMCIENCIAS.

Index

Page references in italics indicate illustrations and t or tt indicates tables.

Aronson, Bernard, 26
Arroyo Mío, Heriberto, 70
Arturo, 115–18, 124, 136
Asháninkas, 66
authoritarianism: of the armed forces, 25, 207n31; the authoritarian divide, 92–95, 202nn4–5; and democratic transitions, 210n6 (*see also* democratic transition); of Fujimori, 15; in the media, 177; public rejection of, 175; of Shining Path, 61, 63–64
Ayacucho, 42, 113–34; ballot boxes burned in, 4; *campesino* responses to Shining Path in, *119*, 119–23; counteroffensive in, 53; death toll in/disappearances from, 5, 46, 146, 184n3, 194n16; demonstrations for free education in (1969), 161–62; education in, 74; introduction/overview of, 14, 113–15; Maoists in, 73–74; people's war launched in, 113 (*see also* war); poverty in, 4, 194n25; public opinion of Shining Path, 57–59, 197n61; resistant adaptation in, 14, *119*, 119–22, 189n22; rural youth in, 114–18, 123–25 (*see also* Arturo; Nicario; peasant patrols); Shining Path and the masses, *124*; Shining Path land cultivation in, 118; Shining Path's defeat in (*see* peasant patrols); Shining Path's social base in, 114–15; Shining Path's structure in, 116–17, *117*; Shining Path violence in, 117–18; Shining Path vs. armed forces in, 123–24, 132–33. *See also* Uchuraccay massacre

Bandera Roja (BR; Red Flag), 73–74, 104
Bastidas, Micaela, 48
Belaúnde, Fernando, 22, 29, 38, 95, 202n5
Benavides, Margarita, 66
Berg, Ronald, 62–63, 115, 122, 137–38
Biondi, Juan, 64
Black Path, 35
blood quota, 142
Bonfil, Guillermo, 95
Bonilla, Heraclio, 65, 196n38
bossism, rural (*gamonalismo*), 115, 137–38, 142–43. See also *patrón*
Bourdieu, Pierre, 52
BR (Red Flag; Bandera Roja), 73–74, 104
burial sites/common graves, 177–78

Buscando un Inca (Flores Galindo), 59, 61, 195n32, 198n65

El Caballo Rojo, 69
cabitos (soldiers), 148, 206n19
CADs (Self-Defense Committees; Comités de Autodefensa), 25, 66, 190n9
Cahuide Agricultural Society, 137
Cajamarca, 160
Calvo, Margie, 36
campesinistas: Indians identified with, 208n4; Marxist, 44; origin of term, 194n21
"La Cantuta" massacre (National Education University), 66, 175
capital punishment, 145. *See also* death
Cárdenas Ruiz, Rodolfo, 36
cargo cults, 164
Carry On, 35
Casa de Cultura (Culture House), 202n5
Castillo, Aracelio, 161–63
Catholicism, 157
CCP (Peasant Confederation of Peru; Confederación Campesina del Perú), 38–39, 63, 115
Central Committee: Plenary of 1980, 81–82; Plenary of 1981, 87, 142; Plenary of 1992, 154–55, 190–91n12
Central Obrera Boliviana (COB), 44
Centro de Estudios y Promoción del Desarrollo (DESCO), 51–52, 196n44
Cerro Corporation, 193n5
Cerro de Pasco (central Andes), 192n2
Cevallos, Noé, 200–201n6
CGTP (General Confederation of Peruvian Workers; Confederación General de Trabajadores del Perú), 77, 170, 193n9, 209n11, 210n9
Chaca, 153
chanas of creation (youngest children of God), 160
chaqwa (chaos or confusion), 60
Chávez de Paz, Denis, 64
chicha (tabloid) newspapers, violence in, 90
Chile, 176, 210n10
cholificación (hybrid cultures), 47, 49, 195n36
Christian Democracy (Democracia Cristiana), 103

Chuschi (Ayacucho), 4, 21, 59, 63, 131–32, 137, 196n47, 198n72, 204n7
chutos (savages), 17, 189n27
Cicatrices de la pobreza (Rodríguez Rabanal), 195n32
citizenship, 49, 75, 179
Civil Guard. *See* GC
Civil Self-Defense Patrols (PAC; Patrullas de Autodefensa Civil; Guatemala), 66, 190n9
civil society, 176
CNA (National Agrarian Confederation), 38–39
CNDDHH (National Coordinating Committee for Human Rights; Coordinadora Nacional de Derechos Humanos), 174–76, 196n42
COB (Central Obrera Boliviana), 44
Cobriza miners' strike (Huancavelica), 193n5
coca production, 24, 125, 156, 190n3
Colina death squad, 67, 175–76
collective individualism, 73
"Collective Memory and Repression in the Southern Cone and Peru," 66
Colombian self-defense organizations, 66
Comentarios reales (Garcilaso), 45
Comisión de la Verdad y Reconciliación (Peru). *See* CVR
communism, definition of, 167
communist parties, development of, 84
Communist Parties of the Third International, 34
Communist Party of Peru, 100–101. *See also* entries starting with Shining Path
Communist Party of Peru–Red Fatherland (Patria Roja), 193n7
community development, 43–44
community of discourse, 71–91; the abolition of the ego, 87–89; "Bases for Discussion," 88; and the cult of death, 87–88; discourse analysis and Shining Path violence, 72–73, 86; and the exaltation of the leader, 87–89; God echoed in, 200–201n6; Guzmán's "For the New Flag," 76–79, 88–89, 200nn4–5; Guzmán's "Let Us Begin to Tear Down the Walls and Unfurl the Dawn," 76–77, 81–84; Guzmán's "On

Three Chapters of Our History," 76–77, 79–81, 88; Guzmán's transition from bureaucrat to prophet, 75–77; Guzmán's transition from prophet to messiah, 87–89, 201n12; Guzmán's "We Are the Initiators," 76–77, 84–87; and ideological and organizational mechanisms of Shining Path, 75; introduction/overview of, 13, 71–72; making of, overview of, 73–74; pledge taken by Shining Path members, 87; and sex/love's devaluation, 87–88; and styles of doing politics, 91; violence of discourse in the media, 90; a Yan'an (revolutionary base) at UNSCH, 74–75
community self-defense patrols. *See* peasant patrols
Complete Works (Mao), 106
"La conducta política" (Granados), 61, 198n71
Confederación Campesina del Perú (CCP; Peasant Confederation of Peru), 38–39, 63, 115
Confederación General de Trabajadores del Perú. *See* CGTP
conquistadores, 160
Consejo por la Paz, 144
Constituent Assembly, 39, 74, 76, 85
Constitution (Peru, 1979), 39
Constitution (Peru, 1993), 174
Constitutional Congress (Peru, 1992), 26, 192n19
Constitutional Tribunal, 191n15
Cooperación Popular (Community Development), 202n5
cooperatives, peasant conflicts with, 62
Coordinadora Nacional de Derechos Humanos (CNDDHH; National Coordinating Committee for Human Rights), 174–76, 196n42
Copernican revolution in Peruvian social science, 41
Coral, Isabel, 65–66
Coronel, José, 140, 148, 204n2, 204n7
corruption, public rejection of, 175
critical idea of Peru, 136, 207n2
Cromotex textile factory takeover (Lima, 1980), 193n8
Cuban Revolution, 100

state spending on, 93–94, 94*t*, 97, 161, 202n4; student profiles, 100–102; truth via, 161–62. *See also* universities

ego, abolition of, 87–89

EGP. *See* Popular Guerrilla Army

Ejército de Liberación Nacional (ELN; National Liberation Army), 103, 191n12. *See also* Popular Guerrilla Army

elites. *See* intellectuals

ELN (Army of the Revolutionary Left), 38

ELN (National Liberation Army), 103, 191n12. *See also* Popular Guerrilla Army

El Salvador, 210n10

emergency zones, 46–47, 195n28

Enlightenment, 166

ESEP (Professional Education Schools), 98, 107

Espinosa, Óscar, 66

Estructuras tradicionales y economía del mercado (Fuenzalida, Villarán, Golte, and Valiente), 59

Eurocommunism, 41

fatalism, 63–64

Favre, Henri: "Perú: Sendero Luminoso y horizontes oscuros," 61–62

FECVRA (Federation of Peasants of the Apurímac River Valley; Federación de Campesinos del Valle del Río Apurímac), 199n85

FEDETA (Departmental Federation of Workers of Ayacucho; Federación Departamental de Trabajadores de Ayacucho), 199n85

felicianistas, 35–36, 192n25. *See also* Ramírez Durand, Alberto

FER (Student Revolutionary Front; Frente Estudiantil Revolucionario), 100–102

fiestas, 123, 157–58

Final Report (CVR), 45, 53, 67–68, 177–78, 180–82, 196n39, 199nn82–83, 211n20

FLN (National Liberation Front), 191n12

Flores Galindo, Alberto, 7, 42, 50, 198n68; *Buscando un Inca*, 59, 61, 195n32, 198n65; *Violencia y campesinado*, 60–61

foquismo, 102

Foreign Language Editions (Beijing), 106

forgetting, 174, 177, 180. *See also* memory

"For the New Flag" (Guzmán), 76–79, 88–89, 200nn4–5

Four Philosophical Theses (Mao), 106

Franco, Carlos, 47

Franco, Francisco, 200–201n6

Frente de Defensa del Pueblo de Ayacucho (People's Defense Front of Ayacucho), 74, 162

Frente Estudiantil Revolucionario (FER; Student Revolutionary Front), 100–102

Frentes de Defensa (Defense Fronts), 39

FUE (United Front of Students; Frente Único de Estudiantes), 199n85

Fuenzalida, Fernando, 53; *Estructuras tradicionales y economía del mercado*, 59

Fujimori, Alberto, 5; authoritarian rule by, 15; Congress dissolved by, 26; Constitutional Congress convened by, 26, 192n19; elections of, 24–25, 174–75; Guzmán's letters to, 28–30; human rights violations under, 176; neoliberalism of, 24–25; pacifying approach to remembering violence, 174; popularity of, 192n19; public support for, 173; as savior of Peru, 91; television under control of, 90

Gálvez, Modesto, 145

gamonalismo, 16

Gang of Four, 75–76, 84–85

García, Alan, 24, 29, 206n24

García Canclini, Néstor, 47

García Sayán, Diego: *Tomas de tierras en el Perú*, 41–42

Gavilán, Félix, 70

GC (Civil Guard; Guardía Civil), 55, 123, 197n54, 203n6

General Confederation of Peruvian Workers. *See* CGTP

genocide, 26, 190n11

Golte, Jürgen, 208n5; *Estructuras tradicionales y economía del mercado*, 59

González Prada, Manuel, 166, 168

gonzalistas, 35, 192n25. *See also* Guzmán, Abimael

Gorriti Ellenbogen, Gustavo, 64, 79, 81–82, 186n12, 200n5

Gramsci, Antonio, 40–41, 194n13
Granados, Manuel: "La conducta política," 61, 198n71
Group of Shanghai, 84–85
Guardía Civil. *See* GC
Guatemala, 176, 210n10, 210n14
La guerra del fin del mundo (Vargas Llosa), 118
Guibal, Francis, 194n13
Gutiérrez, Gustavo, 178
Guzmán, Abimael ("President Gonzalo"): on Belaúnde, 29; on the blood quota, 142; capture of, 5, 27, 71–72, 173; as cosmo-cratic figure (*see under* community of dis-course); deification/stature of, 26–27, 33, 35; destiny embodied in, 200n5; as direc-tor of personnel at UNSCH, 202n6; elec-tions/representative democracy rejected by, 34; escalation of war in Lima by, 190n10; as Fourth Sword, 89; on García, 29; on genocide, 87; iconography of, 15; illnesses of, 83; on infant mortality, 144; influence on Shining Path while impris-oned, 33–34, 36; as an intellectual, 49, 165; international support for, 28; letters to Fu-jimori from prison, 28–30; on the Lucana-marca massacre, 22, 24, 149, 190n5, 190n7; on the masses, 169–70; nickname of, 29, 191n18; PCP–Bandera Roja's Ayacucho Regional Committee led by, 73–74; peace accord urged by, 28–34; personality cult surrounding, 88; realism of, 33–34, 36; religious school training of, 78–79, 200–201n6; on the self-coup, 29–30; on sex, 88; Shining Path militants educated by, 36, 192n26; on the size of Shining Path, 22, 189–90n2; style of texts by, 76; trial/imprisonment of, 27–28, 89–90; turn-around in prison, 30–34; at UNSCH, 69; on violence, 83–85, 141–42, 205n10; on the world revolution, 84; WORKS, 76–77, 81–84; "For the New Flag," 76–79, 88–89, 200nn4–5; "On Three Chapters of Our History," 76–77, 79–81, 88; "We Are the Initiators," 76–77, 84–87

Handbook on Political Economy (Spiridonova), 202n2

Harnecker, Martha, 104, 107–8, 202n2, 208n3
Hernández, Max, 160
Hinojosa, Iván, 68–69, 199n84
Historia del Tawantinsuyu (Rostworowski), 195n31
Hitler, Adolf, 190n11
Holocaust, 180
Huallaga Valley, 22, 24, 190n3
Huamanga, 45, 194n23
Huancasancos, 157
Huancavelica, 194n25
Huanta, 147–48, 152, 161–62, 204n2
Huánuco, 194n25
Huaychao, 157
huayno music, 207n32
Huayopampa, 59–60
human rights survey, 174–75, 179, 209n4
hybrid cultures (*cholificación*), 47, 49, 195n36
hyperinflation, 24, 65, 91, 192n19

ideology/political violence in Shining Path, 159–71; causes of extreme violence, 168, 209n9; and coherence, 164–66; and de-mand for free education, 161–62; elites' role in, 159, 166–71, 208–9n8, 209n10; the hypercult of reason, 15; introduction/overview of, 15, 159; inward-turning re-bellion, 160–61; and knowledge, 161; Marxist-Leninist-Maoist ideology, 163, 165–68, 170, 208n3 (*see also* Marxism); the masses and Shining Path, *124*, 169–70; and myths, 160 (*see also specific myths*); and the proletarian idea, 165; rebellion by appropriating tools of domination, 160–61; truth/escape from deceit via ideology, 160–66
ILA 80 ("initiating the armed struggle"), 84, 86
IMASEN, 174–75, 179, 209n4
Inca, 58, 160
Indians, rights of, 208n4
indigenismo, 42–45, 100, 167
indigenista (redemptive pro-Indian) para-digm/movement, 7, 43–45, 47, 50, 53, 57, 67
inflation, 24, 65, 91, 192n19
Inkarrí myth, 96, 160, 202n8
INP (National Planning Institute), 202n5

insignificantes (insignificant ones or those with no signifier), 178, 210n15
Instituto de Estudios Peruanos (IEP), 9, 10
Instituto de Etnología (Institute of Ethnology; Universidad de San Antonio Abad del Cusco), 93
Instituto de Sociología (Institute of Sociology; Universidad de San Antonio Abad del Cusco), 93
Instituto Indigenista Peruano (Peruvian Indigenist Institute), 202n5
intellectuals: politicization of, 41; role in Shining Path's ideology, 159, 166–71, 208–9n8, 209n10
Inter-American Court of Human Rights (Costa Rica), 191n15
Internationalist Revolutionary Movement (MRI), 191n16
international workers' movement, 84
inversionary discourse, 73, 76
inversion of the world, 59–60, 118, 123, 157
Iparraguirre, Elena, 30, 191n14
Iquichanos, 55, 139–40, 197n55
Isbell, Billie Jean, 63, 115, 137, 208n5; *To Defend Ourselves*, 185n8, 196n47
IVL (Vargas Llosa Report), 53–57. *See also* Uchuraccay massacre

Jelin, Elizabeth, 179–80, 187n16
Junín, 194n25

Khmer Rouge, 63
Khosrokhavar, Farhad, 205n13
kinship ties, 137, 139, 144, 156
Kirk, Robin, 65–66
Konstantinov, F. V., 107–8, 202n2
Kruijt, Dirk, 68–69

La Convención (Cusco), 192n2
Lagos, Edith, 48, 138, 197n61
La Mar, 125, 152
Latin America: democratic transitions in, 176 (*see also* democratic transition); education in, 161; public-intellectual tradition in, 41; state violence in, 45; student enrollment in, 96; truth commissions in, 176, 210n10, 210n12 (*see also* CVR)

Lauer, Mirko, 180
Law 13417 (Peru), 93
Law 17437 (Peru), 93, 101
law of authentic interpretation (Peru, 1996), 175
leader, exaltation of, 87–89
learned city concept, 48–49
the Left: Cultural Revolution's influence on, 75–76; directional changes within, 38–39, 103; mobilizations of, 39, 193n8; politicization of intellectuals in, 41; popularity with voters, 85. *See also specific parties and groups*
Legislative Decree 747, 206n24
Lenin, Vladimir Illich: personality cult surrounding, 201n10; on revolutionary practice and theory, 101; on social classes, 41; on uprising/armed struggle, 200n1. *See also* Marxism-Leninism's expansion in the social sciences
León, Rafael, 104
"Let Us Begin to Tear Down the Walls and Unfurl the Dawn" (Guzmán), 76–77, 81–84
Lévi-Strauss, Claude, 44, 107
Libertad movement, 41
Lima: centralization of wealth/cultural production in, 49, 195n33; dependence on rural areas, 204n8; population of, 49, 195n33; as seat of civilizing/colonizing mission, 7; state of emergency in, 195n28; universities in, 195n28; war's impact in, 5, 25–26
Lima prison massacres (1986), 24
Lirio (Huanta), 139
López, Sinesio, 194n13
López Ricci, José, 67, 205n16
Lucanamarca peasant massacre (Ayacucho, 1983), 22, 24, 149–50, 190n5, 190n7
Lucha por la tierra (R. Montoya), 42

Macera, Pablo, 48, 94
Mama Huaco, 48
Manco Inca II, 161
Manrique, Nelson, 5, 16, 49–50, 63–64, 115, 137; *Violencia y campesinado*, 60–61
Maoism: in Ayacucho, 73–74; on culture as a reflection of politics/economy, 157; divisions within, 35; influence on small Leftist

Maoism (*continued*)
groups, 44; Marxists as Maoists, 44; parties nostalgic for, 191n16; as peasant-centered revolution, 106; of Shining Path, 39, 57–58, 141, 165; on warfare, 123, 139, 147. *See also* ideology/political violence in Shining Path

Mao Zedong: *Complete Works*, 106; death of, 75, 84–85; *Four Philosophical Theses*, 106; as Fourth Sword, 89; on power, 33; on protracted struggle, 151; on rebellion as justified, 205n14

Mariátegui, José Carlos, 58, 80, 89, 167; *Seven Interpretive Essays on Peruvian Society*, 44

marines, 125, 152–53, 206n26

Marxism: analysis of political conjuncture by, 76; elevation to Mao Zedong Thought, 84–85; of elites, 167; Flores Galindo on, 61; Gramscian version of, 41; Leninist, 44; popularity with voters, 85; on practice as the criterion of truth, 170; structuralist, 40. *See also* *campesinistas*; ideology/political violence in Shining Path; Maoism

Marxism-Leninism's expansion in the social sciences, 92–109; and the authoritarian divide, 92–95, 202nn4–5; growth of social sciences, 98–100, 99*tt*, 107, 107*t*; introduction/overview of, 13–14, 92–93; Marxist handbooks/textbooks, 14, 92–93, 101–9, 163, 202n2, 203n13, 208n3; and the social demand for education, 13–14, 95–98, 96–98*tt*; and student profiles, 100–102; university degrees in the social sciences, 93

materialism, historical and dialectical, 92, 104–5, 107–8. *See also* Marxism-Leninism's expansion in the social sciences

Matos Mar, José: *Desborde popular y crisis del estado*, 47

McClintock, Cynthia, 58, 68–69

McCormick, Gordon, 26

memory: active, vs. passive sympathy, 182; Collective Memory and Repression in the Southern Cone and Peru project, 66–67; memory entrepreneurs, 175; of salvation, 174, 181; silenced, 174–75; struggle for, 91; temporalities of, 179–80

mesnadas (troops recruited by feudal lords), 190n6

mestizos. See *mistis*

microdifferentiations, taking advantage of, 63

middle-class sectors, 176, 210n8

military government (Peru, 1968–80). *See* Revolutionary Government of the Armed Forces

military tribunals, 27, 191n15

millenarianism, 58–60, 198n65

MIR (Movement of the Revolutionary Left; Movimiento Izquierda Revolucionario), 38, 100, 103

"Missing the Revolution" (Starn), 52, 60

mistis (mestizos), 61–63, 115, 137–38, 143–44, 157–58, 161, 168–69, 198n70, 204n3, 208n4

mita (mandatory public service), 118, 203n4

modernity, 104, 164–66, 208nn4–5

modernization, 49, 93, 164–65, 195–96n37

Montesinos, Vladimiro, 91, 174–76, 209n5

Montoya, Edwin, 207n32

Montoya, Luis, 207n32

Montoya, Rodrigo, 207–8n2, 207n32; *Lucha por la tierra*, 42

Morales Bermúdez, Francisco, 38

Morote, Osmán, 58, 194n23

Morse, Richard, 44

Movement of the Revolutionary Left (MIR; Movimiento Izquierda Revolucionario), 38, 100, 103

Moyano, María Elena, 70

MRI (Internationalist Revolutionary Movement), 191n16

MRTA (Túpac Amaru Revolutionary Movement), 5, 51, 66, 173–74, 191n15, 196n41, 199n82

Murra, John, 44–45

myth: cosmocrat's role in consolidation of, 72–73; and ideology, 160; of Inkarrí, 96, 160, 202n8; of progress, 96, 136

ñakaq, 153, 206n27

National Agrarian Confederation (CNA), 38–39

National Commission on the Disappeared (Argentina), 210n10

National Coordinating Committee for Human Rights (CNDDHH; Coordinadora Nacional de Derechos Humanos), 174–76, 196n42

National Counterterrorism Directorate (DINCOTE), 5, 27

National Intelligence Service (SIN), 209n5

National Liberation Army (ELN), 103, 191n12. *See also* Popular Guerrilla Army

National Liberation Front (FLN), 191n12

national liberation movement, 84

National Planning Institute (INP), 202n5

National Police of Peru, 27, 138, 174, 197n54, 197n61

naval marines, 125, 152–53, 206n26

Nicario, 14, 123, 145, 150, 156; on Allpachaka, 128–30; on the army, 132–33; background of, 115; on coca production in the jungle, 125; on executions, 117, 131, 146–47; minibusiness started by, 205n17; on new authorities, 131–32; on planting crops, 204n7; in Shining Path, 116, 126–28, 133–34, 136; on Shining Path objectives, 205n11

Nugent, Guillermo, 47

Nun, José, 76

OAS (Organization of American States), 26

occultism, 58

Oliart, Patricia, 136, 207n2

oligarchy, 4, 103, 163, 167

Organization of American States (OAS), 26

organizations, associative, 63

organizations, popular vs. generated, 169, 209n10

Orientalism, 6–8, 17, 60, 186n9

Orozco Huamani, Julio, 70

Othering, 6–7

The Other Path (de Soto), 47, 203n1 (ch. 5)

PAC (Civil Self-Defense Patrols; Patrullas de Autodefensa Civil; Guatemala), 190n9

pachakuti. *See* inversion of the world

Pacucha (Apurímac), 62

Palma, Ricardo, 160

Palmer, David Scott, 58, 65

Pancho, 206n26

Paniagua, Valentín, 209n1

Papua New Guinea, 164, 208n4

Partido Comunista del Perú–Sendero Luminoso (PCP-SL). *See* Shining Path

Pascal, Blaise, 167

Patria Roja (Communist Party of Peru–Red Fatherland), 193n7

patrón (boss or patron), 119, 122–23, 137–38, 143, 147. *See also* bossism, rural

Patrullas de Autodefensa Civil (Civil Self-Defense Patrols; PAC; Guatemala), 66, 190n9

PCP (Peruvian Communist Party), 73, 81–82, 200n4. *See also* Bandera Roja; PCP-UNIDAD

PCP-BR (Red Flag; PCP–Bandera Roja), 73–74, 104

PCP-SL (Partido Comunista del Perú–Sendero Luminoso). *See* Shining Path

PCP-UNIDAD (Peruvian Communist Party–Unity), 73–74, 193n9

Peasant Confederation of Peru (CCP; Confederación Campesina del Perú), 38–39, 63, 115

peasant law, 145

peasant movement (Peru, 1958–64), 38, 192n2

peasant movement (Peru, 1968–75), 38–39, 41–42, 62, 193n4

peasant movements, generally, 16

peasant patrols (*rondas*), 135–58; and Andean culture, 157–58, 207n32; collective crop production, 139, 204n7; first point of rupture, 138–47; formation of, 122–23; introduction/overview of, 14–15, 135, 203–4n1; and kinship ties, 137, 139, 144, 156; peasant support/rejection of Shining Path, 138–39, 145, 149–52, 155, 157, 206n23; and physical security of the population, 147, 205n18; proliferation of, 151, 154, 156, 205n17; and resistant adaptation, 148, 151–52; rural youth and the peasantry, 135–38, 146–47, 149–50, 204nn2–5; second point of rupture, 150–54; and Shining Path as external actor, 149–50, 152; and Shining Path's blind spots/defeat, 138, 151–52, 154–58, 206–7n29; and Shining Path's coercion/violence, 137, 140, 149–51, 153–55; and Shining Path seen as devils, 153,

Critical Human Rights